THE STORY OF THE AMERICAN VICE PRESIDENCY

JEREMY LOTT

THOMAS NELSON
Since 1798

NASHVILLE   DALLAS   MEXICO CITY   RIO DE JANEIRO   BEIJING

Published in Nashville, Tennessee, by Thomas Nelson. Thomas Nelson is a trademark of Thomas Nelson, Inc.

Thomas Nelson, Inc. titles may be purchased in bulk for educational, business, fund-raising, or sales promotional use. For information, please e-mail SpecialMarkets@thomasnelson.com.

Page Design by Casey Hooper

Library of Congress Cataloging-in-Publication data
Lott, Jeremy.
　The warm bucket brigade: drunks, hacks, crooks, and oddballs: the story of the American vice presidency / Jeremy Lott.
　　p. cm.
　Includes bibliographical references.
　ISBN 978-1-59555-082-8
　1. Vice-Presidents—United States—History. 2. Vice-President—United States—History—Anecdotes. 3. Vice-Presidents—United States—Biography—Anecdotes. 4. United States—Politics and government—Anecdotes. I. Title.
JK609.5.L68 2008
973.09'9--dc22

2007033435

Printed in the United States of America
08 09 10 11　QFF　5 4 3 2 1

To my mother, Debbie Lott.

*You can call us Aaron Burr from
the way we're dropping Hamiltons.*

—CHRIS PARNELL AND ANDY SAMBERG

CONTENTS

INTRODUCTION

Q: How is the vice presidency
like the Spanish Inquisition?

A: No one expects the vice president.

It's a groan-inducing gag. But then, according to most folks, so is the vice presidency. The vice president has few formal constitutional powers. He* can break a tie vote in the Senate and ceremonially preside over the nation's most exclusive club. That's it.

Until recently, you could make the case that the vice president was the only U.S. politician appropriately compensated for his efforts. The pomp and paycheck that members of Congress were willing to lavish on the president were extrava-

> * Sorry, ladies but since none of you has ever held the office, I refuse to neuter the vice president.

gances they wouldn't afford the man who was but a heart attack, stained dress, or bungled burglary away from the Oval Office. Ulysses Grant's second vice president, Henry Wilson, had to borrow money to buy a new suit for his own inauguration.[1]

There was no residency for the vice president. Many veeps rented rooms in hotels in D.C., when they bothered to show up at all. A handful of our nation's second bananas decided to take the oath of office elsewhere. It was cheaper, and they didn't have to watch people checking their timepieces, waiting for the real star of the show. To get an idea of how awkward this could be, imagine a wedding singer opening for Tony Bennett.

The president has always been the figure that all eyes are drawn to. On the night of Abraham Lincoln's assassination, the president was sitting in a special reserved box in Ford's Theater. The crowd was packed with local luminaries. Vice President Andrew Johnson was all alone in a hotel on the corner of Pennsylvania Avenue and Twelfth Street.* A civil servant from the patent office broke the news to him that Lincoln had been shot, and Johnson walked alone, through streets filled with angry mobs, to the White House, hoping that Lincoln would pull through.

* Ford's Theater still stands. Johnson's hotel is history.

Like children, vice presidents were expected to be seen— sometimes as "wreath layers" at minor state funerals—but not heard. Not at length, anyway. John Adams took to speechifying in the Senate. The senators threatened to write an official gag rule into the body's rules.

Even in an era that isn't quite so unkind to VPs, there are still several presidential debates to the one vice-presidential match, which is not nearly as widely watched. The satirical cartoon *Futurama* mocked this by advertising a presidential go-round followed by the vice presidential "yo mamma so fat" contest.

Nor have presidents been kinder to their would-be political

heirs. Harry Truman found himself cut off from FDR. Truman was shocked pale and nearly speechless when he was briefed, as president, about how few nuclear bombs the U.S. government had ready to drop. John Kennedy didn't like Lyndon Johnson and rarely communicated with him.

For the most part, the vice president is expected to support his president and party but not upstage them. That's a tough trick to pull off, even for the best of politicians. It's one of the many reasons that our current veep is always retreating to undisclosed locations.

Some vice presidents seem to fall off the face of the earth altogether. In 1965, musical comedian Tom Lehrer uncorked the song "Whatever Became of Hubert?" "Hubert" was, of course, Hubert Humphrey, former senator from Minnesota and vice president under LBJ. Lehrer wondered:

> *Whatever became of Hubert?*
> *We miss you, so tell us please.*
> *Are you sad? Are you cross? Are you gathering moss*
> *While you wait for the boss to sneeze?*

On the grand scale of vice-presidential indignities—and it is a pretty grand scale—Humphrey didn't have the worst experience. At least he had the goodwill of his party and was able to pick up its nomination in 1968 after Johnson quit the race and Bobby Kennedy was shot and killed. That Humphrey lost to Richard Nixon, a former vice president who had failed to win first the presidency and then the California governor's office, was almost fitting.

The Rodney Dangerfield-like lack of respect for the vice president can be comical at times. Comedian and impressionist Vaughn

Meader's best-selling 1962 record, *The First Family*, had a bit in which a young man asked JFK if his daughter, Caroline, could "come out and play?" Answer:

> PRESIDENT KENNEDY: I'm sorry, young mahn, she cahn't,
> she's in Italy with her mothah.
> YOUNG BOY: Oh . . . Well, then what's Lyndon doing?

It can also have serious implications. When Ronald Reagan was shot, Secretary of State Al Haig erroneously claimed that he was third in line for the presidency and, since George H. W. Bush wasn't yet at the White House, he told reporters, "I'm in control here."

The statement went over like a lead geoduck, and Reagan eventually got himself a new secretary of state. However, let the record show that Bush was not really handed control of the government until he was elected president.*

* There was one sort-of exception to this.

That Great Greek Hope, Spiro Agnew, tried to hold off prosecution for taking kickbacks while governor of Maryland by claiming executive privilege. Nice try, said the Supreme Court, but no cigar. Executive privilege doesn't apply to the vice president.

And speaking of cigars, Woodrow Wilson's vice president, Thomas Marshall, is remembered for two things. One, he finished a senator's pompous refrain, "what this country needs . . ." by saying to Senate clerks that America could really go for a good five-cent stogie. Two, he was sidelined and helpless when Wilson suffered a debilitating stroke.

Mrs. Edith Wilson and White House aides ran the government and kept the president's greatly diminished capacity from the public. They also kept Marshall from seeing Wilson. It turns out the inverse of that old saying applies. The veep is but one massive heart attack away from the Oval Office, true. But: while the president has a pulse, his understudy is so out of luck.

THE DUNCE CAP AND DANIEL WEBSTER

One of the reasons we have a low opinion of the vice presidency is that vice presidents have a low view of it—or so they claim. John Adams said that America "has, in its wisdom, contrived for me the most insignificant office ever the invention of man contrived or his imagination conceived." Lincoln's first vice president, Hannibal Hamlin, complained that his office was "a nullity" and said he felt like "a fifth wheel of a stagecoach"—the spare.

Calvin Coolidge stayed in a suite at the Willard Hotel during his vice presidency. The Willard had been evacuated because of fire, and a marshal didn't want to let him in. Coolidge attempted to pull rank by telling the man that he was talking to the vice president. The marshal asked, "What are you the vice president of?"[2] Soon after the calamity of September 11, former vice president Al Gore was selected for the privilege of undergoing "extra screening," twice—on the same trip.[3]

John Nance "Cactus Jack" Garner was Speaker of the House and a contender for the presidency in 1932. He lost out to Franklin Roosevelt and agreed to accept the number-two slot, which he later judged to have been "the worst damn fool mistake I ever made." After all, he could have stayed in the House and run the place. Garner was a Texan and a vulgarian, which may be why his description of the vice presidency has stayed in people's heads.

When Lyndon Johnson called him up to solicit his advice, Garner told LBJ not to settle for the vice presidency. He explained that the job wasn't worth "a pitcher of warm piss."* Even in its

bowdlerized form, a warm bucket of spit, Garner's image proved too apt and too earthy to be forgotten. It gave expression to people's prejudice about the office.

* The newspapermen took the piss out of it.

Granted, they had some reason to think badly of the vice presidency. The vice president of any major corporation—the executive vice president, not the slot for the CEO's daft nephew—has considerably more formal power than the vice president of the United States. The corporate vice president can hire and fire a lot of people and make decisions that affect the future of the corporation. It's not earth-shattering if a private-sector veep has to step in for the boss for a few months. If the vice president of the United States does it, we have problems.

Also granted, the idea of the worthless vice president is deeply rooted in this country's history. John Adams we might be able to write off. He was one of the nation's dourest founders—stubborn, quarrelsome, and almost constitutionally incapable of having a good time. Biographer James Grant was right to call him a party of one. But on the vice presidency, future generations of Americans would agree with Adams.

Daniel Webster was an attorney and statesman who cut a large figure in American politics from the 1820s to the 1850s. He served as a representative, senator, and secretary of state and was thus prime veep material. Webster was twice offered the vice presidency on Whig tickets and twice turned it down.

"I do not propose to be buried until I am dead," he explained.

That remark is trotted out as evidence of Webster's wit and ambition, as well as of the general worthlessness of the vice presidency. But it should instead be used to illustrate Webster's foolish pride and bloody awful bad luck. The men at the top of the tickets he declined to join were William Henry Harrison and Zachary Taylor. They both proceeded to die in office, Harrison after less than a month on the job. In Webster's place, the party nominated John Tyler and Millard Fillmore—that is, *Presidents* Tyler and Fillmore.

IT'S ALWAYS RAINY IN SEATTLE

You could dismiss the vice presidency as a bad joke, a constitutional hiccup, a bit of parliamentary tomfoolery, and an insignificant office to boot. You could also smash your big toe with a hammer. In the long run, turning your back to the vice presidents may be slightly more painful. Adams disparaged his office, but he also said something about it that is far less often remembered: "I am nothing, but I may be everything."[4]

The disparaging pronouncements of our vice presidents tell one story, the facts of history a slightly more complicated and interesting tale. The first two vice presidents were elected president outright, and twelve more veeps would end up, by hook or by crook, in the White House, running things. The vice presidency has supplied a third of our presidents. For that reason alone, it's worth losing sleep over.

The ratio of vice presidents to presidents actually understates the importance of the vice presidency. The office caused two major constitutional crises before a single president had croaked, first when Jefferson's running mate, Aaron Burr, just happened to secure the same number of votes in the electoral college, and then when Burr shot Alexander Hamilton in a duel.

Most savvy political observers will concede that much but then explain that the Twelfth Amendment, which created separate ballots for president and vice president, changed things. Then, the vice president was the heir apparent and a possible political opponent of the president. Now, he's from the same political party as the president, and the vice president can claim no larger constituency.

Somebody forgot to tell that story to the vice presidents, apparently. Our veeps have a tendency to go their own way as president, upsetting political coalitions and the party faithful and reshaping American society in the process.

John Tyler was drummed out of his own party for opposing key Whig legislation. Andy Johnson was reviled by the Republicans, impeached, and nearly removed from office. Teddy Roosevelt started a war within his own party between progressive reformers and the business class. LBJ jettisoned the cautious triangulation of JFK to launch the New Deal Part Deux and also that little misadventure in Vietnam.

In fact, an ambitious poli-sci grad student casting about for a thesis topic to make his faculty advisor's head explode might argue that the real trouble started when we began looking at vice presidents as running mates rather than as institutionalized opponents.

Just think: the Adams-Jefferson rivalry had been right out there in the open, and it had the salutary effect of encouraging opposition to both men's worrisome ideas. Adams signed the Alien and Sedition Acts, but they were hated and didn't last long.* Jefferson was not allowed to drag the United States into the French Revolution. And Adams understood that if push came to shove, he could always count on Jefferson voting against him in the Senate.

* Imagine an alternate history where the Twelfth Amendment was never ratified and the 2000 elections made George W. Bush president and Al Gore vice president, and Vice President Gore proceeded to rail against the PATRIOT Act and the Iraq war, and you can get some idea what this must have been like.

In contrast, Aaron Burr campaigned for Jefferson and helped to secure crucial support in New York. He also, Jefferson believed, plotted and schemed and looked for ways to undermine his president. Thus the tie vote that had to be sorted out by the House of Representatives. Thus the grudging support for Jefferson from his old rival, Alexander Hamilton. Thus the Twelfth Amendment. Thus the duel.

Vice presidents ever since have been more guarded about their ambitions, but those ambitions didn't disappear. Far from it. Veeps have taken to poor-mouthing their own office for roughly the same reason that Seattleites play up how much it rains in their fair city.

Seattleites do it to scare off as many wealthy Californians as possible. Vice presidents do it so that we won't too closely scrutinize them. They want us to vote for or against the top of the ticket and consider the potential vice president just some guy who's along for the ride—and forget that he might just luck into the presidency.

MANCHURIAN MANDATES

You would expect that the vice president's potential power and relatively low profile would breed suspicion, and, lo, it has. Of course, many portrayals of the vice presidents in film and fiction are comical or even tragicomic. In the movie *Dave*—which must have been inspired by Thomas Marshall's dilemma—a president suffers a brain aneurism, and his cronies recruit a nobody (Kevin Kline) who looks and sounds enough like their boss to play the part. They even attempt to pin all of the corruption of the administration on the poor, upstanding vice president.

More recently, the *American Idol* send-up, *American Dreamz*, featured Willem Dafoe as a scheming, bumbling presidential advisor to a George W. Bushian politician (Dennis Quaid)—a cross between key Bush advisor Karl Rove and Vice President Cheney. John Hoynes (Tim Matheson), the first vice president on *The West Wing*, used the position as a salve to treat the pain of losing out to Jed Bartlett (Martin Sheen) for the Democratic nomination and the presidency. He used the office to score with women, announced that there was life on Mars, and eventually resigned in disgrace.

Then there are the darker portrayals of our veeps. At this writing, the wildly popular television drama *24* is being driven by a vice president's attempts to wrest control of the government from an insufficiently militaristic president. It is the second time in the show's six-year run that a vice president has schemed to take over the government.

Nor are things likely to be better in our fictional future. On the sci-fi television novel *Babylon 5*, Morgan Clark (Gary McGurk) was the vice president of the Earth Alliance who rose to the presidency by arranging the assassination of the president—by destroying *Earth Force One* (think *Air Force One* only with booster rockets).

Echoing Johnson's ascension to the presidency, Clark was sworn in on *Earth Force Two*. He proceeded to seize on dubious evidence to make war on everybody under the suns. Clark tried to purge the earth of all extraterrestrial influence, declared martial law, started a civil war, and set a self-destruct mechanism in motion to blow up the Earth right after he had committed suicide.

The harsher treatments of vice presidents owe a huge debt to that paranoid masterpiece of a movie *The Manchurian Candidate*. Based on the 1959 novel by Richard Condon, the 1962 Frank Sinatra vehicle played into the nation's fears of communism and the upper class's obsession with McCarthyism, and succeeded beyond belief.

It had all the elements of great psychological thrillers. A troop of soldiers that had been captured in the Korean War were taken to Manchuria and thoroughly brainwashed, with the intent of affecting domestic American politics. The Communists created a murderous war hero who would shoot the candidate for president, and thus put the vice-presidential nominee of that party—a Joe McCarthy knockoff, who was really the puppet of the Red Chinese—into power.

The movie was groundbreaking because it took all the institutions that Americans were comfortable with and inverted them. A decorated war hero was the gunman, and he escaped suspicion by donning clerical garb. Anti-Communists were really tools of the Red Menace. Angela Lansbury, the strong, kindly mother, was revealed as an evil mastermind. And the greatest threat to the Republic came from a shoo-in candidate for vice president, of all people.

In fact, when *The Manchurian Candidate* was remade in 2004, its bias against the vice president was even more pronounced. Rather than the Communists, the bad guys this time around were defense contractors. The company was clearly a knockoff of Halliburton, the corporation where Dick Cheney served as CEO before he became vice president.

PARANOID PRESCIENCE

Without conceding that paranoiacs are correct in every particular, we might want to admit that they're on to something. The vice president has a lot more power than was given him by the Constitution or by statute. His ability to shape American politics is substantial, and substantially overlooked.

Take the 1960s.* The contestants in 1960 were sitting vice president Richard Nixon and senator John Kennedy, whose surprisingly large showing for the number-two slot among Democrats at the 1956 convention made him a contender for the top of the ticket. Nixon lost, but he went on to a two-term presidency. In 1964, Kennedy's vice president easily won, and LBJ's nearly invisible vice president got the party's nod after antiwar senator Eugene McCarthy shamed the self-assured Texan into retirement.

* Please.

In the 1970s, another vice president (Gerald Ford) would assume the presidency, and two vice-presidential nominees (Walter Mondale and Bob Dole) would each eventually have the nominations of their respective parties. If one even has a reasonable shot at the vice presidency, he can go on to wield considerable influence.

Many a vice-presidential historian will claim that his guy was the one who *really* brought in the modern vice presidency. Nixon was "the first" to play a larger role in foreign policy. Walter Mondale had an "actual office" in the White House. Critics allege that Dick Cheney ordered a plane shot down on September 11 while President Bush was reading *The Pet Goat* to Florida schoolchildren.

These data don't point so much to the creeping power of the vice presidency as its elusiveness. If we wanted to create an office to trade prestige for ambition—a drunk tank for the power mad— we'd probably concoct something like the modern vice presidency.

The vice president is so close to power that he can smell its aftershave. He receives the same briefings every day that the president does, is a statutory member of the National Security Council, sits in cabinet meetings, and presides over Congress, where he can cast historic votes if things get close. But the office comes with frustrations and limitations.

The very act of accepting the vice presidency imposes constraints. In public, the veep has to play the part of loyal soldier, even when that loyalty costs him with constituents. He can't really sponsor legislation or swap votes for special projects, nor can he propose his own budget to Congress. His powers of patronage are limited. The president might seek the vice president's advice, but there's no political reason he should accept it.

And yet, presidents *do* frequently take their number two's advice. Vice presidents *do* play a vital role in lobbying Congress and twisting arms for that crucial vote, and then topping it off with their own ballot.

Vice presidents are in great demand by their parties' apparatuses and civic and policy groups to deliver speeches, and can usually count on a reporter or two taking their words down for posterity. They find ways to use the limitations of their office to their advantage and to collect political chits along the way that come in handy for future runs at the White House—assuming the president serves out his full term.

THE ALWAYS-EVOLVING VICE PRESIDENCY

While it would be an exaggeration to say that the vice presidency is what he makes of it, the vice president's intentions do play a role. Martin Van Buren muscled his way into the office and used it as a springboard to the presidency. Burr might have done the same if he hadn't shot Hamilton.

Henry Wilson used his tenure as vice president to finish and publicize a multivolume history of the struggle over abolishing slavery. Charles Dawes took the occasion of his inaugural address to wag his finger at Congress, which wagged its collective finger right back by engineering an important tie vote in the Senate while he was taking a nap. Andy Johnson used his seventeen minutes of fame to deliver a ridiculous drunken harangue that embarrassed everybody; President Lincoln had the Senate sergeant at arms restrain him from any further speechifying that day.

Richard Nixon performed ably for Eisenhower, serving as a roving superambassador who was nearly torn limb from limb in Venezuela. His memoir of the period was appropriately titled *Six Crises*.

Al Gore and Dan Quayle both took a beating in their first vice-presidential debates but then went on to perform reasonably well, though Gore had to deal with scandal accusations, and Quayle had an entire doe-in-the-headlights "you're no Jack Kennedy" thing to overcome. They also managed to push key issues into the national debate—global warming, in Gore's case; family values, in Quayle's.

These things are hard to measure and are subject to second guesses because the power of the vice presidency can wax or wane within any single administration, but it is one contention of this book that the office of the vice president is becoming more powerful. The average veep today has more authority than the veeps of the nineteenth century, and that trend is likely to continue.

The current vice president is a great example of the office's growing power. Political scientists have compared Cheney's role in the Bush administration to prime minister. There's something to that. His entry at the United States Vice Presidential Museum speaks of the "immense trust that President Bush has placed in him, potentially making him the most active vice president in history." No less an authority, former vice president Walter Mondale has weighed in to acknowledge and to complain about Cheney's great responsibility.

More radical critics of the Bush administration have gone further, painting Cheney as the real power behind the throne—the puppet master, the beast, and the antichrist rolled into one.

Fears of what Cheney would do in the Oval Office have also influenced how congressional Democrats, now in the majority, deal with the executive. Many conservatives balked at handing the federal government over to Al Gore during the Clinton administration's impeachment crisis. Now, some liberal opponents of the Bush administration calculate that President Cheney would be far worse. As one wag put it: "Dick Cheney wouldn't push the button; he *is* the button."

Whether or not the fears are justified, they do give us another example of how the vice presidency is constantly changing. For all their savvy, the American founders never would have dreamt that the president would one day use the vice president as a human shield. They might even have frowned on the idea.

THIS IS REALLY THREE BOOKS FOR THE PRICE OF ONE. FIRST, IT details the history of an office that has been the unacknowledged San Andreas Fault of American politics. Second, it pays close attention to the office's more colorful characters. Third, it looks at the vice president in American culture. It starts where all quests for the vice president should start, with a trip to the Vice Presidential Museum. Welcome, one and all, to *The Warm Bucket Brigade*.

1

SEARCHING FOR NUMBER TWO

How many of you have ever heard of the Soviet Union?

—Daniel Johns

The men's room at the United States Vice Presidential Museum is in fine working order—really—but its patrons are still in for a bit of a shock when they look up to see a large photo of 1980s era Dan Quayle hanging on the wall. Photo Quayle is doing what the Real-Life Quayle would have done here: looking the other way, making the best of an awkward situation.

Your correspondent pulled into the museum in late February. It's not that easy to reach, because the airport at Huntington, Indiana, is too small for commercial airlines to bother. Given the options, it seemed best to fly to Indianapolis, rent a car, and drive northeast about one hundred miles. It had snowed earlier in the week, and the fields and lawns reflected the overcast glare back at me, adding annoyance to the gloom.

So readers can probably understand why the Quayle photo made such a strong impression on me: whenever you travel to some place new, you best remember the first thing you focus on.

The bathroom also had a rather good painting of a bend in the Salamonie River, as well as another vast pic of Quayle and Bush Sr. standing on a porch. I considered venturing into the ladies' room to check out the art there—in the interest of good journalism, of course*—but thought better of it.

I arrived on a Thursday. Executive Director Daniel Johns was going to give me an official tour the next day but I wanted to drop in and case the joint. The museum has two floors. The top floor is devoted to Huntington's most famous son, while the bottom floor strains to contain all the other vice presidents.

* The people have a right to know.

The exhibits downstairs strike a better balance of the high and the low than most political museums, with a mix of original artifacts, campaign trinkets, newspaper clippings, and old magazines from more playful times. Want to read an original account of George Washington's and John Adams's annual salaries?** The Museum of the Vice Presidency has got that, along with typed and handwritten letters by vice presidents, and more.

** Washington: $25,000; Adams: $5,000.

Some of the highlights for me, were

- a vinyl record titled *Spiro T. Agnew Speaks Out*
- an issue of *People* magazine featuring Walter and Joan Mondale sporting matching periwinkle turtlenecks

- a restored porcelain pitcher pitching Levi P. Morton
  for vice president
- a white souvenir jacket from the 1985 inaugural,
  monogrammed for "Tony"—whoever he might be
- a $100 ticket to a 1954 fund-raising dinner in
  Milwaukee. Featured speaker: Richard Nixon

Each vice president has his own exhibit with a description of
his tenure in office and at least one original artifact.

Space is limited. The Gerald Ford exhibit is stuck around an
odd corner, and Nelson Rockefeller's can be found above the water
fountain. A historical timeline of veep lives set against major world
events has been shoehorned in.

THEY GREW UP IN AN INDIANA TOWN

Near the front of the display area, off to the left as you're coming in, is a special exhibit that celebrates Indiana's special status
in the veepstakes. With five vice presidents—Schuyler Colfax,
Thomas Hendricks, Charles Fairbanks, Thomas Marshall, and
Quayle—Indiana is the second most vice-presidential state in
the Union.

State Highway 9 is known as the "highway of the vice presidents" because it connects the historic homes of Quayle, Hendricks,
and Marshall. In 1916, both Republicans and Democrats had
Hoosiers at the bottom of the ticket. Only the far more populous
New York has produced more second bananas.

The vice presidency is a marker both of Indiana's past influence and its frustrations. Not one of its five veeps went on to

become president or even receive presidential nominations. The Indiana Five seem almost cursed in retrospect.

Colfax was finished off by a minor scandal and knocked off the ticket for Grant's second term. Hendricks had a national election stolen right out from under him. Fairfax fell victim to party infighting and then failed to win back the vice presidency. Marshall should have become president, but he was kept out of the White House by a scheming coterie of Wilson advisors and the first lady, as well as his own sense of decency.

D-DAY AND DAN QUAYLE

As I ventured upstairs, the first thing I saw was Quayle's smiling mug again. This one was attached to a body. The life-sized photo mockup, circa 1988, is dressed in a navy blue blazer, white button-down shirt, and red tie with blue ornaments.

It's the sort of carnival prop that people set up so that you can say not so much "I had my picture taken with Dan Quayle!" but rather, "Look, I had my picture taken with this life-size cutout of Dan Quayle!"

The Quayle floor of the Museum has many of the same features as the ground floor but considerably more space. On the whole, it works, but the larger palette produces some oddities. Where the timeline of all the vice presidents is compact, Quayle's is almost garrulous. It sets Quayle family history against world events like so:

D-Day, the allies invade France at the beaches in
Normandy —June 6, 1944

After a massive secret research and development
program, U.S. scientists exploded the world's first atom
bomb in New Mexico —July 1945

James Danforth Quayle was born at Methodist Hospital
in Indianapolis —Feb. 4, 1947

Both floors feature videos that loop continuously. In keeping
with the museum's organizational scheme, the downstairs has a
catch-all documentary about the vice presidency, while upstairs
you get *The Quayle Story: the Boy, the Man, the Vice President*.

The film is upbeat but hardly hagiography—which serves as a
good description of the whole Quayle collection. Visitors can
watch the start of the so-called "battle of Huntington": reporters
peppered the freshly minted vice-presidential nominee with questions about his service in the National Guard as the locals booed
and jeered the effete East Coast snobs. They can learn about Nick's
Kitchen, the local watering hole where Quayle first decided to run
for office and launched all his subsequent, successful campaigns.

MET THE SK8ER BOI

Visitors can also observe Quayle's mother, Martha Quayle, vouch-
ing for her son's determination in a way that only mothers can:
by relating an embarrassing anecdote. When he was a young lad,
Quayle was given a pair of roller skates and was determined to
learn how to use them.

He had a hard time of it and fell a lot. She kept thinking,

Gosh, isn't he going to give up? But he didn't. No matter how many times he wiped out, he got right back up and kept at it until he could skate like a Roller Derby champ.

The display cases are full of items that represent the progression of Quayle's life from child (Little League uniform, second-grade report card) to lawyer (law school diploma—partially eaten by family pooch, Barnaby) to paterfamilias (photo of the Quayles posing with Ronald Reagan in the Oval Office) to politician (decorated golf bag presented to "Senator Dan Quayle") and, finally, to vice president (gavel that Quayle used to preside over the 1992 Republican National Convention).

Quayle's gaffes and failures aren't overlooked. His dismal performance in the first vice-presidential debate is there, as is the National Guard controversy, the "potatoe" incident, the *Murphy Brown* controversy, and every other major flap and farrago.

You are also reminded that Quayle was a giant-killer with unusually good aim. When he entered politics, it was against the advice of all of his friends. He didn't run for an open seat but instead challenged a sitting congressman and won in an upset. In 1980, at thirty-three, he defeated three-term incumbent Birch Bayh, who had been considered presidential timber until the young upstart cut him down. Quayle then went on to win reelection by the widest margin in state history.

Dan Quayle was elevated to vice president in 1989 at forty-one, making him the third-youngest veep ever. The national reaction to his candidacy was surprise and befuddlement. The local reaction tended more toward pride and defensiveness.

In the speech to his hometown, announcing his nomination as vice president, Quayle expressed his gratitude to the people of

Huntington for their basic goodness and decency. He praised them when the whole nation was watching.

LONG ISLAND VICE P

Those words had a lasting effect. Driving into Huntington today, you'll see a blue-and-white road sign that reads "WELCOME TO HUNTINGTON HOME OF THE 44TH VICE PRESIDENT DAN QUAYLE," even though Quayle has long since relocated to Arizona.

There are numerous "Quayle sightings" plaques around town, manufactured at the behest of the Dan Quayle Foundation, to indicate places that the former vice president used to frequent.

At one such haunt, Nick's Kitchen, you can still order a Quayle Burger—half a pound of ground chuck with grilled onions, lettuce, and tomatoes with fries—for $7.25.* The burger wasn't Quayle's regular; it was named by the restaurant owner in 1988 on the theory that every successful politician needs a delicious gut bomb named after him.

* Warning: avoid the butterscotch pie.

And, of course, there's the museum, a former Christian Science church. It's located at the edge of downtown in a handsome, two-story, painted brick building adorned with double classical columns. The multiple doors in front once made it easy for large crowds to enter and exit. Now only one door opens, and an agent of the museum collects entry fees. The upstairs retains the open area, usually filled by rows of metal folding chairs, and an elevated stage with pulpit.

It's hard to imagine that pulpit gets pounded much these days.

Executive Director Daniel Johns is a candid, soft-spoken guy with graying hair and a background in civil war history, public relations, and child education. ("I'm a mutt," he confessed.) One of his previous posts was at a children's museum.

His current place of employment is "becoming known as an educational museum," which means that everything is going according to plan—sort of.

When Johns came to the museum, he considered two facts: first, that Huntington is so remote that it might as well be in Canada, and second, that museums get the bulk of their visitors in the summer. He decided he'd best come up with some way to reach larger audiences for the other nine months of the year.

So: schools. Classes from Indiana schools are regularly bussed in, and Johns also takes the show on the road. He estimates that between the bussing and the road show, about eight thousand students a year learn about the vice presidents through the museum's programs.

The traveling exhibition is very popular in Long Island, New York, for some reason—perhaps because of that state's record number of veeps.

CHECKING OUT THE VEEPS

As Johns walked me through the museum, he filled me in on its history. The Huntington Public Library hosted an exhibit on the vice presidency of Quayle in 1993, and that led to the creation of the Dan Quayle Center and Museum.

The Quayle Foundation decided to expand it into a full museum for all of the vice presidents, which has been largely the product of Johns's efforts. He acquired most of the non-Quayle artifacts and built the wooden display cases himself.

The museum is "not all that well-known" to the "common person," Johns admitted, in part because it can't afford a large advertising campaign. "To do that would essentially break us," he said. The museum's total budget is about $125,000 a year. It is funded in large part by an annual local celebrity golf tournament that Quayle comes back to take part in.

Other recent vice presidents or their estates have been reluctant to pitch in. Johns characterized their collective contributions as "only bits and pieces," though with the minimal acquisitions budget, he's happy to have those bits.

Ford's people sent a few pieces. The library of the University of Maryland chipped in with Agnew items. Cheney has donated the odd item and pledged that he will consider making a larger gift once he's left office.

Johns has enjoyed the challenge of taking a young institution and trying to grow it into something larger. He's had some success. The downstairs gallery feels cramped, true. But that's better than being too sparse. The vice-presidential memorabilia on display represents about half the items available. The Quayle items are about one-tenth of what could be shown.

BOUGHT IT ON EBAY

According to Johns, Quayle wrote a memo to the museum after he had donated his personal papers and such, saying, roughly, "Don't waste time with my baby pictures. People won't care."

However, Johns has found that people respond best to a good

blend of the high and the low. With Quayle and with the other vice presidents, he's tried to find unique stories and colorful items to grab your attention and keep it.

Given American schoolchildren's general ignorance of history, that's not an easy thing to accomplish. Johns told me that when he asks children, "How many of you have ever heard of the Soviet Union?" they look at him blankly.

He illustrated the point by pointing to an official portrait of Mikhail Gorbachev, sans the famous mark-of-the-beast-sized birthmark, and asking, "What's missing?" Few of the students who come through the museum know the answer.

Creative storytellers can break through where historians fail, and Johns is determined to connect with his mostly younger audience. His selection of artifacts evinces a certain playfulness that children are bound to notice and maybe even—who knows?—appreciate.

One item that Johns ranks among his favorites is a cover of *Puck* magazine from 1907. The caricaturist made Charles Fairbanks into a "charlie bear," as a way of contrasting the aristocratic Fairbanks with rival Theodore Roosevelt, after whom the teddy bear was named. The point about Fairbanks is deftly made: there was nothing huggable (or bearlike) about him.

He pointed to some of the other items that he's especially proud of. Charles Dawes wrote the musical number titled "Melody in A Major." It was later paired with words for the song "It's All in the Game," Tommy Edwards's biggest hit.

The record is currently on display along with an original program from Henry Wilson's funeral (which Johns managed to snag for six dollars on eBay) and a letter by William Wheeler, written in ornate, nigh indecipherable cursive that Johns had to translate for me.

HOT PINK RETORTS

Johns uses shtick to make obscure history come alive. During the tour of the Quayle wing, he warns students that something ominous happened to the future vice president while he was at law school and then affects concern about laying such heavy knowledge on impressionable young minds. They of course demand to know what it was.

Johns acted out his response for me, mock biting his knuckle and saying, "He—" dramatic pause—"got married."

He hopes the jokes help young people remember the vice presidents. Of Marilyn Quayle's inaugural ball gown, he tells the kids, "If you stand in front of the dress case just right, it looks like you're wearing it."

I wondered about a photo of Dan Quayle in hot pink shorts, running in a race for a medical charity. "Those were cool colors for that year," he answered gallantly.

Johns sends classes on scavenger hunts through the museum with lists of questions, from the crushingly obvious to real brain teasers. This forces students to invest time and energy, both mental and physical, in the vice presidency, he explains, creating the outside possibility that they will be excited by what has been unfairly assumed to be the world's most boring constitutional office.

I had to ask: Have the students ever broken anything? Johns started to answer but then hesitated. He explained that he was "going to say no," but couldn't say that in good conscience.

Certainly no "exhibit" has so far been destroyed, he said, and then rapped his knuckle on a wooden countertop for good luck. Of course, it helped that all the glass in the display cases is really clear plastic. But for the most part the kids have been well behaved.

One actual glass shelf in the gift shop was shattered, however. Johns had just finished the look-but-don't-touch-or-you-might-hurt-yourself-and-bleed-all-over-the-exhibits spiel. And then, predictably, he heard it:

Smash!

As he related the story to me, Johns looked pained, as though he'd just swallowed a wasp. I wouldn't have wanted to be the accidental vandal that day.

BEYOND THE QUAYLE

Toward the end of the tour, he talked about how people view the museum. Preconceptions play a shockingly large role. For years many visitors—especially those from out of state—came expecting either "a shrine to Vice President Quayle" or a political freak show.

They'd challenge Johns, "I bet you don't have the potatoe," or "So, where's the Quayle-Bentsen debate?" They weren't quite sure how to react when he pointed out that those things were there—loud and proud.

Johns told me that media coverage, at least, has become slightly less silly. Reporters have focused less on the novelty of having a museum devoted to the vice presidents and more on what it has to present.

The editors of the tourism Web site RoadSideAmerica.com went into the museum with a snarky attitude. "The museum's slogan is 'Second to One,' but can any display or artifact disprove the notion that the veep is the vestigial organ of national politics?" they wondered. Johns's collection at least caused them to give some grudging respect to "that happy-go-lucky golfer-son-of-a-gun."[1]

Johns showed me a few reasonably positive mentions, including an *AARP* magazine clip, and related a surprise that he received when he was lecturing to students. A man who poked his head up above the top of the stairs, Johns recognized as Ed Roush—the incumbent Democratic congressman Quayle trounced in 1980.

I asked why he came to work at the museum. Johns gave personal and professional reasons. It allowed him to be close to a sick family member and allowed him the opportunity to shape a growing institution.

He stays because he has more than a passing interest in the subject. He told me that he's one of the last men standing who can name all the vice presidents, though I never thought to make the obvious retort: "Okay, go!"

One of his challenges in crafting the historical narratives of all of the veeps is "keep politics out of it." The future of the museum will have to be less Quayle-centric. For this to happen, other vice presidents will have to step up with donations and even speak there on occasion. The way to secure their cooperation will be to stick around for a while and—more importantly—to tell their stories well.

The museum's task of securing vice-presidential donations is made more difficult for one obvious institutional reason: about one-third of the vice presidents go on to become presidents and get their very own taxpayer-funded library and museum. This gives them little incentive to break up their personal collections.

Vanity and regret are also obstacles. Every vice president is but one heartbeat away from his very own museum. Many veeps who fail to transition to the White House continue to think that political comebacks are imminent—that fate will break their way for once.

Stern-headed realists might want to disabuse them of that notion, but it would be the realists who are full of it. As the story of the vice presidency shows, almost anything is possible.

A TITLE IN SEARCH
OF A JOB
DESCRIPTION

*A more tranquil and
unoffending station could not
have been found for me.*
—THOMAS JEFFERSON

*If he is elected, murder, robbery,
rape, adultery and incest will
be openly taught and practiced.*
—JOHN ADAMS

The Constitution originally gave the vice president, as vice president, precisely one duty. He shall be "the President of the Senate but shall have no Vote, unless they be equally divided." It did not spell out what being president of the Senate meant, which proved highly embarrassing for our first vice president, John Adams.

Adams had helped to edit the Declaration of Independence and served his country ably as an advocate, bureaucrat, and the diplomat who gained America its first formal recognition, from the Netherlands.* Perhaps his greatest gift to America was the

* You take 'em where you can get 'em.

model of three distinct branches of government, which was imported from the state constitution of Massachusetts that he had drafted.

Our first veep was worldly-wise and Harvard educated. He had hobnobbed with royalty and gotten the better of sharp-tongued Parisian ladies.[1] But if Adams thought he could decide what duties the office of the vice president entailed, he had another thing coming.

He went in thinking that his position of the president of the Senate meant that he was in charge. The Senate thought other-wise, especially after Adams made it a top priority to devise grander titles for Washington. "What will the common people of foreign countries, what will the sailors and soldiers say?" he thundered. "George Washington, president of the United States, they will despise him to all eternity."[2]

After forty minutes of this, senators concluded that Adams was not only a closet monarchist but also something of a buffoon. As it turned out, "president" was grand enough for Mr. Washington, thank goodness. Just imagine what the foreigners, sailors, and soldiers would have made of "His High Mightiness," just one of Adams's highfalutin titles.

As the drafter of the Massachusetts constitution, Adams should have seen one of the problems of his office a mile away. There is supposed to be a separation of powers between the three branches of government. However, the veep is a creature both of the executive and legislative branches.

Senators objected to Adams introducing legislation as vice

president, rather than as president of the Senate, and they were infuriated by his incessant oratory from the floor. While George Washington was setting one precedent after another for the presidency, Adams was trying to do the same for the vice presidency and getting slapped down.

By 1790, Adams had admitted defeat. He agreed to style himself "John Adams, Vice President of the United States and President of the Senate." Also, faced with the threat of being officially gagged, he agreed instead to hold his tongue.[3]

A minor constitutional crisis was thus averted. From that point onward, every vice president has been president of the Senate only from a procedural point of view, though a few veeps have flexed those procedural muscles.

PARTY HEARTY

Adams did excel in one vice-presidential role: he was a tie-breaker the likes of which the Senate has never seen since, casting 31 in all. He could cast that many decisive votes because (1) important questions were being hashed out in those early days of the Republic, and (2) the various and sundry factions were trying to pretend that they weren't organized factions.

In his farewell address, President Washington warned against "potent engines, by which cunning, ambitious, and unprincipled men will be enabled to subvert the power of the people, and to usurp for themselves the reins of government; destroying afterwards the very engines, which have lifted them to unjust dominion."[4] In other words: political parties are bad and will lead us to our ruin. Avoid them, people.

Washington was a great unifying figure, certainly. He was the only president ever elected unanimously by the electoral college. Twice. But his purpose in warning the nation against the "potent engines" of political parties was to shore up what amounted to a party. Those pols that wanted a strong national government became known as the Federalists, and Washington was their nominal leader.

That hadn't been his intent. Washington's first administration was something of a national unity government. But most of the president's most contentious decisions—to allow a national bank, to put down the Whiskey rebellion—had broken in a direction that many onetime supporters couldn't abide. Secretary of State Thomas Jefferson's decision to leave the cabinet at the end of 1793 signaled the unstoppable rise of faction.

Jefferson became the head of the Republican Party—not to be confused with Abraham Lincoln's party—which over time became the Democratic-Republican Party and then just the Democratic Party.

COME THE REVOLUTION, WHAT?

In his parting words, Washington also famously warned against "entangling alliances" with foreign nations. That warning was much more closely related to the lament about parties than you might imagine.

The problem was, Britain and France were at war. The United States had won its independence from Britain with the help of French money and support, and many in Jefferson's party wanted the United States to come to the aid of France, even though the monarchy that had funded the colonial upstarts had been deposed and, well, decapitated.

The French Revolution made some Republicans more likely to press for taking France's side. To be fair to them, it took some time for the Revolution to descend into the godless horror show that it became, and accounts of atrocities weren't always reliable. Besides, it's not as if there wasn't some unpleasantness in the United States after the Revolutionary War. The Tories were stripped of their possessions and exiled to Canada.

Federalists seized on Republican support of the French Revolution to paint them as a bunch of dangerous, bloodthirsty anarchists. Adams warned that if Jefferson was elected, "murder, robbery, rape, adultery and incest will be openly taught and practiced."[5]

It was an unfair jab, but Jefferson had led with his chin on the subject. About Shay's Rebellion, a violent debtors' revolt in Massachusetts in the 1780s that was one of the causes of the con-

stitutional convention, he had written, "A little rebellion now and then is a good thing . . . What signify a few lives lost in a century or two? The tree of liberty must be refreshed from time to time, with the blood of patriots and tyrants. It is its natural manure."[6]

The Federalists could have replied, "Well, manure is one word for it." The Republicans' support for revolution in the

Adams: Returned fire

abstract helped to reinforce the charges that Federalists worked to perpetuate about them: they were reckless; they were lawless; they were Jacobins. They were the French party.

The Federalists, because of their tilt away from France, their pomp, and their efforts to create a powerful central government run by a strong executive, found themselves disparaged as monarchists. First we had King George; then we had George Washington.

However, in one surprisingly nonmonarchial gesture, Washington had insisted on retiring after two terms. That made the election of 1796 a referendum on the Federalist vision for the future of the country with all its warts versus the Republican vision with all its uncertainties.

Public opinion had initially been rather pro-France, but then two things happened. First, the French overplayed their hand. Edmond-Charles Genêt was dispatched to the United States to ask our government for support. Instead, he worked to raise a private army. Second, the Terror changed many Americans' minds about the nature of the French Revolution.

The struggle looked increasingly to voters like a fight that we'd best stay out of. Washington's government declared neutrality and pursued treaties with Britain and Spain that were unrelated to the war. Adams promised more of the same; Jefferson was an uncharted course. It was a close-run thing in the electoral college, but Adams came out on top.

KNEW WHEN TO HOLD 'EM

Jefferson took the narrow loss well. It helped that he got the vice presidency as a consolation prize. Our second vice president mused to Benjamin Rush, "A more tranquil and unoffending station could not have been found for me."[7]

He wasn't just turning that frown upside down. Unlike Adams, he didn't fret too much over the paucity of formal powers of his office. He was happy to have the needed income that it provided along with a job that had an inside track on the presidency. To pass the time in the Senate, he put together the *Manual of Parliamentary Practice* that is still consulted today.

Give the man credit—he knew when to hold 'em. Jefferson knew that the Federalists had no one to replace Washington in the public affection. He knew that Adams was "distrustful, obstinate, excessively vain, and takes no counsel from anyone," and would likely overreach.[8] A canny student of human nature, he also must have guessed that personality conflicts in the Federalist Party were likely to tear it apart.

The overreach didn't take long. In a frenzy of anti-French activism not matched until the Freedom Fries farrago, Federalists passed the Alien and Sedition Acts in 1798.

The Acts extended the waiting period for citizenship from five to fourteen years, enabled the president to expel any alien from a country with which America is at war, enabled the president to expel any alien judged a risk to the United States, and—despite the First Amendment—made it a crime to diss the government, with one really big exception. I'm normally against long block quotes, but I beg the reader's indulgence, because you've really got to see this one for yourself:

> That if any person shall write, print, utter, or publish, or shall cause or procure to be written, printed, uttered or published,

or shall knowingly and willingly assist or aid in writing, printing, uttering or publishing any false, scandalous and malicious
writing or writings against the government of the United
States, or either house of the Congress of the United States,
or the President of the United States, with intent to defame
the said government, or either house of the said Congress, or
the said President, or to bring them, or either of them, into
contempt or disrepute; or to excite against them, or either or
any of them, the hatred of the good people of the United
States, or to excite any unlawful combinations therein, for
opposing or resisting any law of the United States, or any act
of the President of the United States, done in pursuance of
any such law, or of the powers in him vested by the constitution of the United States, or to resist, oppose, or defeat any
such law or act, or to aid, encourage or abet any hostile designs
of any foreign nation against the United States, their people
or government, then such person, being thereof convicted
before any court of the United States having jurisdiction
thereof, shall be punished by a fine not exceeding two thousand dollars, and by imprisonment not exceeding two years.[9]

Now, what major figure is missing from that list of protected
politicians? I'm sure that Federalists in Congress left the Republican vice president off the list entirely by accident.

Ultimately, twenty-five Americans were arrested for sedition,
and ten were convicted. One man was fined for wandering into
the wrong bar in Boston during some festivities and loudly, drunk-
enly wishing that one of those cannonballs going off in the background would "hit Adams in the ass."[10]

Jefferson and father of the Constitution James Madison*
worked behind the scenes to overturn the Acts, which they held to
be unconstitutional, under both the Tenth
and First Amendments. They engineered the
Kentucky and Virginia Resolutions, which
advanced the theory that the United States
was a compact between the states, and that individual states had the
right to nullify unconstitutional federal legislation. The theory of
nullification became popular in the South and, after many twists
and turns led three generations later to the Civil War.

* Boy, there's a duo that you wouldn't want to have working against you.

Madison and Jefferson's behind-the-scenes efforts helped to
end the Acts. There was also, of course, the presidential election
of 1800.

HAMILTON'S REVENGE

The controversy over the Alien and Sedition Acts put President
Adams on the ropes, but it was his long-standing feud with
Alexander Hamilton that delivered the knockout punch.

The two had hated each other at least since the presidential
election of 1788. Electors had been only too happy to give George
Washington, commanding general of the American Revolution,
their unanimous support. Hamilton, Washington's former *aide de
camp* and future treasury secretary, however, insisted that in the
contest for vice president, there should be genuine competition.

Many of the electors in 1789, and again in 1792, cast their
vice-presidential ballots again for Washington or for other candidates, which Adams took as a slight. He thought it a deliberate
plot on Hamilton's part to cause him embarrassment.[11]

That wasn't the sort of thing that Adams was likely to get over, and it was made worse by gnawing jealousy. Adams almost got himself officially gagged by the Senate by advancing what he took to be the interests of President Washington, but he was in no way a player in Washington's government.

Adams didn't help draft the president's speeches, nor did he help to hammer out a lot of the early compromises that came to define the American government. He didn't have the president's ear, as Hamilton did. He loyally supported Washington's policies but believed that his repayment for this was only abuse and more abuse.

This frustration came out in Adams's response when Hamilton was caught in a sex scandal. Adams called Hamilton a "bastard" (true) and a "Creole" (not even close). He also charged that this one case was only one of many indiscretions, for Hamilton emitted "a superabundance of secretions which he could not find whores enough to draw off."[12]

Hamilton gave back as good as he got, albeit unintentionally. He wrote a letter that was intended for private circulation among Federalists. It led off with a lengthy condemnation of Adams and then ended with a surprise endorsement of the condemned. Jefferson's running mate, Aaron Burr, got hold of it and publicized its contents.

With the feud out in the open, Hamilton decided to try to make the Federalist candidate for vice president, Charles Pinckney, president instead of Adams. The maneuver didn't work, but it likely put the Republicans over the top in the must-win state of South Carolina.

The result was a kind of chaos that we'll explore in more detail next chapter. The short version is that Jefferson and his vice presidential candidate, Burr, ended up tying during the first round of ballots in the electoral college. That threw the election to the House of Representatives to decide.

Jefferson never admitted it, but he accepted the deal Hamilton offered him. In trade for becoming president, he would agree to maintain neutrality between France and Britain and would maintain the Bank of the United States and the Navy. After seven days and thirty-five ballots, Hamilton convinced key Federalists to abstain, break the deadlock, and elect Jefferson.

In a show of bad manners that wouldn't be repeated until his own son decided to leave town before Andy Jackson got there, Adams didn't stick around for the inauguration.

Adams came to regret that slight. In a final flourish that would seem corny even in a Frank Capra movie, after the political passions had cooled, the retired Adams and Jefferson struck up a correspondence that bloomed into a friendship, writing each other as often as several times a day.[13] They died almost simultaneously on July 4, 1826, the fiftieth anniversary of the Declaration of Independence. Adams's final words were "Jefferson survives!"

3

WEEHAWKEN WEEKEND WARRIORS

Contemptible, if true.

—AARON BURR

When Hamilton shot Burr, I made a sort of shocked guttural sound from behind the camera: "Iiiieeeepp! . . . What?"

Michael Brendan Dougherty—Alexander Hamilton in our little reenactment—looked back at me with his mischievous grin, pumped his arms and his squirt gun into the air, and yelled, "Alternate history!" He pointed the gun at the camera and repeated the rationalization: "Alternate history."

Rather than argue with him, I called for another take, this time without the revisionism, thank you.

We waited in the parking lot of the ferry terminal in Weehawken, New Jersey, for a helicopter to pass overhead, and then I called: "Ready! Set! Wait!"—the last to caution against Dougherty's hair trigger and sure aim.

Burr: Almost president

And then: "Present!"

Shawn Macomber—playing a dyspeptic Vice President Aaron Burr—fired, but he hadn't pumped enough air into his Super Soaker knockoff. The arc of water barely made it five feet from the nozzle.

Macomber pumped air into the squirt gun to increase his range, and Dougherty inched forward. In a few seconds, they managed to meet in the middle.

Drops of water landed on Dougherty's striped purple-and-black polo shirt, whereupon he mock fell to the ground and delivered a variation on Hamilton's would-have-been final words with all the halting melodrama that William Shatner would have breathed into them:

"It is"—pause—"a mortal wound."

He was such a ham that I couldn't help but laugh. The outcome of that duel that we were reenacting, however, was grim business.

FORGIVING BURR

Hamilton's judgment was correct. The shot did kill him, though not immediately; it took about thirty-six hours. In old Western movies, the worst possible outcome of a gunfight is the "gut shot." Those tended to kill people slowly. The best medical care of the day could only moderate the pain; the poor bastards were almost better off reaching for the Scotch.

When Burr fired the dueling pistol early on the morning of July 11, 1804,[1] the ball hit Hamilton in the stomach, bounced around his organs, and lodged next to his spine. Hamilton pronounced his own fate and passed out.

Dr. David Hosack came running from the nearby brush as soon as the shots rang out. The physician had been hiding because it was necessary for legal reasons that he not actually see the duel, just as it was necessary that the dueling weapons be smuggled there in a container in a secret chamber. Plausible deniability, they call it.

Once the deed was done, the two parties broke up and hurried back across the river to New York. Hamilton's "second" for the duel, Nathaniel Pendleton, and Dr. Hosack revived the critically injured man and brought him to the mansion of William Bayard on Jane Street in Greenwich Village.

Hamilton was given the last rites by Benjamin Moore, president of Columbia College and Episcopal bishop of New York. Before Bishop Moore would give Hamilton Communion, he forced him to consider the gravity of dueling and "the delicate and trying situation in which [Moore] was placed."[2]

Historian Richard Brookhiser writes, "The dying man abjured dueling, confessed his faith in God's mercy through Christ and forgave Burr."[3] Whether or not he was sincere in forgiving Burr, he could be fairly certain the nation never would.

Dueling was serious business then, but not for the reasons that you might suspect. The *Code Duello*[4] forbade deliberately wasting one's shot, as Hamilton did, but that's usually how the game was played. U.S. Vice Presidential Museum executive director Daniel Johns told me that students today have a hard time wrapping their minds around the notion that this wasn't about killing the other guy but restoring honor.

Most duels stopped short of gunfire actually being exchanged, and most duelists deliberately missed. If that was not the case, many of our founders would have died violent deaths.

Hamilton took part in ten bloodless duels, which included such illustrious opponents as John Adams and George Clinton. Hamilton also acted as a second on several occasions.

Then again, every time someone wasted his shot, he had to understand that there was a possibility that his opponent wouldn't. Hamilton had advised his son Philip to deliberately miss before a duel in 1801. Philip fired wide; his opponent's bullet found its mark.[5]*

* Here's a macabre footnote for you: the pistols that Burr and Alexander Hamilton used in the duel were the same set that had been used in the duel that claimed Philip Hamilton's life. Like son, like father.

PLAYING FOR BLOOD

It was no small thing for Bishop Moore to grant absolution. Both ecclesial and civil authorities hated dueling and tried their best to stamp it out.

The Council of Trent had anathematized dueling, condemning the duelists, their seconds, and advisers to automatic excommunication. Pope Benedict XIV forbade Christian burial for duelists, even if they did not die on the dueling field and even if they had been given absolution.[6]

Dueling was condemned or forbidden by James I of England,

Louis XIV of France, Frederick the Great of Prussia, and Joseph II of Austria. In America, Benjamin Franklin condemned the practice, and George Washington disdained it and urged his officers to do the same.

Burr and Hamilton fought the duel in New Jersey rather than in New York, because it was tolerated there, but that didn't stop a New Jersey grand jury from indicting Burr on murder charges.

I went to Weehawken and recruited friends, fellow ink-stained wretches, to reenact Burr-Hamilton because, like Johns's students, I was having a hard time wrapping my mind around this dueling thing. Unlike the students, I understood the not shooting. It was the elevated sense of honor I found vexing.

Where today men might sue, in the past they at least threatened to shoot. So-called gentleman were possessed of a touchy and irritable sense of honor not much different from the Oriental concept of "face." Insults and slights—real, imagined, or manufactured for political reasons—demanded satisfaction, which could not be denied.

The immediate cause of the duel was a letter that the *Albany Register* published on April 24, 1804. It claimed Hamilton had uttered a "despicable" slander against Burr at a political banquet without spelling out the alleged slander.*

* Because, as J. Jonah Jameson reminded us, then it would be libel.

Escalating demands for satisfaction then came from Burr. Hamilton claimed not to know exactly what he had said. How could he be expected to apologize for remarks (1) that he didn't remember and (2) that were never specified?

Burr wasn't having any of it. He pressed his claim to the point of blood, and he got it. It says something about the man's character that when he was informed Hamilton had wasted his shot, which struck a tree branch instead of his opponent, Burr called the act of mercy "contemptible, if true."[7]

AMERICAN CAESAR SALAD

Virginia politician John Randolph wrote that the Burr-Hamilton duel "reminded [him] of a sinking fox pressed by a vigorous old hound."[8] It's a good way of explaining it, but there are complicating details.

First, the explanation: Burr had every reason in the world to want Hamilton dead. To start with, Hamilton was the chief reason Burr was not elected president.

Under the Constitution, each state had two electoral votes. To prevent the concentration of power, no elector could vote for two men from the same state. The candidate with the most electoral votes became president; the candidate with the second-highest total became vice president. But a vote was a vote was a vote. The Constitution provided no way to distinguish between presidential and vice-presidential ballots.

That might not have been a big deal, but the election of 1800 was the second most contentious in our nation's history, and the final count had Jefferson and Burr tied for first with seventy-three electoral votes. It was one of those forehead-slapping moments, where it suddenly became obvious that Article II of the Constitution had "always" been a disaster waiting to happen.

There was no doubt that Jefferson was at the top of the ticket. That's how the campaign had been conceived; that's what people thought they were voting for. But a vote was a vote was a vote, and

Burr, without whom the Republicans wouldn't have won New York, had as much right to be president as Jefferson.

The deadlocked election was turned over to the House of Representatives. For years Hamilton had fulminated against Jefferson as the American Robespierre, and his warnings had had some effect. Many of the Federalists wanted to intervene for Burr to keep Jefferson from power, but Hamilton was determined to prevent this.

Hamilton and Burr were almost mirror images of each other. They were both successful New York lawyers and Revolutionary War heroes, financial profligates, and sexual libertines. Hamilton saw in Burr an empty and corrupt version of himself.

The former treasury secretary detested Jefferson's politics but had respect for him as a man. Burr he condemned as a scoundrel with "no principle, public or private."[9] He believed Burr was a would-be American "Caesar," which was ironic—as the kids say—because that was the very charge Jefferson leveled against Hamilton. When he threw his support to Jefferson, that cinched it.

LIBELLEE GENERAL

As vice president, John Adams complained that he was the country's "Libellee General,"[10] but he rarely suspected the false charges had come from President Washington. He had remained loyal to the president, and Washington had been reasonably loyal in return. The Adams-Jefferson relationship had been one of open rivalry. They hated each other and worked to undermine the other, but at least there were no surprises.

The Jefferson-Burr relationship was different still. It soured. Publicly, Burr denied he wanted to be president. Privately? Many people suspected that Burr had negotiated with the Federalists to try to win the presidency and might have won if only Hamilton hadn't come out swinging.

You could count Jefferson in the something-smells-funny camp. After the election had been decided, Burr begged the president to publicly defend him from some of the attacks. Jefferson refused. When it came to his reputation, Burr was on his own.

Even after that, Burr's great polish and charm might have redeemed him. His conduct as president of the Senate was distinguished and impeccable. However, the vice president's obsessive interest in patronage appointments—government jobs for his friends and allies—threatened Jefferson with charges of "sleaze," while his fair dealings with Federalists in the Senate exposed him to charges of treachery from his own party.

Those were strikes two and three. Jefferson had Burr replaced on the 1804 ticket with his New York rival, Governor George Clinton. Burr decided he wanted to replace Clinton. He ran as an independent for governor, and Hamilton worked against him one last time.

Burr lost. He wanted revenge, and there was Hamilton—a hothead and an inveterate duelist with a big mouth, who had worked to hand him one political defeat after another. Relentlessly, remorselessly, the forty-five-year-old Burr wove a trap of honor that ensnared the fifty-six-year-old Hamilton. They met on the morning of July 11 on the Weehawken Heights, and the rest is history.

TAILS, YOU DIE

Now for those complicating details. It's hard to know Burr's mind, but the duel seems out of character. For all the supposed personal animosity between the men, Hamilton wrote during the 1800 election debacle that they got along well enough. He distrusted Burr because he had known Burr—and, he might have added, because they had so much in common.

Hamilton thought his fellow New Yorker a man of low character, but that moral reprobate happened to be the same moral reprobate who had intervened to stop a duel between Hamilton and later president James Monroe.

Burr inquired into Hamilton's health in New York after the duel and was barred from seeing him. Hamilton's words of forgiveness for Burr might have been calculated, but they came at a time when he was readying his soul for whatever comes next. It's possible they were sincere.

Then there was Hamilton's own situation. After his son's macabre demise, which also grew out of a quarrel with a Republican over an insult, he grew increasingly gloomy and fatalistic. A sex scandal had destroyed his political ambitions, and his Federalist Party was falling apart. He was taking on debt faster than he could bail.

When he came to, Hamilton said that he hadn't meant to fire on Burr. By every reasonable indicator we have, that is correct. And yet, put yourself in Burr's shoes for a minute. Before the call to "present," your opponent makes a big production out of adjusting his glasses and appears to take careful aim at you.[11] And . . .

"Present!"

You don't have much time to think about it.

"Present!"

Hamilton hasn't ever killed someone in a duel but . . .

"Present!"

His gun is just as loaded as yours is.

"Present!"

He knows how to use it.

"Present!"

You are extremely angry.

"Present!"

So is he.

"Present!"

It would be a stretch to label it suicide on Hamilton's part. He hadn't insisted on the duel; Burr had. And Burr could have wasted his shot as well. Most political duels were bloodless because of an elaborate set of deceptions that both parties adhered to.

Bloodless duelists had learned to pretend they were going to kill

Hamilton: The shot heard 'round the world

each other, feign poor marksmanship, and declare honor restored. The point was in showing up and risking it all. In so doing, you gained back the respect of the offended party. Hamilton followed this convention; Burr did not.

We live in a postdueling world, but to the extent that modern Americans are likely to take any side in this fight, my money's on Burr.

I say this, admittedly, based on the sketchiest of anecdotal evidence. When we were in Weehawken shooting the reenactment, I realized I hadn't assigned the two parts to my actors, so I flipped a coin. Shawn Macomber called heads, and that's how it came up, so I gave him the choice, "Burr or Hamilton?"

"Ahhh, I'll do Burr," he said.

THE CURSE OF BURR

After he had killed Hamilton, Burr briefly became a fugitive. There were three different unsuccessful attempts to try him for the duel. He got to stay vice president until the end of the term and even deliver a farewell address to the Senate.

According to one contemporary account of that speech, Burr "challenged [the senators'] attention to considerations more momentous than merely their personal honor and character"— which was a good gambit, because few people at that point believed he had either.

Burr did his best to change their minds by speaking of "the preservation of law, of liberty, and the Constitution." This house, said he, "is a sanctuary; a citadel of law, of order, and of liberty; and it is here—it is here, in this exalted refuge—here, if anywhere, will resistance be made to the storms of political [frenzy] and the silent arts of corruption; and if the Constitution be destined ever to perish by the sacrilegious hands of the demagogue or the usurper, which God avert, its expiring agonies will be witnessed on this floor."[12]

He spoke for twenty minutes. When he finished, he departed the Senate alone, closing the door on the way out. The scene after that in the Senate must have been something to behold. There were several minutes of "solemn and silent weeping."[13]*

Burr may have delivered the speech of his life, but he left the Senate a cursed man. Two years later, he would be tried for treason on charges that he wanted to carve his own personal empire out of the Southwest. He beat the rap, but that hardly mattered. It cemented his reputation as one of America's greatest villains.

* Crybabies.

He eventually returned to New York and beavered away at a private law practice. It kept Burr solvent, barely. With his political fortunes exhausted, his personal financial prospects also withered. There was one brief bright spot. At age seventy-seven, he married the wealthy widow Eliza Jumel. She decided that he cost too much, however. They were separated after only four months and divorced soon after.

The ratification of the Twelfth Amendment in 1804 seemed to institutionalize the curse of Burr. The next several vice presidents inherited a much smaller office. Fittingly, the next man to make anything of it was nicknamed the "Little Magician."

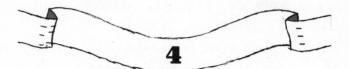

4

KICKED IN THE
KNICKERBOCKERS

*Mr. Senator, allow me to be
indebted to you for another pinch
of your aromatic Maccoboy.*

—MARTIN VAN BUREN

George H. W. Bush's campaign for president in 1988 was
haunted by the ghost of Martin Van Buren. The questions
were probably as irksome to his staff as they were inevitable. They
became more so after he reclined with his Texas ten-gallon boots
on the Oval Office desk.

Wasn't it true that no sitting vice president had been elected
to the presidency since Van Buren pulled off that trick in 1836?
Well, yes. Didn't both men run on the coattails of popular-
but-divisive presidents. *Yes, they did*—Bush's "kinder, gentler"
rhetoric notwithstanding.

It was the right bet, too. Vice President Al Gore would try to
tack the other way, charting out his own identity wholly apart
from President Clinton, and fail. Bush and Van Buren both won,

albeit with smaller showings in the electoral college than their presidents had managed.

In office, both men suffered several of the same slings and arrows of outrage and misfortune. There were recessions and unflattering comparisons with the men whose coattails they rode in on, sure. But what really stung was the charge that they'd lost touch with the common man.

In Bush's case, a *New York Times* reporter tagged along with him and mistook his unfamiliarity with an experimental scanner for unfamiliarity with "even basic [supermarket] scanner technology."[1] *Reality check on aisle one!*

It wasn't true, but that was almost irrelevant. As the Urban Legends Web site says, "Even if Bush *had* been in a grocery store or two since the advent of scanners, everybody *knew* he had 'people' to do his shopping for him."[2] *Of course* he'd be shocked to see how an honest-to-goodness modern checkout line worked.

GOLD IN THEM THAR SPOONS

In Van Buren's case, the story is even more absurd, and more deliciously unfair. A rumor had circulated around D.C. that Kentucky congressman Landaff Andrews, while enjoying the president's hospitality at a White House party, had spied a gold spoon on the table.

He was supposedly so outraged by this gross excess that he declared, "Mr. Van Buren, if you will let me take this spoon to Kentucky and show it to my constituents, I will promise not to make use of any other argument against you; this will be enough."[3] Andrews was a Whig; Van Buren was a Democrat; and it was a presidential election year, when these things tend to take on a life of their own.

And by "take on a life of their own," I mean "partisans exploit them shamelessly." Whig congressman Charles Ogle decided to go on about the alleged gold spoon at length on the floor of the House of Representatives. Congressman Andrews tried to stop him in his tracks. It turned out there was no gold spoon, and he hadn't actually insulted the president.

Ogle wasn't going to allow such small considerations to get in the way of a good harangue. He'd been through the White House accounts and discovered that the nation had been billed more than three thousand dollars for improvements, including the "purchase of furniture, trees, shrubs and compost and for the superintendence of the President's grounds."[4]

The congressman was a master of his material. He took Van Buren apart for three whole days, to the amusement of those spectators in the peanut gallery. Ogle knew what Dr. Johnson knew: "Of all the griefs that harass the distress'd / Sure the most bitter is a scornful jest."[5]

Ogle conjured a fantasy of a decadent and effete president of monstrous dimensions. Of "the superintendence of the President's grounds," he mocked, "the survey of smooth lawns and gently sloping meads, covered with rich coats of white and red clover and luxuriant orchard grass, made no delightful impression on their eyes.

"No, sir; mere meadows are too common to gratify the refined taste of an exquisite with sweet sandy whiskers. He must have undulations, beautiful mounds, and other contrivances, to ravish his exalted and ethereal soul. Hence, the reformers have constructed a number of clever sized hills, every pair of which,

Van Buren: Has golden spoon right here

it is said, was designed to resemble and assume the form of an Amazon's bosom, with a miniature knoll or hillock on its apex, to denote the nipple."[6]

As for Van Buren himself, Ogle alleged that he strutted "by the hour before golden-framed mirrors, nine feet high and four feet and a half wide." The president dined on "fricandaus de veau and omelette soufflé," and afterwards he cleaned his "pretty tapering soft, white lily fingers" by immersing them in "Fanny Kemble Green finger cups."[7]

Short of saying, "You're so gay," it's hard to imagine how the congressman could have been more obvious. After he published his "Gold Spoon Oration" and distributed it at his own expense, the whole country was chuckling.

Van Buren's response was a day late and about three thousand dollars short. Commissioner of Public Buildings William Noland certified that "no gold knives or forks or spoons of any description have been purchased for the President's house since Mr. Van Buren became the Chief Magistrate of the Nation."[8]

THE NICK OF NAMES

The charge was groundless and effective. Van Buren argued in his *Autobiography* that the "Presidential Canvas of 1840 and its attending occurrences" were "subjects of regret with ninety-nine hundredths of the sober minded and well informed people of the United States."[9]

He pressed the point further, saying that "no one of that number"—not a single solitary soul—"can now hesitate in believing that the scenes through which the Country passed in that great political whirlwind were discreditable to our Institutions and could not fail, if often repeated, to lead to their subversion."[10]

One can sympathize with Van Buren, but that sympathy will probably be limited by the knowledge of practical politics of the time—a politics that he helped create. In fact, he practically *invented* American political demagoguery in the 1828 election. Back then it was the simple, homespun war hero Andrew Jackson putting the boot to the decadent and effete President John Quincy Adams. It wasn't until the boot was on another foot that Van Buren would decide this was a bad thing.

Politics was more nickname heavy then. Van Buren was given four of them: "Old Kinderhook," the "Red Fox of Kinderhook," the "Little Magician," and "the American Talleyrand."[11] There was also one jab that was popular during the 1840 election but didn't quite stick in the long run: "Martin Van Ruin."

Each nickname said something important about the man. Kinderhook, New York, was where he was born, raised, and educated until he was apprenticed to a lawyer at the age of fifteen. No Harvard or Yale for this son of poor Dutch stock. "Old" was then an affectionate term (thus Andrew Jackson's nickname, "Old Hickory"). Foxes are clever and cunning, especially where self-preservation is involved.

"Little Magician" was a backhand compliment given to him

once he had made it into the Senate. His colleagues were practiced at the art of misdirection, but they were surprised to see him work his black arts on voters. On all of the great, divisive issues of the day, he managed to keep people guessing what shell his true position was under. He was against expanding the franchise, then for it. He was for internal improvements, then against them. He was for high tariffs, then against them, then for very high low tariffs. How *did* he do it?

The comparison of Van Buren to Talleyrand was the most contemptuous of all. Charles Maurice de Talleyrand was the notorious cleric, statesman, and sellout who had endorsed first the ancien régime, then the French Revolution, then Napoleon, then the return of the Bourbons, and benefited under all four governments.

Talleyrand was a faithless bishop who betrayed his own church. He accepted bribes from foreign governments to sell out Napoleon's secrets to European leaders. He was particularly loathed by Americans because he had very nearly started a war between the United States and France by demanding bribes during the so-called "XYZ affair."

What had Van Buren done to earn such a standing rebuke?

BUCKTAILING THE SYSTEM

One thing he hadn't done was extend the family dynasty, because there wasn't one to extend. Van Buren's father was a tavern keeper who had married a widow with children. Between her two marriages, she had eight kids. The family's scarce resources were stretched thin.

Van Buren, as you might guess from his name, was a member

of the Dutch Reformed church. His religious beliefs, like his politics, were elusive. Publicly, he maintained what he wrote in one Annual Message to Congress: "All forms of religion have united for the first time to diffuse charity and piety, because for the first time in the history of nations all have been totally untrammeled and absolutely free."[12]

The answer was like most modern poll-tested pieties: calculated to appeal to the broadest number of people and give the least offense. With instincts like that, Van Buren took to politics early on. By the time he qualified for the New York bar, he had already attended the local Democratic convention and worked on the campaign of fellow Dutchman Peter Van Ness.

Martin and his half brother, James Van Nes, began a practice of defending the interests of common folk against one group of local bigwigs, the Livingston family. This ingratiated Van Buren to the rival, powerful Clinton clan, who made use of his political expertise. He was appointed a Columbia County probate judge in 1808 as a reward for his role in the successful 1807 gubernatorial campaign of Clinton ally Daniel Tompkins, who later became vice president under James Monroe.

He broke with De Witt Clinton, former mayor of New York City, lieutenant governor, and future governor, over the War of 1812. Clinton, along with most of New England, hotly opposed the war, but Van Buren supported it. His support for the war didn't seem to slow him down. He became a state senator and then attorney general in rapid succession.

Then he took over the place. His faction of the party, known as the "Bucktails" for their plumed hats, created the first modern machine that encompassed all of New York. The New York City arm of the machine, which held court in the Tammany Hall club, would become a byword for political corruption in the decades to follow.

The new spoils system that Martin Van Buren created was extra-ordinarily effective. The Bucktails finished off the remnants of the Federalist Party and more than offset the influence of the Clintons. They managed this through the power of patronage. Loyal sup-porters of the Democrats were rewarded with jobs, and they were expected to finance future victories. The party came first, last, and always.[13]

VOX ALIBI

His success in state politics translated well into national affairs, after a rough start. In 1824, Van Buren supported Treasury Secretary William Crawford for president, a candidate with a big problem—he'd been utterly incapacitated by a stroke.

Crawford, like the three other candidates—Andrew Jackson, hero of the battle of New Orleans; House Speaker Henry Clay; and Secretary of State John Quincy Adams—belonged to the party with the unwieldy name Democratic-Republican, the Federalists having collapsed nationally as well.

Tennessee's Jackson received a plurality of both the popular and electoral votes, but he did not win outright. That made it the House of Representatives' call. Clay knew that he could not win, but he wasn't about to let Jackson have it. He supported Adams and secured his election. Clay was then named secretary of state of the Adams administration.

Jackson denounced Clay as a "Judas" and the alleged Clay-Adams quid pro quo as a "corrupt bargain."[14] Clay had given the nod to Adams, and then Adams had given him the job that had been an inside track to the presidency. Jackson's constant reiteration of the theme that the voice of the people had been thwarted made him even more of an American idol than he was already.

After 1824, it became clear that America was becoming much more of a populist democracy, with a few drapes from the old Republic left over. Van Buren, true to his nature, decried the "corrupt bargain," then voted to approve Clay as secretary of state.

Secretary of War John Calhoun was elected vice president in 1824. Both Calhoun and Van Buren saw that Jackson was now an unstoppable force, and both planned to succeed him. They had been allies but fell out over two things. First, Calhoun realized Van Buren shared his ambition to be president. Second, Van Buren voted in 1828 for the "tariff of abominations," a massive tax on most imported goods. Southerners like Calhoun believed it would devastate their region and leave it at the mercy of the industrial North.

Van Buren claimed his hands were tied, as the New York legislature had ordered him to vote for it, but he also suggested the tariff would be relaxed when Jackson become president.[15] The Little Magician was never a man to be caught without an excuse or an escape clause up his sleeve.

He was returned to the Senate in 1827 and then elected governor of New York in 1828. From Albany, he spearheaded Jackson's presidential campaign. He created a series of symbolic but substanceless gimmicks, including the mass plantings of Hickory trees and the distribution of "Hickory sticks." By necessity, Van Buren revolutionized campaigning by inventing the practice of intensive local politicking under centralized control—because he couldn't be on scene to control it.

PETTICOAT VICE PRESIDENCY

Having resigned the Senate to take up the governorship, Van Buren resigned that post to become Jackson's secretary of state in 1829. He had already gained Jackson's trust, but he endeared himself to him by taking the president's side in the so-called "Petticoat Affair."

Secretary of War John Henry Eaton had scandalized Washington with his marriage to the widow Peggy Timberlake, who had allegedly driven her former husband to suicide by her adultery with Eaton. Jackson was especially sensitive to the issue because of an unintentionally bigamous marriage to his first wife.

Van Buren, almost alone in the cabinet, stood with Mrs. Eaton, further infuriating the upright Calhoun, whose even more upright wife was the leader of the anti-Peggy faction. He provided further service to Jackson by resigning in 1831, which allowed Jackson to purge his cabinet of Calhoun supporters.

He was then appointed ambassador to Great Britain, pending the Senate's approval. After Van Buren had arrived in London, he learned that Calhoun had engineered his rejection. He'd cast the tie-breaking vote against the appointment in the Senate.

This infuriated Jackson, who showed remarkable restraint by not challenging his vice president to a duel. Calhoun jumped before he was pushed and returned to the Senate. Van Buren bided his time in Europe and returned to take the number two slot on the ticket in 1832. Jackson and Van Buren of the Democratic Party mopped the floor with Henry Clay and John Sergeant of the National Republicans.

Van Buren was easily the most powerful vice president the

United States had yet seen and an invaluable running mate. He was a counselor to Jackson, writing speeches, accompanying him on horseback rides, guiding his "kitchen cabinet," and frustrating Jackson's now-bitter enemy, Calhoun, in the Senate.

After the 1832 victory, Jackson's enemies (who would soon coalesce as the Whig Party) didn't let up. They called him "King Andrew," and displayed the sort of antiroyalism that had been characteristic of most Americans since the Revolutionary War. The pro- and anti-Jackson forces clashed repeatedly. Often, the spats were serious. The Senate, led by Henry Clay, would vote to censure the president in 1834.

Other times, they were comical: Van Buren, presiding over the Senate, grew tired of listening to Clay drone on and on. One day, he decided he'd had enough. He stepped down onto the floor and walked to Clay's desk. Clay stood up and wondered what was going on. He wasn't alone. The gallery held its breath.

Van Buren bowed and said in a parody of refinement, "Mr. Senator, allow me to be indebted to you for another pinch of your aromatic Maccoboy."[16] Clay, who looked as if he'd been hit upside the head, gaped in silence, while Van Buren leaned down and took a pinch of his snuff and then returned to his perch. Spectators let out hoots of laughter.

JACKSON TAKETH AWAY

The yuks covered over a conflict that Van Buren worked very hard to mitigate, with some success. A few historians charge that Jackson was the first "Imperial President." They have half a point. He believed that his election by the people gave him plenary powers to act for them—within constitutional limits, certainly, but limits as *he* interpreted them.

Jackson's second vice president convinced him to become more modest in his claims, thus dodging a constitutional crisis. It didn't hurt that the midterm elections of 1834 went heavily for the Democrats, proving yet again that praising Athens to the Athenians is good politics.

A grateful Jackson ensured that Van Buren would be the Democratic presidential nominee in 1836. Jackson's endorsement helped Van Buren immensely, as did the fact that the Whigs ran four different candidates against him and Richard Johnson.

Johnson, forced onto the ticket by Jackson, was one of the most eccentric characters ever to hold the office—and that is saying something. He was rumored to be a non-bather who had lived openly with his black slave and de facto common-law wife, Julia Chinn, who bore him two daughters.[17]* To say that he wasn't a net gain for the ticket would be an understatement.

His vice president wasn't the only liability that Van Buren inherited from the Jackson administration. There was also the small matter of the Panic of 1837. Jackson had abolished the Second National Bank because he saw it as a pawn of corrupt "monied interests." That may have been true, but it turned out those interests knew what they were doing. Jackson's decision to place treasury funds in state banks, and to allow money to be printed in excess of what could be redeemed in gold, set something awful in motion.[18]

* Here's a great example of how the past really is a different country. Johnson's contemporaries thought that his de facto marriage to a slave was weirder than his nonbathing. Of course, the fact that he could become vice president also confounds a lot of modern notions about pre–Civil War, pre–civil rights America.

First, there was the speculative bubble, then a currency crisis, and finally, the worst financial meltdown in the history of the United States to that point. The economy collapsed only weeks after President Van Buren had been sworn into office.

It nearly paralyzed Van Buren's presidency from the get-go. You could say that the people abandoned him, but that's a bit off because they were never really "with" him. The good feelings that were attached to Jackson didn't translate to his closest advisor and successor. Jackson could play the part of outsider and rebel taking on a corrupt establishment; Van Buren *was* the corrupt establishment.

The new president muddled on as best he could, which is to say, he failed. He tried to annex Texas but couldn't swing it. He later came out swinging against it when he tried for the Democratic nomination in 1844.

Van Buren made two racially tinged decisions for which he is probably best remembered today, and not fondly. He stood with the Spanish government and the slaveholders in the *Amistad* case, in which several slaves en route to Puerto Principe mutinied and eventually landed on American soil.[19] He also stood with Jackson in forcing the brutal uprooting of the Cherokee Indian tribe in 1838 in the Trail of Tears.[20]

THE PRINCE AND THE PAUPER

The take-away lesson from the Van Buren administration is best summed up by that famous passage in *The Prince*, where Machiavelli asks, "Is it better for a leader to be loved or feared?" Feared, the perceptive author answers by way of his alliterative translator, because the people are "fickle, false, cowardly, and covetous."[21] Any politician who trusts in their gratitude is liable to have his head lopped off when things go bad.

Van Buren was to learn this firsthand after the Panic of 1837. It was no good for him to point out that the panic and the economic devastation it caused weren't really his fault. As Machiavelli reminds us, friendship that is bought—not by secured "greatness or nobility of mind"—is counterfeit currency in a crisis.

And Van Buren's political capital was based almost entirely on the favors he bestowed on others. He was the first great "fixer" in American history. He had a thousand friends but no real allies. We'll run into him several times in the next few chapters, but I don't think it will ruin any suspense to say that he spent much of the rest of his life trying to regain his former glory; George H. W. Bush, perhaps seeing where that had gotten his distant predecessor, decided to quit with his dignity intact.

5

AND TIPPECANOE TOO

Go you now, then, Mr. Clay, to
your end of the avenue, where
stands the Capitol, and there
perform your duty to the country.

—JOHN TYLER

After walking back from the Williamsburg Lodge, I discovered that my rental car* was illegally parked in the lot where John Tyler's house used to stand. The law office of his brother, Nicholas Tyler, was still there next to the lot—a small, two-story, white building with black shutters. The Lightfoot tenement building continues to defy gravity across the street.

> * If you can call a PT Cruiser a car. It's really more of a large retro plastic toy with wheels and a working engine.

But the home where Vice President Tyler learned that something terrible had happened to President William Henry Harrison? And the Knocker That Changed History? They paved it over to put up a parking lot.

It's hard to understand that decision. Demolishing the past is not standard practice for Williamsburg, Virginia, to say the least. The town's motto is "Where history comes to life," and it's not an empty boast like, say, L.A.'s "City of Angels." Period tourism is a big deal for the local economy, as well as for local amusement. When I had driven into town, a large-scale reenactment of some sort was in full swing.

The main drag of downtown is called "merchant's square." It looks like a cross between converted, pedestrian-friendly malls of college towns such as Ithaca, New York, and Burlington, Vermont, and more explicitly cutesy locales like Leavenworth, Washington. Visitors can stop by the toy store, the cheese shop, the peanut shop, the J. Fenton Gallery, or one of the many cafés, restaurants, and pizzerias that dot the square.

That odd mix makes sense if you consider the likely customers. Williamsburg is both a tourist magnet and a college town. The Kimball Theatre targets out-of-towners and the thousands of students at the College of William and Mary with a mix of historical plays, live music, and art-house movies.

Nearly everything about the town only works to deepen the Mystery of the Parking Lot. History is big business here. The Tylers played an important role in that history. William and Mary, for instance, was vastly expanded under the stewardship of Lyon Tyler, one of John Tyler's many offspring.

One reason that it might have been knocked down is that it was quite large, and the lodge needed the space. In its current incarnation, the hotel has 323 guest rooms, and most of that is spread out rather than up.

Only a purist would deny that trade-offs have to be made between historical preservation and historical tourism. But . . . a parking lot? All men of goodwill should find themselves scratching their scalps over that trade-off.

You don't even have to have a particularly hallowed view of history to think that. Some things are inherently more marketable than others. If someone wanted to push over the Statue of Liberty to make way for a new extra-large museum of American immigration, people* would be understandably upset; the new structure would also receive fewer visitors.

* Including the French.

Then again, there's no denying that business is booming at the lodge. To get into the building, I had to make my way past a wide variety of people, including a group of state troopers on their choppers. According to a computer signboard, the center was hosting events for Owens & Minor, the Women's Health 2007 Conference, ECR Pharma, the Goodwin Society, and the National College of Probate Judges. All that day, if I read the screen correctly.

TOO MUCH HARD CIDER

While business proceeded more or less as usual at the Tyler household in the fall of 1840, the Whig Party did something new in American politics. Andrew Jackson had helped to break down the reticence that kept candidates from aggressively "running" for office, rather than relying mostly on surrogates and free booze, but they had still campaigned to do specific things.

Whig ambition changed all that. The opposition party had two things going for it in the 1840 campaign. First, there was a widespread recession that Van Buren was associated with, caused in part by Jackson's canceling the National Bank. Second, the personal popularity of candidate William Henry Harrison—a politician and military leader most famous for winning the battle of Tippecanoe—was off the charts.

The organizers of the Whig campaign figured, why ruin a perfectly good campaign with issues? It would only divide the loosely held-together party and give Democrats something to aim at. Instead, the policy pronouncements at political events were subordinated to an intentional carnival-like atmosphere. One Democrat newspaper took a snobbish shot at Harrison; the Whigs embraced the criticism and created the "Log Cabin and Hard Cider" campaign.

The house that Harrison then lived in was spacious, but subordinates and even the candidate himself referred to it as a "log cabin." At every rally, Whigs set up makeshift log cabins, often with a coonskin cap nailed to the door. The point was to cast their party as the one of the common man, even though their nominees for president and vice president were wealthy and came from relatively patrician backgrounds.

Most of the speechifying went over the large crowds' heads, but it hardly mattered. The music had the real effect. One campaign song called "What Has Caused This Great Commotion?" was particularly popular. The chorus says it all:

For Tippecanoe and Tyler too—Tippecanoe and Tyler too,
And with them we'll beat the little Van, Van, Van,
Van is a used up man,
And with them we'll beat little Van.

And beat him they did, like a redheaded stepchild. The electoral college totals were 234 to 60, advantage Whigs.

Sympathetic Tyler biographer Oliver Chitwood mounted a partial defense of the crowds' enthusiastic reaction to the Whig campaign. It was a different time then, he explained, with fewer opportunities for entertainment, and people flocked to the Whigs like they might go to the county fair.

Chitwood found it necessary to concede, however, that it "is certainly not to the credit of the American people that they allowed themselves to be swept off their feet by this long-continued exhibition of political clownishness."[1]

Because of their success in 1840, Whigs had every reason to be happy as the spring of 1841 rolled around, and to expect more happiness yet. When Harrison delivered his inaugural address on March 4, 1841, they controlled the House, the Senate, and the presidency. The Democrats could carp, but the Whigs would get their way. After twelve years of Democratic rule, they'd won.

Then something wholly unexpected happened. Harrison caught a bad cold after his inauguration, and it congealed into pneumonia. He took to bed, and his condition only continued to worsen. After only thirty days in office, at the age of sixty-eight, the president died. He appears to have mistaken his doctor for the vice president, for his last words were, "Sir, I wish you to understand the true principles of the Government. I wish them carried out. I ask nothing more."[2]

DEAD PRESIDENTS

Which brings us back to Tyler's Williamsburg home that I was illegally parked in. John Tyler learned of President Harrison's death sometime on the morning of April 5. The principal bearer of bad news was Fletcher Webster, son of Secretary of State Daniel Webster. He came banging on the door that used to stand here to summon the vice president to Washington.

Legend has it Tyler was shocked speechless, but historian Edward P. Crapol casts doubt on the stories by pointing out that any surprise was gotten over quickly. Tyler and several slaves and family members made the 230-mile trip from Williamsburg to D.C. in about twenty-one hours—by boat up the James River and then by train from Richmond.

Tyler immediately met with Harrison's cabinet and told the secretaries they were welcome to stay on in his administration. He swore an oath before a federal judge in their presence.

That sounds routine and humdrum to a modern audience, but it was groundbreaking. Vice presidents had died in office before. The funerals of the fourth and fifth vice presidents, George Clinton and Elbridge Gerry, helped to sell the idea that the Twelfth Amendment had made the office into something of a dead-end job. But no president had ever croaked in office.

There was no precedent for succession, and the exact wording of the U.S. Constitution was not clear on the subject. It only speci-fied that the vice president would in some sense fill in for the deceased executive. Still up in the air, explains Crapol, was whether the "vice president became president in his own right, or whether he was to be the acting president until a new chief executive was duly elected."[3]

Nobody knew for sure, except John Tyler. The letter that the young Webster delivered was addressed to the "Vice President," which must have irked Tyler. The judge who administered Tyler's second oath of office recorded that the first oath should have been sufficient, "yet as doubts may arise, and for greater caution, [Tyler] took and subscribed the foregoing oath before me."[4] The Virginian then delivered an inaugural address in which he referred to himself several times as the "chief magistrate" and the "president," to a stunned audience.

Tyler insisted on being treated as nothing less than the legitimate head of the executive branch, and Congress was made to respect this fact. He returned any correspondence addressed to the "vice president" or "acting president" unopened. In order to do business with Tyler, you had to refer to him as the president, full stop.

It was such an effective precedent that seven more vice presidents would follow it before two-thirds of the states got around to ratifying the Twenty-Fifth Amendment—in 1967. When LBJ put his hand on that Bible and was sworn in, on *Air Force One* in Dallas, the country had John Tyler to thank (or blame) for it.

THUNDERBOLTS AND LIGHTNING

When Tyler asked the cabinet how his predecessor did things, he was told that Harrison had them vote on issues and followed the majority. They may have been putting the new boss on. But, if true, Harrison had been content to drift along because he was ill but also because he saw himself as a caretaker president whose party was running things.

The most powerful man in Washington then was not the president but Henry Clay, the famed senator from Kentucky. Clay had a vision for internal improvements, banking, and tariffs that he reasonably expected to become law under a unified Whig government. Harrison went along with it; Tyler would balk.

Tyler and Clay had been friends and sometimes allies when they were senators. In fact, Tyler had been a delegate pledged to vote for Clay at the 1840 Whig convention. But President Tyler found Senator Clay to be overbearing and rude. In part, this was because of Clay's theory of congressional supremacy. Even if he did not regard Tyler's presidency as illegitimate, Clay thought of the executive as far inferior to Congress.

The Kentucky senator's massive ego and bad temper didn't help. When fellow Whigs had nominated Harrison over Clay because they correctly thought him more likely to win a national election, Clay had gone on what Crapol describes as a "drunken rampage" that shocked his supporters. Those impulses put him on a collision course with the proud, refined new president.

It finally snapped during a meeting at the White House. Tyler wanted to come up with a compromise for chartering a new national bank that would respect states' rights. Clay was so disdainful in his disagreement that the president threw him out, saying, "Go you now, then, Mr. Clay, to your end of the avenue, where stands the Capitol, and there perform your duty to the country as you shall think proper. So help me God, I shall do mine at this end of it."[5]

Tyler's problem was that he was what some modern wag might call a WINO—a Whig In Name Only—and even that only lasted for so long. He'd found a place in the newish party almost by accident. He described himself as "a Jeffersonian Republican" and his positions were much closer to the Democrats than his own party.

While in the Senate, Tyler had voted against federal funds for road construction, insisting that things hadn't gotten so bad in Virginia that they had to take "charity." He tolerated tariffs for the sake of raising government revenues but, like so many Southern farmers, he balked at high tariffs to shelter expensive northern industries.

On the subject of the National Bank, the new president proved intractable, which nearly proved his undoing. He vetoed Senator Clay's uncompromising bill, and then he vetoed the compromise bill. Every member of his cabinet except Secretary of State Webster resigned in protest.

The president was formally expelled from the Whig Party; burned, hung, strangled, drowned, stabbed, kicked, and karate chopped in effigy; censured by the House; and almost impeached. The Whig paper, the *Kentucky Intelligencer*, editorialized, "If God-directed thunderbolts were to strike and annihilate the traitor, all would say, 'Heaven is just.'"[6]

TAKING OFF THE WHIG

The creation of a national bank was a small and fairly technical idea, but the conflict over it was epic. It was one of those signaling issues that speak to the party faithful. A modern equivalent might be the opposition to partial-birth abortion bans by Democrats. When politicians cross their supporters on these sorts of issues, they risk denunciations, primary challenges, and fund-raising woes galore. Opposing a national bank was just not something that any respectable forward-looking Whig would do.

Historian M. Boyd Coyner Jr. argued that the Whigs realized the bank was more important for intraparty politics than for appeals to the public and thus excluded it from the party platform in 1844. This "erosion of interest in such an institution," he wrote, was evidence that "on this one issue, at least, Tyler spoke with the voice of the people."[7] They distrusted both the banks and the government and thought the combination of the two dangerous.

Tyler had a markedly different notion of respectability than many of his contemporaries, largely because of his aristocratic Southern upbringing. He was the son of John Tyler Sr., a governor and judge of Virginia. He attended William and Mary, where the Old Dominion's future leaders were cast in the mold of George Washington, Thomas Jefferson, and James Madison.

Like his idols, the younger Tyler saw himself as a farmer-statesman. He shared their skepticism of most government schemes, and he hated and feared Great Britain. Also like the previous Virginians in the White House, he accomplished an awful lot during his single term. Here is a short list:

- Set a lasting precedent for succession to the presidency
- Negotiated the northern boundary between Maine and Canada
- Established a steamship navy
- Initiated and signed a treaty with China, giving U.S. merchants a leg up on the competition
- Forced Britain and France to recognize Hawaii's independence
- Annexed Texas

He managed all of this in a single term, against formidable obstacles, without ever taking the country to war. The Whig-dominated Congress hated the president and tried to impeach him over his *vetoes*—six over a four-year period. He was derided as the "man without a party," "His Accidency," the bastard child of Benedict Arnold and Marie Antoinette. Some abolitionist critics came right out and called him an agent of Satan.

Worse, the president went through more cabinet secretaries than Spinal Tap went through drummers. There were a lot of resignations, to be sure, but his employees also had an unfortunate tendency to die on him.

Two of Tyler's four secretaries of state died less than a year apart. The second fallen secretary of state, Abel Upsher, bought it in a cannon-firing accident on a presidential cruise that also killed a secretary of the navy; a commodore; two regular seamen; Tyler's personal slave, Henry; and David Gardiner, the father of Julia Gardiner, whom the widowed president had been courting for two years after his first wife died in the White House.

He narrowly missed being blown up himself. According to Crapol, Tyler had "hesitated at the bottom of the stairs to hear a song his son-in-law . . . had just begun singing." When Julia learned what had happened to her father, she fainted. The president carried her "across a gangplank to a rescue vessel that had come alongside to take the wounded and so many dazed passengers ashore."[8]

After Julia mourned her father, the two decided to set another precedent: Tyler became the first president to marry while in office. He was fifty-four; she was twenty-four. They eventually had seven children, bringing the total number of his sons and daughters to fifteen and making him the clear winner in the presidential fertility sweepstakes.

MORE AND PEACE

Tyler's accomplishments as president tended toward the social and diplomatic, which makes sense: the two are often related. Even his harshest critics, such as congressman and former president John Quincy Adams, privately admitted that the man's social graces were considerable. When the president made a swing through the North, the huge crowds that came out to greet him in Boston and New York attested to his personal popularity.

They were reacting to more than his Southern courtesy. In order to survive in high society then, one had to have manners, true. To thrive, he also needed something that the president had in spades: boldness.

We can see this bravado in one of his early diplomatic initiatives. When he assumed the presidency, a British subject was on trial in a capital murder case that resulted from the constant border skirmishes between Canada and Maine. Tyler later admitted that the "peace of the Country . . . was suspended by a thread." If the verdict came back guilty and the sentence was death, the Brits promised to withdraw their ambassador and declare war.

The president's short-term solution was described by Sir Robert Peel to Queen Victoria as "a perfectly novel one, a measure of hostile and unjustifiable character adopted with pacific intentions." He could have added, ". . . I hope."[9]

Tyler threatened to short-circuit the normal diplomatic process if the British subject hanged by holding the ambassador hostage. It was a perfectly crazy idea—after all, Britain could go to war without withdrawing the ambassador—but it convinced the Crown that the president was serious about keeping the peace.

Special envoy Lord Ashburton was dispatched from London to settle all matters of dispute between the two countries, including the Maine border, the British claim of a right to search American vessels, and an issue that had the South up in arms: the freeing of slaves on ships that mutinied and made it to the shores of British colonies.

The president went to extraordinary lengths to make peace with Her Majesty's government while salvaging some honor for his country. He paid twelve thousand dollars out of a secret State Department contingency fund to fund a secret propaganda campaign to convince the Maine locals to settle the border dispute. Lord Ashburton paid even more for his own propagandists. The locals were still reluctant to go along.

At one point, Ashburton got so fed up with Maine's negotiators that he announced he was going back to London, but Tyler flattered him back to the table. The president's persistence and appeals to the patriotism of Maine residents eventually effected a compromise that both sides could stomach.

On the issues of right-to-search and slave mutinies, Tyler exacted concessions and apologies that sufficed for most Southern senators to vote for the treaty's ratification. Abolitionists were shocked to learn that the treaty also included a proviso that established joint U.S.-British patrols to stamp out what remained of the African slave trade, and puzzled that this Southern slaveholder president had signed off on it.

Tyler employed methods that were iffy constitutionally to twist the arm of Maine residents, because the alternative was war with Britain. He thought that conflict would be militarily and politically ruinous, and it's hard to argue with that judgment. Congress had spent little money on armaments over the last decade, and the new navy fleet was still being built.

Then, with the country's eastern flank secure, Tyler looked west to Texas and spent the last two years of his term bringing the Lone Star republic into the Union. Annexation had been proposed and failed before, but no one had ever been so determined or so politically savvy.

Tyler knew the Whigs would be reluctant to add Texas to the Union, so he came up with a backup plan that tapped into the expansionist sentiment of the American public. He created a dummy third party that nominated him for the 1844 election. That placed necessary pressure on the Democrats just in time for their convention. They nominated dark-horse candidate and unabashed Texas expansionist James Polk.

The president then withdrew from the race and endorsed Polk, who went on to win the White House. Crapol allows that Tyler's support "may have been a decisive factor in providing the Democrat his slim edge in the popular vote." The victory was made sweeter by the fact that the Whig candidate was none other than Tyler's rival, Senator Henry Clay.

The Whigs had insisted that annexation should be treated as a treaty, requiring a two-thirds vote to pass—a threshold that was nigh impossible for a controversial measure to clear. Tyler argued that a joint resolution, requiring only bare majorities in both houses, should suffice. Polk's victory settled the question, and in February of 1845, Congress passed a joint resolution for the annexation of Texas. Tyler signed it and gave the "immortal golden pen" to his new first lady as a present, which she wore around her neck.

The first couple went out in style. The handover of administrations was marked by two weeks of elaborate banquets and galas,
including a final "glorious dinner" in honor of James and Sarah
Polk, where "the champagne and wine flowed like water." One
guest complimented the outgoing president on a successful event.
Tyler took the compliment and gave it a twist. He said, "They cannot say *now* that I am a President *without a party*."[10]

ROBIN HOOD RETIREMENT

President Tyler's story is one of hardship, death, tears, drama, and
accomplishment. Hazard a guess: where do eminent historians rank
our tenth president against his competition? Seventh? Tenth?
Fifteenth?

Not even close. In February 2007, Tyler made one of his rare
public appearances these days on the cover of *U.S. News & World
Report* as one of "America's Worst Presidents." The deck promised,
"From Richard Nixon to John Tyler, a fresh look at our most dismal commanders in chief."

"Most dismal" on an epic scale. Literary biographer Jay Tolson
introduced the readers to the magazine's list of eleven contenders
for a "negative Mount Rushmore," based on an averaging of five
recent polls of "historians and other custodians of the long view"
that rated all of the U.S. presidents. Tyler came in sixth worst,
after Millard Fillmore and just ahead of Ulysses Grant. It's a judgment that's barely budged since Arthur Schlesinger Jr. kicked off
such rankings for *Life* magazine in 1948.

His successor, Polk, was a one-term president whose achievements were roughly comparable (Tyler annexed Texas; Polk won

the Oregon territory and much of the Southwest; they both got the better of Britain), though historians seem to like Polk better. Tyler tends to rate sixth or eighth from the bottom of the barrel; Polk's average ranking is about twelve from the top. Why the large disparity? It's almost as if we're getting the Whig version of history.

To solve the Mystery of the Low Rankings, along with the Mystery of the Parking Lot, I drove twenty miles outside of Williamsburg along the John Tyler Memorial Highway, conveniently enough, to an old plantation in Charles City.

After I parked and walked through the gate, I saw a pet cemetery. There were a few dozen crosses and small headstones for pets ranging from "Beppo" ("1985–2002; My buddy; Good old doggy woggy") to one larger stone that really commanded my attention:

> *Here lie the bones of*
> *My old horse, "General"*
> *Who served his master*
> *faithfully*
> *for twenty-one years,*
> *And never made a blunder.*
> *Would that his*
> *Master could say*
> *The same!*

General was Tyler's favorite horse. He was buried on these grounds because, when the retired president returned to Virginia, he didn't return to his old home in Williamsburg. My tour guide, Tim Coyne, hazarded one explanation as to why: often a new wife has a hard time living in the home of her predecessor. It's possible, though, the estate was purchased early in Tyler's presidency (in 1842) while he and Julia were, at best, interested parties.

For both of them, the estate came to represent a new start and a reaction against many of the political currents of the time. The place was named "Sherwood Forest" in celebration of the former president's outlaw status among Whigs. A big knocker on the front door, which Tyler had specially made, advertises this fact.

It was an ambitious undertaking. By bits and pieces, Sherwood Forest became the longest frame house in the United States, at more than three hundred feet long. Downstairs, the kitchen, dining room, receiving room, study, ballroom, and law office are all in a line—one continuous room divided by doors. The place has been preserved and occupied by Tyler's remarkably long-lived descendents. It's currently owned and occupied by Harrison Tyler, son of Lyon Tyler, son of John and Julia Tyler.[11]

It was here that Julia threw parties that lasted for a week or more, drawing visitors from all over the country. It was here that a new branch of the Tyler clan was born. It was here that Tyler's slaves, children, and farmhands grew high-quality wheat, rather than more punishing crops, like tobacco. And it was from this place, perhaps while Tyler gazed out on the paradisiacal vista of the James River, that he grew increasingly worried about the sectional divisions of his country.

After the surprise election of Abraham Lincoln in 1860, Tyler chaired a special peace conference that tried to hammer out an accommodation between North and South. Almost nobody liked the compromise, including Tyler. He resigned his leadership position, voted against the conference's recommendations, and came back here with the prospect of war almost certain.

REVISING TYLER

Tyler is today known as our only traitor president (or the only president to become a citizen of another country, as my tour guide Coyne put it—fair enough). After the failed peace conference, he didn't stay here at Sherwood Forest; he took a more active role in his state's affairs. He negotiated Virginia's entrance into the Confederacy, changing the new would-be nation's capital from Montgomery, Alabama, to Richmond, Virginia.

We can't know what he thought of the outcome of the Civil War because he died in Richmond in January 1862, before he could serve in the Confederate Congress. His body was laid to rest in that city's Hollywood Cemetery.

The plantation survived—just. In restoring the place, Tyler's descendants have left some cracks here and there—in the front door, in a wall panel—to show the Union troops' forced entry and vandalism. The place was looted. Mirrors and windows were smashed. The library was torn up, and personal papers were destroyed for spite. Julia and her children fled the country.

After the war, she came back to Sherwood Forest and worked to put things back together. Her return focused all of the Tyler family's preservationist energies on the plantation in Charles City rather than the house in Williamsburg.

The attachment of the Tyler family seems to have bled into the recollection of the nation. When people think of our tenth president, this is the place they associate with that memory. That makes it a little bit easier to understand why the preservation efforts in Williamsburg didn't extend to a building of great historic import.

As for the historians' negative assessments of Tyler, they tend to give reasons that I suspect are only a fig leaf to disguise the real motivations behind their censure. In his book *John Tyler: The Accidental President*, Crapol—who is more sympathetic than most historians—plays up Tyler's many inconsistencies in a way that seems almost trifling. He complains, for instance, that Tyler ignored some of his own scruples about executive power in order to annex Texas.

That judgment ignores the unwritten rules of the game of expansion. President Jefferson, normally a stickler about such things, had been convinced that the Louisiana Purchase was unconstitutional. He went ahead with it anyway, because he wasn't willing to make perfect the enemy of the common good.

It's a way of judging Tyler down without really giving good reasons, which is a shame. In the presidential-rankings game, historians claim to base their assessments on the president's performance in office, rather than his behavior afterward. It may be admirable that Jimmy Carter has spent his retirement helping to build houses for the disadvantaged, teaching Sunday school, babysitting lepers, and walking on water. Ronald Reagan is usually rated the better president, for good reason.

Revisionism is too popular nowadays, but John Tyler, the first vice president to be thrust into the presidency, deserves a second look.

MILLARD FILLMORE AND THE TEMPLE OF DOOM*

The nourishment is palatable.

—MILLARD FILLMORE

Pity the poor Whigs. Twice they managed to elect presidents. Twice those presidents died in office. The first eight commanders in chief had been blessed with rude good health, but a cold—a cold!—finished off Old Tippecanoe only a month after he was sworn in. Then there was the John Tyler fiasco, party infighting, and Texas expansion—all of which worked to keep the party out of the White House in the presidential go-round of 1844.

---

* Note to readers: There was an epic six-volume editorial struggle over the chapter title. It was either this or "A Short, Obligatory Millard Fillmore Chapter." I lost. Proceed accordingly. Or, as Yoda would put it: "Warned you, have I. Proceed at your own risk, will you." Then he'd cock his head in that knowing, puppet way.

With the election of 1848, the Whigs had decided not to take any chances. The successful formula was: (1) take one old military leader, preferably an Indian fighter; (2) strike a position on slavery that split the difference between North and South; (3) add water. And, presto: instant president!

Granted, it was slightly more complicated than that. But Harrison's previous success does help explain the Whigs' choice of Zachary Taylor from Louisiana. His troops had nicknamed him "Old Rough and Ready" for his tendency to throw together something approximating a uniform. It was rarely obvious to people who didn't already know that this was a general, but he did get results.

Taylor was the winner of the battle of Fort Harrison, the first U.S. land victory in the War of 1812; a veteran of the Black Hawk War; and one of the prosecutors of the recent Mexican-American War. His military bona fides were substantial; they were also his only qualifications for office. He had never even voted in a presidential election.

In the matchup of 1848, Democrats and Whigs were both divided over slavery, and an Athena emerged from the splitting migraine of the two-party system. Antislavery Democrats and so-called "conscience Whigs" formed the Free Soil Party to oppose the expansion of slavery into U.S. territories. They put up as their candidate the heavyweight, but controversial, former president Martin Van Buren.

Taylor's lack of political experience turned out to be a huge asset to Whigs. Though the general was both a Southerner and a slave owner, he wasn't Martin Van Buren. Surrogates for the general insisted to Southerners that he would protect slavery and to Northerners that he would not expand it.

WINK AND NUDGE AND ELECT

An integral part of this wink-and-nudge routine was the nomination of Millard Fillmore for vice president. Other than the normal Whig priorities, Fillmore's politics could be summed up with three antis. He was anti-Mason, anti-Catholic, and moderately anti-slavery. He was on record as having opposed Texas's admission into the Union as a slave territory, and he was therefore highly skeptical of the war over Texas.

His home state was one selling point. Whigs needed to find some way of fogging up the issue of human bondage; they also needed "regional balance," which is a fancy way of saying that they needed a vice president who could deliver a swing state. And without New York, they wouldn't have a prayer.

Fillmore fit that bill perfectly. He was a successful New York comptroller who'd reformed the state's banking laws. He had been a state legislator, congressman, and candidate for governor. His Yankee, non-slavery-expanding ways would complement the Southern slaveholding general of the Mexican-American War—a conflict that many critics charged had been a "war for slavery."

Running two gentlemen so different together would be a perfectly dotty idea today—imagine if some wiseacre proposed an Alan Keyes–Barack Obama ticket. The country was so divided over the issue of slavery that the only way the Whigs could have a prayer of winning was to put up a ticket that embraced those contradictions.

Inconsistency triumphed at the ballot box. The final electoral college showing was 163 Whigs; 127 Democrats. The Free Soil Party didn't receive any electoral votes but garnered about 10 percent of the vote nationally.

The real difference came in Fillmore and Van Buren's home state of New York. Van Buren managed to do especially well there among Democrats, which siphoned crucial votes away from Democratic nominee Lewis Cass. At the same time, Fillmore on the ticket kept most of the New York Whigs from bolting.

In other words, Fillmore's candidacy pulled it out for his party. It put Taylor in the White House and —when Taylor died of gastroenteritis* sixteen months into his term—it kept the executive branch in Whig hands until the next go-round.

* A particularly painful way to go, involving inflammation of the stomach and gastrointestinal tract. Not recommended.

SPLISH SPLASH

That much is fact, but let's wade into the murky waters of historical conjecture: was Fillmore an architect of his party's victory, or a more-or-less passive recipient of good fortune—a Lee Atwater, or a nineteenth-century Forrest Gump?

The question matters because Fillmore is remembered today mostly for not being remembered. The syndicated comic strip *Mallard Fillmore*, about a Republican anthropomorphic duck whose name is a play on our thirteenth president, is about as familiar as most people will ever be with Fillmore. The title is a piece of political esoterica. Historians consistently rank him low on their presidential lists, but unlike, say, John Tyler, his name does not inspire passion.

Fillmore was a vice president whose presidency lasted just over half of one term—a footnote, a blip, not even an afterthought. In the book *The Remarkable Millard Fillmore: The Unbelievable Life of a Forgotten President*, author George Pendle passes along this harsh judgment from *American Heritage* magazine: "To discuss Millard Fillmore is to overrate him."

Pendle then goes on to discuss Fillmore by making up a series of outrageous claims. Pendle's Fillmore had a life that was so hardscrabble that he made the rest of the presidents who were born in log cabins look like robber barons. His achievements were similarly exaggerated. Here was the first man to vulcanize rubber. He fought at the Alamo and prevented Vice President Andrew Johnson's assassination.

His feats of strength and bravery and wisdom put "those of Washington and Lincoln completely in the shade." The cover features the subject of the book reading a book while astride a small white unicorn, but I wouldn't be surprised to see some of the book's claims reported as fact.

There is a venerable tradition of making up great lies about Fillmore. Most famously, the newspaperman H. L. Mencken, facing a daunting deadline in December of 1917, wrote up a fake history of the bathtub in the United States, including the "fact" that Fillmore was the first president to bring one into the White House. Mencken explained that the president's choice to install a bathtub helped to beat back a series of harsh antitub laws, which should have been an obvious sign to readers that he was having a bit of fun.

It was a joke that all kinds of people didn't get. Mencken saw one "learned journal" after another pick up his fake history—especially the bit about Fillmore—and run it as fact. It was too good to check, because it confirmed all kinds of prejudices about our backward forebears.

Mencken issued two loud recantations of the bathtub hoax, to little effect.[1] It continued to pop up in history books and news accounts and continues still. In a 2001 article for the *Washington Post*, reporter Sandra Fleishman explained that the two-and-a-half bathrooms of most modern homes represent an entirely "different planet" from the one that existed in 1851, "when President Millard Fillmore was criticized for indulging in 'monarchical luxury' when he had a bathtub installed in the White House."[2]

NOT A DUMB HUNK

But back on planet earth, the non–Bizarro World version, we're left with real historical questions about Fillmore and his legacy. In a "Straight Dope" column, alt-weekly, all-purpose answer man Cecil Adams wrote that "Millard faced up to the responsibilities of [the presidency] by doing, as far as anyone could tell, nothing at all," which is a pretty good summation of how people think about the subject.*

* *If* they think about the subject.

The column also reiterated the dumb hunk theory of Fillmore's success. According to Adams, the veep had been tapped to bring "aesthetic" balance to the ticket: "Taylor, a Mexican War hero, was short, fat, grubby, and crude. Millard was athletic, handsome, and polite."[3] It's the same charge that would be deployed against Warren Harding and Dan Quayle by high-minded critics: he only got to be somebody because he looked the part.

That assessment of Fillmore rings false. George H. W. Bush once said that few people have sought the vice presidency, but few turn it down. Fillmore sought it, first in 1844 and again in 1848.

He managed to swing the election his way the one time he was on the ticket.

Dumb luck? Could be, but Fillmore didn't lose many elections. He "retired" from politics no fewer than three times, usually because he could see political storms brewing on the horizon, and he understood that every lost election can be a fatal sign of weakness.

Politically, Fillmore was highly opportunistic. He started out as a member of the Anti-Masonic Party. He disassociated himself from them as he saw the movement losing steam, and joined the Whigs while he looked for a way to build a viable third party. Finding none, he decided instead to take the Whig Party over. He came within a few votes of beating Henry Clay for the speakership in 1841 and after a few setbacks became vice president and president.

Fillmore was immensely important to the country for his role in the debate over slavery. As president, Taylor had proved to be a serious disappointment to the Whigs. As a Southerner, he resented high tariffs and opposed them. He was not in favor of another national bank. With declining Treasury revenues from territorial land sales, he informed Congress that there would be little money for those much-sought-after "internal improvements." But nowhere was the disappointment more keenly felt than on the slave question.

Taylor proved to be a bull in the china shop of sectional relations. He didn't want the dreaded institution expanded into the new territories acquired during the Mexican-American War, including New Mexico and California, and he had little patience for the normal back-and-forth of congressional debate.

The president urged California and other territories to settle the question quickly by opting for immediate statehood. They

should draft constitutions and submit them for congressional approval forthwith. Congress should accept the new states and take
no other actions. When Southerners threatened secession, Taylor
threatened to stretch their necks until dead.

As vice president, Fillmore opposed this get-it-done-quick-and-
dirty approach and promoted a series of laws designed to unruffle
feathers. As president, he signed off on several measures that
became known as the Compromise of 1850.

The deal allowed for the admission of California as a free
state. The federal government took on $10 million worth of Texas
debt in exchange for the state giving up any claims to New
Mexico. The compromise also codified the idea of "popular sover-
eignty" for settling the slave question in the existing territories,
ended the slave trade in D.C., and gave Southern slave owners the
right to recover slaves that had escaped to the North.

Fillmore issued an explanation for why he had backed the
compromise, even though he found parts of it unappealing. "God
knows that I detest slavery," he wrote, "but it is an existing evil,
for which we are not responsible, and we must endure it, till we
can get rid of it without destroying the last hope of free government in the world."[4]

HAD THEIR FILLMORE?

Historians tend to take a dim view of the compromise because it
didn't fix the slavery problem. On the other hand, they also recognize that short of secession or war, there might not have *been* a fix.

It's popular but wrong to describe politics today as especially
polarized. Modern pols can't hold a candle to the burning rage of

the mid-nineteenth century. Abolitionist Northerners had moved from condemning the institution of slavery to condemning the slave owners, and also insinuating that there must be something deeply wrong with a region and a people that would tolerate this injustice.

Southerners, being Southerners, did not turn the other cheek. There were multiple fistfights in Congress over slavery in the territories. In 1856, Congressman Preston Brooks would take his walking stick and beat the abolitionist senator Charles Sumner unconscious on the Senate floor, inflicting so much damage that Sumner's seat would be vacant for three years while he recovered.

Fillmore's compromise did work for a few years to reduce this kind of sectional conflict. It provided a period to calm down before the shouting started again. However, in the election of 1852, his party decided it could do better without him. Whigs returned to form, nominating another general of the Mexican-American War, Winfield Scott, whose troops had given him the unfortunate nickname "Old Fuss and Feathers."

It didn't work, in part because Scott had a reputation as being antislavery, and in part because the party couldn't find the right vice president to help them fudge the issue. Out of power, the Whigs fell to pieces. The Southerners started supporting the Democrats, and the Northerners broke up into disparate political movements.

Northern Whigs of a more abolitionist bent founded the Republican Party. Fillmore was not among them, for personal and political reasons. In 1856, he ran as the candidate of the anti-Catholic, anti-immigrant American Party (aka, the Know-Nothing Party). He won only one state in the electoral college but received more than 20 percent of the popular vote. We can't know if he would have pulled it out for the Whigs, but that was an awfully good showing for a third-party candidate.

As far as national politics went, that was Fillmore's last hurrah. From the sidelines, he disliked President Lincoln but took a shine to his vice president-cum-embattled president Andrew Johnson.

After his presidency, Fillmore traveled some and returned to Buffalo, New York, where he served as chancellor of the University of Buffalo. After the death of his first wife, Fillmore married the very wealthy and childless widow Caroline McIntosh. The two purchased a large house, where they frequently entertained friends and former supporters.

Fillmore suffered a stroke in 1874 and died on March 8 of that year. His alleged last words, after being fed a bowl of soup, were "The nourishment is palatable." The house chef, wanting to do better than "palatable," asked the former president if he would like fries with that.

The chef reported, sadly, "He just stared at me blankly."

HOW WAS THE PLAY, MRS. LINCOLN?

*Damn the Negroes. I am fighting those
traitorous aristocrats, their masters.*

—ANDREW JOHNSON

The capitol grounds of the state legislature in Nashville, Tennessee, admit that Andrew Johnson was here, but they do so almost grudgingly.

One's eyes are drawn to a huge, magnificent likeness of Andrew Jackson on his steed, charging into the battle of New Orleans. ("Well, in eighteen and fourteen we took a little trip / along with Colonel Jackson down the mighty Mississip. / We took a little bacon and we took a little beans / And we caught the bloody British near the town of New Orleans.")

Nearby is the tomb of James and Sarah Polk. When I visited the city, I saw evidence that people still lay flowers for the Polks. Both monuments contain elaborate explanations for why these figures were worth memorializing.

Johnson's statue, by contrast, is more modest. It's about life-sized and has a less prominent placement than even the statue of Sam Davis, legendary "boy hero of the Confederacy," who chose to hang rather than betray his friends. Several cedar trees, planted in remembrance of the Holocaust, do a better job competing for your attention.

The statue is of a man in a three-piece suit and cape. One of Johnson's hands clutches the hem of his cape; the other fist balls up around his coat at chest level. The look on his face is dour, determined, almost a scowl. The placard simply explains that he was a U.S. president and gives us the dates.

It's an odd bit of statuary understatement from a city that makes a big deal out of these things. A short drive from the capitol (or a long walk) to Centennial Park will bring you to a near-exact replica of the Parthenon, complete with a creepy reproduction of the statue of Athena, Greek goddess of war—with spear and shield—which towers more than forty feet tall.

A few blocks from the capitol sits the Tennessee State Museum. The main branch is arranged to tell the story of the state from prehistoric times to the turn of the twentieth century.

Visitors might learn about the early attempts by Western settlers to break off from North Carolina and form their own state of Franklin. They can watch videos about Andrew Jackson and the rise of the "common man," see James Polk's sword cane, and browse the historic portrait gallery of some of the state's prominent citizens.

Johnson makes out slightly better at the museum. Most of his political CV is here. Several items highlight his controversial career, including a ticket to the Senate gallery for the impeachment trial in 1868 and the epitaph on his tombstone: "His faith in the People never wavered."

SHOOTING HIS MOUTH OFF

"The People" certainly voted for Johnson enough times. In his adopted hometown of Greenville, in east Tennessee, locals elected him alderman, mayor (at twenty-six), state representative, and state senator before sending him on to the House of Representatives. On the way up, he only lost one election—for state representative —over a reform bill that he correctly predicted would be a boondoggle. So when the Whigs in the state legislature gerrymandered him out of his House district, it should come as no surprise that Johnson decided not to retire early and putt around the garage.

Instead, he ran hard against the favored Whig candidate for governor, Gustavus Henry. For two long months in the sweaty, unforgiving summer of 1853, large crowds came out to watch the two orators have at it. Henry had polish, but Johnson had something that all Americans would eventually be obliged to respect— the force of his determined personality.

It went well for Johnson. At the end of July, Henry approached him with a problem: Henry was exhausted, and there was a serious illness in his family. Would Johnson be willing to stop campaigning? He agreed to stop stumping, but continued to wheel and deal. Come election day, the underdog Democrat pulled off an upset by just over two thousand votes.

In the next go-round in 1855, Governor Johnson again ground his opponent down with his relentless speechifying. Where the first campaign had been hard fought but mostly polite, the second

gubernatorial contest against Merideth Gentry was far more vitriolic. Just a few decades earlier, the insults would have led to a duel.

Johnson's opponent, and many of Johnson's detractors, were
associated with the anti-immigrant, anti-Catholic Know-Nothing
movement. Rather than trim his sails to pick up nativist votes,
Johnson diabolized them—literally. "Show me the dimension of a
Know Nothing," he said, "and I will show you a huge reptile upon
whose neck the foot of every honest man ought to be placed"[1]—a
clear reference to the snake that tempted Eve in the Garden of
Good and Evil.

The governor reminded crowds that immigrants had fought
and died in the Revolutionary War. More controversially, he also
stuck up for the state's tiny Catholic population. He charged that
the Know-Nothings were trying to set one sect of Christian
against another and were thus in league with "the Devil, his
Satanic Majesty."[2]

His defense of Catholics cost the governor votes but didn't
finish him off. At the time, only Johnson could have staked out
the principled position he did in Tennessee politics and still win
here. It wasn't so much that voters agreed with him as that he was
that rare politician who can turn a disagreement into a thing of
defiant beauty.

In the early twentieth century, for instance, the British Catholic
writer and candidate for Parliament Hilaire Belloc spoke to the
voters in the Salford South riding. Responding to "papist"
taunts from a predominantly Protestant audience, Belloc pulled
a rosary out of his pocket, and explained, "Sir, so far as possible
I hear Mass each day and I go to my knees and tell these beads
each night. If that offends you, then I pray God may spare me

the indignity of representing you in Parliament." Belloc also won the election.

The campaign against the Know-Nothings wasn't the only time that Johnson's fiery political oratory would put his career, or even his life, in jeopardy. The wonderful book *The Avenger Takes His Place* recounts a campaign story with an utterly Johnsonian twist. The Tennessee governor had received several death threats contingent on him speaking at an event, but he showed up anyway and took his turn at the podium to speak.

"Fellow-citizens," Johnson began, "it is proper when freemen assemble for the discussion of important public interests, that every thing should be done decently and in order." He had been informed that "part of the business to be transacted on the present occasion" was his assassination. He proposed "that this be the first business in order," and continued, "if any man has come here tonight for the purpose indicated, I do not say to him, 'Let him speak,' but 'let him shoot.'"

Johnson stood there for half a minute, surveying the crowd with his right hand on his pistol, daring somebody to reach for it. Nobody drew on him. After the long pause, he said, "Gentlemen, it appears that I have been misinformed." He holstered his gun and began his regularly scheduled speech.[3]

THE OTHER ANDY

There was one other important reason that Johnson could beat Gentry, even when his position was not held by most. Then, as ever, he framed his argument to appeal to the poor, the dispossessed, the lower class, the common man. He knew how they thought and so could state unpopular things in ways that were palatable to them.

Johnson never was a member of any church, but he professed to be a Christian who venerated the Bible. He attended Baptist and Methodist services and also, much more controversially, Catholic Masses. In defense of his occasional Mass attendance, Johnson offered the explanation that Catholic services were more democratic than many of the alternatives. Unlike Protestant churches of the time, Catholic churches didn't allow rich families to buy reserved pews.* The rich and the poor were seated together, though they wouldn't be forced to shake hands until the 1960s.

* That wasn't quite as snobbish as it sounds. Many Protestant churches sold reserved pews in advance to finanace the construction of churches.

Political opponents who attacked Johnson for his modest beginnings always came to regret it. He didn't run from his poor past; he cultivated it; it hung about him like the dirt cloud that follows the Charlie Brown regular, Pigpen. Attacks and whispers against him simply made him more determined to out-poor his pompous political foes, even though he person-ally accumulated a small** fortune, including property and slaves.

** By which I mean, large.

Rare was the Johnson campaign speech that didn't include an account of his dirt-poor childhood—father drowned when he was young; apprenticed to a "mudsill" tailor at age ten by a mother who could no longer support him; wholly unschooled; learned to read and write through his own efforts and through the tutelage of his wife, Eliza.

Johnson once called himself not a "pseudo, hermaphroditish Vallandigham [Democrat] but a Jacksonian Democrat."[4] Clement

Vallandigham was an Ohio politician who represented everything that Johnson abhorred. Colonel Jackson was the Indian fighter, war hero, and first Democratic president so memorably memorialized at the Tennessee capitol, and practically the only influence that mattered when Johnson entered the political arena here.

It made sense for Johnson to model himself after Jackson, and not just in the sense that modern Republicans claim to worship at the shrine of Reagan the Great. There really were a lot of similarities. Both men were often referred to as the more informal "Andy"—today, they might be called "Drew." Both embraced mass democracy and populist ideas in a way that put them out ahead of their contemporaries. Both also inspired loyal followings and intense hatreds.

If you had to locate the point of departure in the two men's character, it *might* be Johnson's resentments, though Jackson wasn't entirely lacking in that department. Johnson steamed and boiled and consumed his politics. Popular historian Howard Means writes that his struggle "was a lifelong fight against the swells, the blue-bloods, the pocket liners and influence wielders and schemers."[5]

During his first term in Congress, Johnson denounced his would-be social betters as an "illegitimate, swaggering, bastard, scrub aristocracy," and he wasn't just whistling Dixie. He struck back at them throughout his career with blistering rhetoric (one of the articles of his impeachment would be for "intemperate, inflammatory and scandalous harangues") and with leveling legislation.

Some of Johnson's proposals were the sort of vaguely progressive things that wouldn't raise an eyebrow today—the direct election of senators, for instance, and more state funds for public education. Some made sense in a country still spreading across the continent. The Homestead Act, a bill that granted land to settlers who would build houses on and maintain sizable tracts of land, was a piece of legislation that Johnson championed and rejoiced to see signed into law.

And some of his ideas were just kooky proposals—populism on steroids. Johnson wanted to limit all federal employees to eight years of service so everyone could have his turn. The desire to limit the bad effects of patronage may have been admirable, but his solution would have stripped government of whatever vital expertise it had managed to hold on to through the changeover of several administrations. He also opposed prisoner work details on the grounds they took work away from noncriminal craftsmen, such as . . . well, Johnson.

EMANCIPATION PROCRASTINATION

This Tennessee man of the people was also like Jackson in his basic outlook toward national politics. Johnson believed devoutly in an assertive executive, territorial expansion, states' rights, the Constitution, and the permanence of the Union. So while the unexpected election of Abraham Lincoln as president in 1860 convinced many Southern politicians, including former president John Tyler, to head for the exits, it only stiffened Johnson's resolve to keep the United States united.

Several of Johnson's enemies had attacked him as an abolitionist during earlier phases of his career. It wasn't true—he was a slave owner, for crying out loud—but he believed there were greater goods than slavery. Having been appointed to the Senate, Johnson became the only Southern senator to buck the drive to secession.

His impassioned speeches kept Tennessee "in" until

Tennesseans understandably balked at sending troops to fight fellow Southerners. When the state decided to leave, it did so over the objection of a sizable minority, including a majority of the voters in Johnson's base of east Tennessee.

Parts of the state were easily recaptured or held by the Union, but Tennessee was still a staging ground for conflicts as well as a bloody crossroads for armies. President Lincoln sent Johnson back to Nashville as the military governor, and he did what he could to cope with famine, disease, overcrowding, disloyalty, and Baghdad-level civilian violence. During one particularly close call with Confederate forces, he warned his staff, "I am not a military man but anyone who talks of surrender I will shoot!"[6]

His thinking during the war about slavery evolved, perhaps out of necessity. He went into the conflict *for* slavery and *for* the Union. He dismissed charges that the war was about slavery by saying, "Damn the Negroes. I am fighting those traitorous aristocrats, their masters."[7]

In Johnson's populist-Manichean worldview, it all made perfect sense. The *South* wasn't in revolt—at least not as a whole. It was all a matter of a few rich and powerful men exploiting sectional tensions in both the North and the South to bust up one perfectly good Union. And his job as a politician in this time of tumult was to sock it both to the abolitionists and to the secessionists.

On the one hand, he fulminated against well-heeled "traitors" and threatened to stretch a few necks when this little revolt was put down. On the other, when Lincoln was drafting the Emancipation Proclamation, Johnson succeeded in having Tennessee left off the list of states that were technically considered "in rebellion" and thus subject to having slaves emancipated by executive order.

But as the war wore on and Johnson tried to figure out how to reconstitute an elected government in Tennessee, he started to realize just how impossible it would be to return to the status quo. Once the Emancipation Proclamation took effect in those states that continued to fight, government couldn't very well unfree the slaves.

Both North and South used carrots and sticks to get blacks to help support their armies or fight outright. Slaveholders in Tennessee and elsewhere were paid by the Union for the "use" of several thousand slaves. The transaction amounted to one-half of that old hard-core abolitionist demand, "emancipation without compensation," and Johnson knew it.

He eventually turned against slavery and turned hard. He would paint himself after the fact as someone who had always been against the institution, even though he had owned slaves and defended slavery. As Senator John Kerry might put it, he was against it *while* he was for it. (Or there's always "personally opposed, but . . .")

In Greenville, Confederates had forcibly ejected Johnson's wife and children and seized all of his property there, including slaves. Two of them escaped and made their way to Nashville. Johnson told crowds that the slaves had asked him if they could work for him for pay, and he accepted the deal. It was his way of edging them up to the fact that the peculiar institution was toast with a side of marmalade.

THAT'S THE TICKET

Johnson's late conversion to the antislavery cause is one reason that he became vice president. When he announced his new position, President Lincoln wrote to him, "I see that you have declared in favor of emancipation, for which, may God bless you."[8] The other reason is rather more crass but no less true: Lincoln needed the votes.

With most Southern states excluded from the electoral college, you'd think the Republicans could win reelection in a walk, but that wasn't obvious at the time. A large number of Northerners were so-called copperheads—Democrats who wanted the war to end and for the South either to be allowed to secede or to reenter the Union on its own terms. Cities such as New York erupted in deadly draft riots.[9] Though the North had a superior economy to crank up the war machine, Southern soldiers continued to fight as though their lives depended on it.

The Republican Party was only one of several parties that had emerged from the breakdown of the Whigs and the fisticuffs over slavery. Republicans had only won one national election, and that one by default. In 1860, Lincoln had secured a plurality in a four-way race, with less than 40 percent of the popular vote. The result: civil war.

It was conceivable that Lincoln could lose in 1864. And it became clear that if he did win, he'd have to win convincingly, in a way that told Southern states they should stop fighting. That was going to be a hard trick to pull off with a ticket that was tied to, and representative of, the Republican Party. The solution to this problem turned out to be a two-step affair:

Step one: switch parties. Lincoln supporters worked to create a shell party called the National Union Party. It was supposed to be a wartime unity ticket composed of Republicans, pro-war Democrats, and unaffiliated Unionists. They had to come up with some way of proving that this wasn't just the GOP in drag, however, so . . .

Step two: switch veeps. Lincoln's first vice president, Hannibal Hamlin, had been a senator from Maine. If the president couldn't win there on his own strength, he might as well have packed it in. Hamlin was also a teetotaler and a Radical Republican whose instincts on what to do with the South made Lincoln seem like Snuggles the Bear. The president once joked, "I have an insurance on my life worth half the prairie land in Illinois."[10] The "insurance" policy was Hamlin.

Hamlin's chief virtue was also his vice. He was far too prickly to extend an olive branch, which was exactly what Lincoln needed to do. What he wanted was a running mate who was stoutly committed to the war but who could broaden the president's national appeal. In 1860, Lincoln hadn't even been on the ballots of most Southern states. In the next election, he put a Southerner on the ticket to help bring the South back in.

LANDING ON CEREMONY

Many Republicans would come to bitterly regret that decision, starting with the swearing-in ceremony. Johnson's first act as vice president was an abject embarrassment, though it's only fair to point out that he'd tried to avoid it. Johnson was recovering from typhoid fever and tried to beg off attending the inauguration.

Lincoln pressed him to attend, and so Johnson reluctantly made the trip. The night before, he drank too much and showed up on the morning of March 4, 1865, sickly and with a raging hangover. Seeing his dour condition, out-going vice president Hamlin broke with his normal policy (he had banned spirits from the Senate) and sent an aide to fetch a bottle of whisky to help steady the vice president-elect's nerves and calm his hangover.

It worked too well. Johnson quickly downed about half the bottle. By the time he was called to give a short speech and take his oath of office, you could have driven a nine-inch nail through his left earlobe and he wouldn't have felt it. He rambled on for seventeen long minutes about his lowly origins and the wellspring of power in a democracy—poor people like Andrew Johnson.

It was one of those awkward moments that we all hope to avoid. Senator Charles Sumner hid his face under his hands. Hamlin yanked at Johnson's coat in a failed attempt to make him shut the hell up. Senator Zachariah Chandler, a Johnson supporter, captured the mood of the room. "Had I been able to find a hole I would have dropped through it out of sight," he admitted.[11]

Johnson's one additional task that day was to oversee the swearing in of new senators, but he was too incoherent to manage it and fobbed the task off on a clerk. Lincoln walked out to the steps of the Capitol to deliver his famous second inaugural. He ordered the Senate sergeant at arms to keep the vice president from any further speechifying that day, for his own good.

The incident would be nothing more than a historical footnote—"Oh those wacky vice presidents!" people would say. Except that on April 14, not two months after the inauguration, an intruder lied and then forced his way into the bedroom of the ailing Secretary of State William Steward and stabbed him several times in the face and neck. That same night, the star actor John Wilkes Booth barged into the reserved box at Ford's Theatre and shot the president in the head.

Steward eventually recovered, though he was scarred for life, and the deaths of his wife and daughter not long afterward were probably hastened by the bloody horror show. Lincoln never awoke and was pronounced dead the next morning. Johnson found out about this on the night of the fourteenth, when a civil servant from the patent office came knocking at the door of his hotel room.

Johnson would later find out that he was also on the hit list—which at least had the salutary effect of quieting a lot of the conspiracy theories. Booth had offered money to one George Atzerodt to kill the vice president. Atzerodt took the money and checked into a room at Whitlow House, where Johnson was staying, but he couldn't work up the nerve.

While Booth and knife man Lewis Powell plunged the capital into chaos, Atzerodt imbibed and nervously wandered the streets—a troubled soul condemned to death by his own greed and cowardice.

NOT A LINCOLN

As president, Johnson quickly learned how difficult it is to follow a martyr. Lincoln had come around to emancipation and even mused about voting rights for some of the former slaves, but as war wound down, he had faced daunting problems which were now Johnson's problems.

Lincoln had been far less radical, and less vengeful, than many of the Republicans in Congress. They didn't want him to let the South up easy; he wanted to find some way of convincing the South that this was a victory for the Union, not just for the North.

But it was difficult to pursue both at the same time or even to split the difference. If he'd lived, it's possible that his second term would have been a total flop.

After his death, Northern preachers, politicians, and poets turned Lincoln's moderation into a trait that was good for him, at the time, but no longer enough for the country. Herman Melville composed the poem "The Martyr" about the assassination of Lincoln, the mourning of the Unionists ("There is sobbing of the strong / And a pall upon the land"), and their demands for vengeance. Older readers might remember the repeated lines "Beware the People weeping / When they bare the iron hand" from grade school. Melville captured popular expectation when he wrote of the changeover from Lincoln to Johnson, "They have killed him, the Forgiver— / The Avenger takes his place."

For the first few weeks of his rule, it looked as though Johnson would live up to that billing. He gave fiery speeches about making treason "odious," and he assured many Republicans that he understood their concerns, and shared them. They could breathe easy, and the rebel leaders should worry about having their air supply cut off by rope.

He wasn't lying exactly, but he was shaping his message to the audience. Johnson did believe that slavery was finished. He made it clear to Southerners that an end to human bondage was one of the costs of the war. He also advocated limited suffrage for blacks. He thought that those who owned property and had significant assets should have the right to vote, though he didn't insist on this as a condition for recognizing state governments as properly reconstructed.

Johnson was willing to blame Southern plantation owners and

other moneyed men for what had gone wrong, not the people. He might have been able to sell Congress on a watered-down version of this approach, but he chose to grab the unruly bull of Reconstruction by the horns and wrestle it to the ground all by himself.

The president announced a general pardon for most Southerners who were willing to swear a loyalty oath, excluding members of the Confederate government, high-ranking military officers, and very rich Southerners, and allowed that even those groups could appeal their case directly to the White House. He also put forward generous terms under which the federal government would recognize the states as having been brought back into the company of equals.

That choice meant two headaches for Johnson. Because a large number of people were excluded from the pardon, waves of petitioners came to see him to ask for mercy. The queues to see him got to be so long that people who had some way of expediting the process could demand tidy sums from petitioners.

Worse, Congress, not having been consulted on this, was furious. Enraged Republicans tried to pass all manner of legislation, by overriding Johnson's vetoes, to beef up the federal Reconstruction effort and limit Johnson's powers. When Southern states elected delegations and sent them to Congress, the body exercised its right of refusing to seat them.

DEATH OF JOHNSON

Lincoln might have been able to deal with the Republicans. He was their first president, and he knew how to work a room of his peers. But Johnson had started out all wrong and was proud and stubborn and combative. He was also a Democrat.

The refusal of Congress to seat the Southern politicians so incensed Johnson that he endorsed most of the opposition to the Republicans in 1866 and campaigned for them. When the voters in the Northern states returned an increased Republican majority, it was only a matter of time before the confrontations escalated. Even otherwise unobjectionable actions, like the purchase of Alaska from Russia, raised hackles.

Congress passed the blatantly unconstitutional Tenure of Office Act over Johnson's veto to keep him from removing Republican appointees. He responded by waiting until Congress was out of session and removing and replacing Secretary of War Edwin Stanton.

That led to the president's impeachment in the House and a lively trial before the Senate in 1868 that lasted nearly three months. Johnson missed being removed from office by a single vote. In his book *Profiles in Courage*, John Kennedy celebrated the man who'd been billed the swing vote, Senator Edmund Ross from Kansas, but also acknowledged "those who stood with him."[12]

Ross's vote was the most dramatic, but he wasn't the lone dissenter. Several Republicans, who otherwise opposed the president's policies, thought that to remove him from office over a piece of legislation that the Supreme Court would later, predictably, find to be unconstitutional was a bit much. The dissenters were just numerous enough to keep Johnson from being removed from office.

It wasn't likely that Johnson would have another shot at the presidency, but the long impeachment trial completely finished off his chances. It did not, however, finish off his desire to poke at the powers that be, stick up for his people, or run for office. In fact, he found a way to leave the White House with a bang.

Ulysses Grant was elected in the fall of 1868. In the lame-duck phase of his presidency, on Christmas Day of that year, Johnson issued a blanket pardon of all Southerners who took part in the rebellion, including former Confederate president Jefferson Davis.

Then he returned to his state and three times sought seats in the House and Senate. Eventually the people came through for him, if by "people" you mean state legislators. In 1874, they appointed the old pol for one more term in the country's most exclusive club.

Johnson was seated in the Senate in the spring of 1875 and gave one rabble-rousing speech denouncing the corruption of the Grant administration, which was interesting considering that Grant had been Johnson's first choice to replace Stanton.

The former president died that summer of a stroke near Elizabethton, Tennessee, and was buried in Greenville with a copy of the Constitution.* Historians tend to take a dim view of Johnson's legacy, but their criticism comes with its own built-in irony. Improbably, history has remembered our seventeenth president badly for playing the part of "the Forgiver."

* The joke almost writes itself: Johnson didn't think of it as a living document.

BANG, YOU'RE
PRESIDENT

If it were not for the reporters,
I would tell you the truth.

—CHESTER ALAN ARTHUR

The predicament that made Chester Arthur into president may be hard to wrap your head around. On July 2, 1881, President James Garfield arrived at a train station in D.C., to go on a long summer vacation. The president was accompanied by Secretary of State James Blaine and met a few other government officials and well-wishers at the station. Without warning, two shots rang out.

Both bullets, broadly speaking, found their mark. One went clean through Garfield's shoulder and exited out his back. The other bullet lodged itself somewhere near his pancreas, we now know. Surgeons continued to prod at the wound in search of the .44-caliber slug from the Webley "British Bulldog" revolver. They never did find it.

It's hard to say for sure, but Garfield may have been able to survive with the bullet stuck in him; one of his predecessors, Andrew Jackson, had lived half his life with a dueling round lodged near his heart. What is known is that the doctors didn't bother to scrub down or use sterilized implements as they poked at the president. That made infection well-nigh inevitable, as did the fact that one physician managed to damage Garfield's liver.*

* See Hippocratic Oath, the.

Infections ravaged his body for nearly three months. The doctors' ministrations weren't helping things. Inventor Alexander Graham Bell brought in a prototype metal detector just to locate the bullet. It didn't work for the tragicomic reason that the underside of the bed that the president was resting on was metallic.

The ailing Garfield was moved to Long Branch, New Jersey. The official reason was that doctors thought the sea air could do him good. Unofficially, it was a much more pleasant place to expire than the nation's capital, especially during the long, hot, scorching summer and early autumn.

Garfield died in Long Branch on September 19. His once-formidable body had wasted away. The day the bullets struck him, the six foot two man weighed north of 200 pounds. Only about 120 pounds of flesh were left to bury.[1]

The president's final words were a puzzle: "The people . . . trust." Presumably, "the people" were the American people, which raised questions. Were they object or subject? If subject, what or whom did they trust? Was it a warning (the people *are wrong* to trust); an imperative (the people *should* trust); or the scattered, incoherent utterances of a fading man? In other words, were they *words* but not really *thoughts*?

All of those interpretations are possible. So is this one: the words were sage advice to Vice President Arthur. After all, the president had had a long time to ponder what he wanted to say. Soon after he had been shot, a physician on the scene tried to downplay the injuries. Garfield replied, "I thank you, doctor, but I am a dead man." He saw it coming, and he knew that his successor would have a crisis of credibility on his hands.

GONNA SHOOT YOU RIGHT DOWN

The vice president's problem was simple and horrible. A relatively unknown lawyer named Charles Guiteau was the assassin. He surrendered his gun and his person to authorities, announcing proudly, "I did it! I will go to jail for it! I am a Stalwart of the Stalwarts, and Arthur will be president!" In a letter, he also called the vice president "my friend Arthur."

To gauge how poisonous those words were, imagine the political fallout if the Democrats had had tapes of Lee Harvey Oswald proclaiming "Nixon's the one" or got hold of footage of John Hinckley stumping for George H. W. Bush. It was without question the least welcome endorsement in the history of the republic.*

In Guiteau's mind, the shooting was entirely political. Garfield and Arthur were thought to belong to two different factions of the Republican Party, with the awful nicknames the "Stalwarts" and the "Half Breeds." Stalwarts believed in mom, apple pie, and patronage—in reverse order. The Half Breeds believed in the first two and had a few ideas about reform.

* With the possible exception of the time Jim Jones endorsed Jimmy Carter.

The governing parties at federal and state levels then ran what amounted to massive job programs for supporters. Civil-service positions were political appointments. That meant employees could be terminated at will or would be fired en masse if their horse lost an election. The parties in charge tried to keep that from happening by demanding "assessments" from government workers to finance the campaigns.

Letters demanding assessments were phrased as "requests" but, as on *Jeopardy*, the form-of-a-question thing was purely for show. These were really nonnegotiable fees—a cross between union dues (for collective bargaining, with the voters) and protection money. Parties would ask for a fraction of the worker's income, and he'd pay up and not gripe too loudly about it if he wanted to keep his job.

The mandatory fees were only the thin, green shell on the iceberg lettuce of corruption. Assessments were perfectly legal, but the monies raised financed some things that weren't, including bribery and vote buying. Legal violations of sense and propriety went well with more serious transgressions. Kickbacks were commonplace. Enterprising office holders and government workers constantly found new ways to drain the Treasury of excess revenues.*

Most voters may not have liked the patronage system, but it created a level of cynicism about government that was hard for critics to overcome. Would-be reformers were often those parties out of power. They were very likely to quietly change their positions once they were in charge and supporters came a-calling in search of jobs.

Fired jobholders could complain that they were trod on by an unfair system and insist that government service should be based

* As opposed to today, when they find ways of spending money that we don't have.

more on what you know than who you know, but who would listen? However admirable these men might have been, they had benefited from that system in the first place, so the amount of sympathy their sob stories could generate was limited.

You say you got a plum job because of your connections and then lost it because you angered a political boss? *What did you expect?*

TILDEN AT WINDMILLS

What nobody expected was that the ferocious fights over patronage would lead to the assassination of a president. It had been thought that, unlike European nations, America had purged all the political violence from its system during the Civil War.

Yes, postwar rhetoric could be vitriolic and overblown, but it had the quality of a soap-operatic melodrama. Most of the Great Questions had been settled. The country used to rend its garments over secession and slavery. Now the great question was, who gets a cut?

Nationally, the answer was, Republicans. After Andrew Johnson left office, a Democrat wouldn't live in the White House again until 1885. Memories of the war and Reconstruction made it difficult for the opposition. However, that didn't mean it wasn't a fight.

At the presidential level, immensely popular war hero Ulysses Grant* racked up two commanding electoral victories before things hit a rough spot. In the election of 1876, the Democrats' Samuel

* Q: Why not "General" Grant?
A: Because Garfield, Arthur, and pretty much everybody else involved in this story also have the title "general."

Tilden and Thomas Hendricks bested Republicans Rutherford Hayes and William Wheeler by a quarter of a million votes in the popular total, but didn't clearly win in the electoral college.

The result was a little bit like the 2000 Florida recount debacle—on crack. Bedlam reigned and poured in the electoral college. Four states issued contested slates, or multiple slates, of voters to cast ballots for president. The matter was eventually thrown to Congress, which created a commission that included members of Congress and the Supreme Court to sort it out.

Commissioners ruled in favor of the Republicans on a party-line vote, which did not go over well with angry voters and office-holders. The politicians made their peace—Democrats finally agreed to let Hayes and Wheeler be president and veep in exchange for the federal government withdrawing all of its remaining troops from the South. But many, many voters were still boiling over with anger. Hayes first took the oath of office privately, just in case the public swearing-in was disrupted by riots.

Arthur: Opposed the president

Hayes's administration didn't fare much better. In an effort to win over Democrats, the new president threw them some appointments, which made Republicans wonder why they had gone to the trouble. If the point of a Republican president was to squeeze as many jobs out of the government as possible, he wasn't delivering.

MAKING HAYES

Worse, unlike the Stalwart former president Grant, that Half Breed Hayes wanted to reform the civil service. To do so, he had to make an example, and in Chester "Chet" Arthur, Hayes thought he had the perfect target. The political calculation was simple:

- Arthur had been appointed by President Grant as collector of the Port of New York at the urging of the political boss, New York senator Roscoe Conkling.
- Arthur ran the Customs House—the agency responsible for collecting tariffs on goods that came into the country through New York harbors, and seizing smuggled goods.
- Arthur was extremely well compensated for his efforts, he had stuffed the Customs House with Republican Party workers, and his office hours were a running joke.
- Arthur's wealth and refined taste were conspicuous. He dressed in tawny suits and took his meals and entertained at Delmonico's Restaurant and the Fifth Avenue Hotel.

Ready, aim, fire the guy, right? Here Hayes had the chance to send a signal about what his government expected from its bureaucrats. Arthur owed his livelihood to the very kind of politics, and the very kind of politician, that the president was dead set against. The reformer from Ohio almost didn't have a choice in the matter.

When President Hayes attempted to fire Arthur and replace him with Theodore Roosevelt Sr., however, Congress balked. The Stalwarts, led by Senator Conkling, led the charge against the firing, as expected. But support for Arthur turned out to be fairly broad.

The case for Arthur wasn't difficult to make: he was tied to Conkling but had none of the senator's bombast. He was a good organizer who had served as quartermaster general for New York during the war—a job that made him responsible for feeding, housing, and supplying several hundred thousand troops. And unlike previous controllers, he didn't take bribes or find other illegal means to feather his bed.

Moreover, he was a pleasant fellow. Republicans from the different factions of the party genuinely liked Arthur, and they were willing to stick up for him. Senators speechified against the firing. Several GOP-leaning newspapers, including the *New York Times*,* took his side.

* No, that's not a typo.

The Tenure of Office Act—the piece of legislation whose violation had led to President Johnson's impeachment and near removal—was invoked, which was a sign of just how contentious the issue had become. The Act was meant to keep a hated Democratic president from removing Reconstructionist Republicans without the consent of the Senate, not to keep a Republican president from being able to appoint his own men.

President Hayes finally did manage to can Arthur in 1878, when Congress was in recess. It was a bloody nose for all Stalwart Republicans, and it heralded doom for the whole party in the midterm elections. The GOP lost control of both House and Senate, and for the last years of his term, the president found himself warring with a party whose candidate should have rightly been president.

Hayes had promised during the 1876 election that he would only serve one term, which was just as well. If his loss of the popular vote and jury-rigged electoral college hadn't finished off his chances, the electorally poisonous fighting between powerful factions of the Republican Party would have been the coup de grâce.

LUCK OF THE ENGLISH

Arthur's nomination for vice president would otherwise have been a complete mystery. The former controller had never run for office nor seriously contemplated running. It would simply have been out of character. He preferred to wield influence in the presence of fine meals, brandy, and cigars.

In the primaries of 1880, Stalwarts had tried to secure the nomination for Grant for an unprecedented third term. They narrowly failed. The Half Breeds were likewise unable to nominate their standard-bearer James Blaine. After three dozen rounds of balloting, delegates to the Republican national convention settled instead for the mildly reformist James Garfield—and adopted a mildly reformist platform to go with him.

That unexpected choice left the slot of vice president open, but not wide-open. The nominee for veep would have to be able to get the Stalwarts on board without being completely objectionable to the Half Breeds. He'd also have to deliver a state that was teetering. Arthur fit the bill. It didn't hurt that his name was fresh in the minds of the delegates because of the controversies of the last few years.

Arthur shocked and offended his mentor Senator Conkling by saying yes when Garfield's men asked if they could submit

Arthur's name to the convention. He carried the nomination on the first ballot; then he returned to New York to go to work for what most people thought would be a doomed campaign.

The Republican vice-presidential nominee coordinated the effort with ruthless efficiency. Arthur "requested" the assessments of government workers, hit up Republicans of every stripe for money, brokered a truce between warring factions of the party, and disbursed funds and talking points. He also dispatched the party's best operative, Stephen Dorsey, to Indiana with enough money to contest a state that should have been an automatic pickup for the Democrats due to the fact that they had nominated local pol William English for veep.

On election day, the Republicans scored a major upset. In the legislative races, they took back the House of Representatives. In the presidential contest, they won the popular vote by a sliver of 1 percent, which was a whole lot better than the quarter-million vote deficit of the previous Republican ticket.

They also managed to get the votes where they counted. The GOP held New York and the rest of the Northern states, poached Indiana, and confined Democratic wins largely to the solid South. Their majority in the electoral college was a respectable 214 to 155.

A party was held at Delmonico's after the election to honor Dorsey's achievement. The guest list included John Jacob Astor, J. P. Morgan, and Ulysses Grant. Booze flowed freely into the night, and the drunken guests began hinting at the sorts of things that Dorsey had engaged in to win what even Arthur conceded had been a de facto Democratic state.

Finally, the vice president-elect noticed that the journalists present were madly scribbling, and cautioned the guests: "I don't

think we had better go into the minute details of the campaign."
He then proceeded, in the words of biographer Zachary Karabell,
to "taste his own shoe leather." Arthur alluded to some of the dirty
tricks of the election and said, "If it were not for the reporters, I
would tell you the truth."[2]

ALL ABOARD FOR ALBANY

The opening months of President Garfield's administration did
not give Arthur's faction great cause for celebration. During the
campaign, Garfield had made some vague promises about appointing Stalwarts, and those pledges were rarely carried out. The cabinet officers were all Half Breeds, with the exception of Thomas
James for postmaster general.

In order to placate Senator Conkling, Garfield deferred to
him on the nominations of a number of judges and other appointments, especially those in and around New York. Stalwarts were
not enthusiastic about the concessions, but they'd take what they
could get. Memories of how a divided party had been swept out in
the midterm elections made them cautious about openly feuding.

Enter Secretary of State James Blaine. He argued to Garfield
that the concessions to Roscoe went too far and threatened to
resign if some of the appointments weren't withdrawn. Garfield
took the threat seriously. He sacked the head of the New York
Customhouse and nominated Half Breed William Robertson to be
the new collector.

This was "perfidy without parallel,"[3] Conkling alliterated, and
many other Stalwarts joined their voices to the outrage. It signaled that the fights between factions of the Republican Party

would be just as fierce during the Garfield administration as they had been under Hayes's tortured tenure.

Arthur didn't hesitate before siding with Conkling against Blaine and the president. He tipped his old mentor off when he learned of the nomination. Then Arthur lobbied to defeat Robertson's nomination in the Senate. When it became clear that a combination of Republican Half Breed support and Democratic calculation would put Robertson in the Customhouse, Conkling and fellow New York senator Thomas Platt came up with an idea that has to rank right up there with automotive ejector seats, Rabbit Jerky, and New Coke: they resigned.

It's hard to explain their resignations. We can look at the gambit now as the height of hubris; there was more to it than that. One charge the Half Breeds could always throw at the Stalwarts was that their agenda lacked popular support. In a sense, it was true. Americans were already suspicious of government. Pile patronage on top of suspicion and people had even less of a reason to be interested.

Another way of looking at it was more practical. *Popular support?* Stalwarts could ask, *Who got the votes out?* The Half Breeds tried and failed in 1876. The Stalwarts pulled it out for them in the next presidential go-round, and now the ungrateful reformers were acting too good for their own coalition partners. They knew the truth that Arthur had refrained from blurting out, but they thought that the Stalwarts would ultimately have to suck it up and go along.

By resigning and forcing the New York legislature to vote on their reappointments, Platt and Conkling were looking to radically shift the debate. The effect that they were after was similar to a snap election in a parliamentary democracy—called when the ruling party finds itself hopelessly divided on an important question.

The Stalwarts wanted to prove that they enjoyed popular support and that Republicans would be foolish to follow James Blaine and company on their high horses, charging over an electoral cliff. They went to Albany to convince state legislators to return them to the Senate.

Arthur supported their effort in word and in deed. He traveled with them to the state capital to help lobby the state legislators, and covered much of the bill. It must have been an odd spectacle to see the vice president picking up the tab for countless rounds of drinks and meals, over which two former senators tried to talk state legislators into helping them embarrass the president.

The trio stumbled over formidable obstacles, including Half Breed resistance in the legislature, parliamentary delaying tactics, and a sex scandal. We'll never be sure how it would have turned out, because while they were trying to secure the reappointments to undermine Garfield, Charles Guiteau shot the president.

NOT A VULTURE

Arthur understood almost immediately what Conkling never quite got. The shooting changed everything. It didn't matter that Guiteau was a "lone gunman," in modern parlance—that nobody had put him up to it. Nor was it terribly relevant that the man was a religious nut who believed that God had told him to kill Garfield, and who composed a manifesto titled *The Truth: A Supplement to the Bible*.

The fact remained: Guiteau had shot the president with the

intention of making Arthur president. And he had been egged on in his deadly quest by the public attacks of several Stalwarts on the president.

The minds of normal people could take in all the pomp and moralizing and discount for political rhetoric. Guiteau didn't have that filter. In the fights between the Stalwarts and the Half Breeds, he saw a political crisis that could only be resolved by murder. Worse, the assassination embodied both madness and self-interest. He had been a chronic "office seeker," like the thousands of people who cycled through D.C. in search of patronage jobs, which was exactly the sort of striving that Arthur and his political allies stoutly defended.

The vice president and Conkling were assigned police guard to protect them from angry mobs. Conkling bristled at this; Arthur pondered. When he spoke to reporters, he chose his words carefully. The shooting was horrible, he said. Whatever differences he'd had with the president, he never wished for anything like this. In his own quiet Episcopalian way, he would be praying for Garfield's life.

Arthur wanted to stay in New York, so as not to create the impression that he was waiting and hoping for the president to die. He may have been many things, but he was not a vulture.

It took a request from political opponent James Blaine to convince the vice president to come to D.C. To Mrs. Garfield, he offered support and condolence. To the cabinet and to anybody who would listen, he said that he did not want to be president—and meant it. Visitors described a man who looked tormented and had to fight back tears.

When Garfield finally died, Arthur was as ready for the presidency as he'd ever be. In fact, in some ways he was a changed man.

SEVENTY-FIVE CENTS

President Arthur met with former Senator Conkling, but it did not go well. The New York pol proved to be less interested in any appointment for himself than with taking care of business, so to speak.

To understand just how petty Conkling's request was, it might be useful to consult the great George Costanza. On a memorable episode of *Seinfeld*, he talked to a customer representative at an automotive dealership. She was trying to apologize because he had paid for a Twix bar that was caught in the vending machine and then eaten by a mechanic. He replied magnanimously: "All I want is my seventy-five cents back, an apology, and for him to be fired!"

Conkling's demand was simple: Arthur must fire Controller Robertson. The president's response was equally simple: no way, José.

Arthur may have thought back to when he was fired and decided to do unto others, or he may have figured that too much political capital had already been squandered fighting over that particular position. As much as he had not wanted Robertson for the job, this was where his two immediate predecessors had stumbled. It was a mistake that his new administration could not afford.

There was also the shift of perspective that usually comes with being president. Arthur thought his new office—which he had never wanted—demanded disinterestedness from its occupants that the office of the vice president does not. It was now his job to rise above faction or at least try to take the needs of the whole nation into consideration. Consequently, his record as president was worlds removed from the naked Machiavellian maneuvering of vice president:

- President Arthur called for civil-service reforms, including the groundbreaking Pendleton Civil Service Reform Act.
- He outlawed assessments of federal employees.
- He extended an olive branch to Garfield's cabinet and kept on Robert Todd Lincoln as secretary of war.
- He vetoed an internal improvements bill that was one of the earliest examples of pork-barrel spending.
- Stephen Dorsey had engaged in a scheme to use postal contracts to defraud the federal government of hundreds of thousands of dollars. Rather than turn a blind eye to his old friend's alleged crimes, Arthur instructed the federal attorneys to prosecute— twice.*

  * It was a bit like George W. Bush ordering the Justice Department to throw the book at Karl Rove.

- He used his own funds to have the White House repaired and stylishly redesigned.
- He began the repair and modernization of the naval fleet that had fallen into disrepair after the Civil War.

His presidency was a mixed blessing for Republicans. In the 1882 elections, there was a general revolt of the voters against corruption and "bossism." The lame-duck Congress broke the logjam that had held back civil-service reform, which at least cut down on Democratic opportunities for patronage.

By the time the 1884 elections rolled around, Arthur enjoyed enough popularity that he might have had a shot at reelection. Republicans thought otherwise. They opted instead to nominate James Blaine, who went on to lose to the popular New York governor and Democrat, Grover Cleveland, and his running mate, the once-jilted Thomas Hendricks.

It was just as well, because Arthur was dying. During his presidency he had gone to great pains to disguise what doctors had diagnosed as Bright's disease. His body did a horrible job of filtering toxins out of his system. The food that he ate—and he was a man of considerable appetites—was slowly killing him.

Garfield had withered away over a few months; for Arthur, the process lasted for at least the last year of his life. He died on November 18, 1886. Had he been president at the time, the nation would have experienced more loss, and another vice president would have been called into service.

MADMAN IN THE WHITE HOUSE

*Mr. President, I can no longer
hold back the Senate.*

—GARRETT HOBART

*I would a great deal rather be anything, say
professor of history, than vice president.*

—THEODORE ROOSEVELT

People tell me that Garret "Gus" Hobart had many good qualities, and I believe them. Unfortunately, it turns out, robust,
good health wasn't one of them.

The New Jersey pol had been selected as William McKinley's
running mate in 1896. The Republicans managed to get more
votes than Democratic candidates William Jennings Bryan and
shipbuilding magnate Arthur Sewall, and they got the votes where
they mattered.

Party-building mastermind and Ohio senator Mark Hanna had
raised a record amount of money from businesses. He used those
funds to make the Republicans competitive even in urban areas.

Bryan stumped everywhere, muttering something about crucifixions and crosses of gold and freeing the Lone Ranger's horse; McKinley affected to campaign from his front porch while the Republicans purchased mass advertisements and organized rallies that were really more like parades. After the two nonconsecutive terms of popular Democrat Grover Cleveland, it looked as though the Grand Old Party had righted itself.

McKinley and Hobart were perfect running mates. McKinley was a former Ohio governor, a man of the people, who played well in Peoria. Hobart, a long-term occupant of the New Jersey legislature and a lawyer for the railroads, added necessary regional balance to the ticket, as well as a touch of class. The result was a clean sweep of the Northeast and Midwest, with California thrown in as the electoral cherry on top.

The two Republicans weren't friends before the campaign, but that changed once they decamped to D.C. Hobart became a regular in the White House, which was unheard-of for a vice president. President McKinley visited the house that the Hobarts leased on Lafayette Square so often for dinners, parties, and afternoon smoking sessions that it became known as the "Little Cream White House."

In part, the closeness was due to the saintly efforts of Mrs. Jennie Hobart. She befriended McKinley's wife, Ida, who wanted to shirk most of the duties of First Lady because she was epileptic and therefore reclusive. Jennie would visit the White House every day to check up on Ida and would look after her when the president was out of town. At Ida's urging, she also served as the stand-in First Lady for most official events.*

* It wasn't the only time Jennie's influence played a role in Garrett's political fortunes. He had been a Democrat, but her family was staunchly Republican, so much so that he switched parties right about the time they were wed.

Vice President Hobart's long experience in the state legislature—he had become the highest-ranking officer in both houses—helped him to get along in the U.S. Senate. Hobart took his duty to serve as the president of that body seriously and issued rulings with an authority that few of his predecessors could match.

GAINING GITMO

There was one hitch in Hobart's get-along. The U.S. government had dispatched naval forces to Cuba to protect American interests during an insurrection and to discourage Spanish troops from committing more alleged atrocities. On February 15, 1898, a mysterious explosion rocked the battleship USS *Maine*. It sank to the bottom of Havana harbor, taking more than two hundred sailors with it.

The newspapers went nuts. Media critics have subsequently tut-tutted that the journalism during that period was the ugliest shade of school-bus yellow. On some details, they have a point, but I contend that (1) the outrage of the press over the *Maine* accurately reflected the outrage of the country as a whole, and (2) the notion that the ship was attacked was not ridiculous.

More than one hundred years and several investigations later, we're *still* not sure what sank the vessel: an internal explosion of some kind, or a mine, or a third, still unexplored cause.[1] Soon almost the whole nation took up the battle cry, "Remember the *Maine*! To hell with Spain!"

President McKinley was an admirable holdout. He wasn't convinced that the Spanish had sunk the boat and dispatched fact finders to get to the bottom of it.* He did not want war with Spain and indicated as much.

* Unintentionally morbid pun alert.

Some business and religious groups voiced support for the president, but the Coalition for Prudence and Caution was fighting a losing nonbattle. The people were convinced that an act of war had been committed against their country. Several hundred of their fellow citizens were dead, their bodies lying at the bottom of a foreign harbor, and the living weren't about to roll over.

In the Senate, Vice President Hobart watched opinion swing sharply, then irreversibly, in favor of war. After a speech by Illinois senator William Mason, a demonstration broke out that Hobart was unable to gavel down. He advised McKinley, "Mr. President, I can no longer hold back the Senate. They will act without you if you do not act at once."[2]

That report seems to have broken McKinley's will. He asked Congress for a declaration of war. The pen that he used to sign the declaration was sent to him by his trusted vice president.

The Spanish-American War was a multifront effort that lasted about six months, all told. U.S. victories ranged from comic and bloodless, as when the Navy took Guam because the Spanish officers hadn't been told they were at war, to the hard-fought bloody victories at the battle of El Caney and the battle of San Juan Hill. When the dust had settled, the United States had won Cuba, Guam, Puerto Rico, and the Philippines. And, as a side note, the annexation of Hawaii happened that same year.

Cuba got its independence subject to some annoying U.S. oversight. The now-infamous military base on Guantánamo Bay was one of the conditions of the country's freedom. Guam and Puerto Rico were taken over by the Americans, but the Philippines were more controversial. Hobart cast a tie-breaking vote in the Senate against an amendment to a bill that would have cut the islands loose. His vote reflected a general shift in how part of the country thought about itself. America was now heir to an overseas empire; it was not in any hurry to dismantle that empire.

Hobart might have gone on to a second term as veep or taken over an important cabinet department, but he didn't have the heart for it. Throughout 1899, the vice president suffered fainting spells that marked the slow onset of heart failure. He left the capital to try to recover in his home in Paterson, New Jersey, and wouldn't be talked back to D.C. for any reason. He died on November 21 of that year at the age of fifty-five.*

* He was the sixth of seven vice presidents to die in office. For extra points, name those vice presidents.

ROUGH RUNNING MATE

That left the vice-presidential slot open for the election of 1900. The party faithful wanted one man, and only one man, to fill the role: New York governor Theodore Roosevelt Jr.

McKinley's campaign virtuoso, Senator Hanna was just as determined that "that damn cowboy"[3] should not be vice president. He buttonholed, twisted arms, begged, and cajoled, all to no avail. After the nomination, he asked some Republicans, "Don't any of you realize that there's only one life between this madman and the White House?"[4]

Hanna may have had his own self-interested reasons for opposing Roosevelt. The senator's presidential aspirations were well-known. The fact that both he and McKinley were from Ohio kept him off the ticket, but there was always 1904.

As it was, Roosevelt nearly refused the nomination. He had

ruled it out in advance, saying, "I would a great deal rather be anything, say, professor of history, than vice president." He didn't want to be a mere "figurehead." He thought that the job would be a "bore" and worried that his influence on policy would be "infinitesimal."[5]

But both Hanna and Roosevelt eventually bowed to the inevitable. In Roosevelt's case, his friend Senator Henry Cabot Lodge talked him into accepting it. The ticket of McKinley and Roosevelt walked all over William Jennings Bryan, who came back for a rematch, this time with Cleveland's second vice president Adlai Stevenson.*

* The first. Stevenson's grandson, Adlai Stevenson II would go on to get his clock cleaned by Eisenhower in two successive elections.

In March of 1901, the president and new vice president were sworn in. As expected, Roosevelt found himself sidelined and bored but, alas, not for long.

On September 6 of that year, President McKinley was at the Pan-American Expo in Buffalo, New York. There was a line to shake the president's hand, and so the Polish immigrant and revolutionary anarchist Leon Czolgosz got in line and waited his turn. When he got to McKinley, rather than shake his hand, Czolgosz produced an Iver Johnson revolver and shot the president twice.

One of the bullets did real, but not immediately fatal, damage, puncturing McKinley's stomach, colon, and kidney. The president's doctors tried not to repeat the same mistake that President Garfield's doctors had made and risk infection by looking for the second bullet.

Infection came anyway, in a big way. McKinley died eight days later in Buffalo from septic shock, caused by the gangrene around the bullet wounds.[6] The life that had been standing between Roosevelt and the White House had quit this veil of tears.

GET READY FOR TEDDY

To understand why Senator Hanna would have called the man who would become president mad, watch director John Milius's great made-for-television movie *Rough Riders*. There is Roosevelt, played ably by Tom Berenger, as the number-two man of the navy, making the case for war. There he is, at high-society parties in D.C., buttonholing senators and bumping into anyone who gets in his path. There he is, resigning his post and volunteering to help raise a civilian army and help take Cuba from Spain. And there he is, leading the cavalry charge along with his motley crew of "Rough Riders" up San Juan Hill.[7]

That was par for the course for Roosevelt. He despised the "cold and timid souls who knew neither victory nor defeat," the kind of accommodation that is the stuff of practical politics. He wrote that while criticism "is necessary and useful" and "often indispensable," it cannot "take the place of action, or be even a poor substitute for it. . . . It is the doer of deeds who actually counts in the battle for life."[8] More: "I have a perfect horror of words that are not backed up by deeds."[9]

After the death of his first wife, Alice, in 1884, Roosevelt had entrusted his one young daughter (also named Alice) to the care of his sister Bamie and moved to the Dakota Territory to start a cattle ranch. This was not an easy move for an upper-class city slicker from New York, but Roosevelt claimed that he handled the transition okay. He wrote in his autobiography, "There were all kinds of things I was afraid of at first, ranging from grizzly bears to 'mean' horses and gun-fighters; but by acting as if I was not afraid I gradually ceased to be afraid."[10]

The ranch was not a success. Roosevelt moved back to New York a changed man, having been reborn in nature. He became one of America's founding conservationists. More important, he became a best seller. His books about the life in the West— *Hunting Trips of a Ranchman, Ranch Life of the Hunting-trail*, and *Winning of the West*—were devoured by eager readers.

Almost everything Roosevelt did was infused with a manic energy:

- In 1886, he returned to New York, ran unsuccessfully for mayor of New York City, married childhood friend Edith Kermit Carow, and published the first volume of his western trilogy.[*]

- In 1895, Roosevelt was appointed commissioner of the New York police department and turned it into the first truly modern police force.

  [*] He wrote thirty-five books in all during his lifetime, including two before he had graduated college and one while he was president. No jealousy here.

- In 1897, he was appointed assistant secretary of the navy, which gave him effective control over that branch of the military.

- In 1898, he won the governorship of New York during a victory lap from his heroics in the Spanish-American War.

- The whole time, Roosevelt read two books a day, often tearing the pages out of them as he went. He was also an avid sportsman and boxer. He was very nearly blinded in one eye in a bout during his presidency.[11]

Roosevelt could be a bit odd, but most voters found his eccentricities endearing. One of his verbal tics was the frequent use of the word *bully*.[12] A century ago, this meant what "sweet!" means today, but many of his contemporaries figured anybody that charismatic and that determined would not have to operate with the normal restraints of most presidents. That is, they thought he would be a bully in the modern use of the term—with the military at his beck and call.

PEACETIME PRESIDENT

As president, Roosevelt surprised most of the doubters in matters of affairs of state. Granted, he sent American gunboats to block the Colombian Navy from attacking the province of Panama, thereby creating a separate nation that the United States could do business with. And, sure, he bragged afterward that he "took Panama without consulting the Cabinet."[13]

It was only a splashier way of doing what McKinley or even Hobart might have done. Americans wanted a canal built to make passage from East to West Coasts cheaper and safer. By negotiating an agreement whereby the United States would take over the Panama Canal's construction in 1904, Roosevelt wasn't leading domestic opinion: he was following the rising tide of American adventurism.

But he didn't follow that tide too far. Internationally, Roosevelt, that dangerous cowboy, that warmonger's warmonger turned out to be a . . . peacemaker, the Jimmy Carter of his day. He even got the Nobel Peace Prize to prove it. He arbitrated disputes between France and Germany and Russia and Japan. In the latter case, he helped to end the Russo-Japanese War.

When Roosevelt was up for reelection, he did make some noise challenging Morocco to rein in a local bandit who had seized a Greek who had at one time held American citizenship. The tough-sounding slogan that the president adopted was "Perdicaris alive or Raisuli dead!"[14] He dispatched several gunboats and Marines to the area, but nothing much ever came of it.

Why he proved to be so restrained is a tough question. Before going to war with Spain, Roosevelt had admitted, "I should welcome almost any war, for I think this country needs one,"[15] and he thought the Spanish-American War a "splendid little war."[16] Why, once he had the influence and the power to do it, didn't he launch a "splendid little war" with Morocco or any other easy-to-pick-off target?

It's possible he was only being a prudent imperialist. Some of the gains that the United States made ended up giving this country indigestion. The Philippine-American War, which consisted of several battles and ongoing guerrilla violence, resulted in the deaths of thousands of American troops. He may have thought it best to consolidate the country's gains.

My own pet theory is that the presidency often changes people. When they were congressmen or private citizens or even vice presidents, they felt that they could advance their own parochial interests, but then they became president and realized the awesome responsibility they bore.

Just think: Andy Johnson preached vengeance but ended up a

failure for his pardons. Chet Arthur, spoilsman extraordinaire, reformed the civil service. And Teddy Roosevelt, man of war, gave peace a chance.

If my crackpot conjecture is correct, then it only applies while one is president. After he left office, Roosevelt clamored for America's entrance into World War I. He endorsed Republican candidate Charles Evan Hughes because he had vowed to take us into war while Woodrow Wilson had vowed peace.

When Wilson took us into war anyway, Roosevelt tried to reenter the army but was turned away. All of his sons served with distinction. Kermit served in the Middle East, and Archibald won the Croix de Guerre. Theodore Jr. won the Distinguished Service Cross in World War I and died in 1944, shortly after leading the troops ashore on Utah Beach, for which he was posthumously awarded the Medal of Honor. Youngest son Quentin was shot down and killed over France in June 1918.

AGAINST THE MALEFACTORS

Another strike against the presidency-changes-people theory can be found in the man's domestic policies. He went into the White House a progressive Republican, and a progressive Republican he remained.

As president, he commenced battle with the trusts and America's leading plutocrats—the Rockefellers, Carnegies, and Mellons, et al.—who held dominant positions in banking, oil, and railroad markets. Where Jefferson and Jackson had railed against the monied interests, Roosevelt inveighed against "the malefactors of great wealth."[17]

Before the New Deal, there was the Square Deal. "We must treat each man on his worth and merits as a man," he declared. "We must see that each is given a square deal, because he is entitled to no more and should receive no less."[18]

He was the father of American regulation, initiating federal control of food and drugs. He gained the power to set railroad rates. He established the Forest Service and laid the groundwork for the National Parks system.

Roosevelt thought of himself as a progressive most likely because progress involves action, movement. Arguments that the federal or local governments ought not to do something carried very little weight with him. Those were words.

What Roosevelt valued, in government as in all other spheres of life, were deeds. The complacent critic could construct elaborate arguments for inaction, and he might listen to those with one ear. What he really valued was a decisive leader who could make things happen.

The presidency offered him plenty of opportunities to do just that. When a mine strike threatened to lead to coal shortages, he ordered both the miners and the mine owners into the White House and forced a settlement. When Congress dragged its feet on antitrust legislation, he instructed his Justice Department to launch antitrust lawsuits against large companies.

One bit of inaction that he surprisingly observed was President Washington's example of serving only two terms. Roosevelt stood down for the 1908 election and then toured the world, engaging in exotic hobbies, such as big game hunting in Africa. Eventually, he got bored and got a bug in his bonnet and decided to run for president again. In 1912, the Republican Party refused to oblige, so he started a third party and had a run at it.

If he meant to win, it didn't work. A Roosevelt would eventually shatter Washington's precedent all to pieces, but his name wasn't Teddy.

10

THE THOMAS MARSHALL INTERLUDE

If you look upon me as a wild animal,
be kind enough to throw peanuts at me.
—THOMAS MARSHALL

With the number of constitutional crises America has faced over the years, critics often make the argument that the framers should have seen X coming and done a better job of preparing for the problem.

The criticism is usually valid, but there are some scenarios that are so far out of left field that nobody could have predicted them—such as the wife of the president deciding that the little problem of her husband's debilitating stroke did not bear on his fitness for office.

That was the call that Edith Wilson made in 1919. The scary thing about it is that, almost a century later, we still don't know all of what really happened.

We do have pieces. On September 25 of that year, Woodrow

Wilson was in Pueblo, Colorado, arguing for American member-
ship in the League of Nations, when he briefly lost his capacity for
speech. A week later, on October 2, he was going
through his normal morning bathroom routine
when he pitched face-forward into the edge of the
White House bathtub.*

* Curse you,
Millard Fillmore.

Smack!

Edith found him half an hour later, unconscious. There was
blood everywhere.[1]

She decided the most important thing was to keep a lid on the
situation. She made a private call to a White House usher, Ike
Hoover. He summoned the president's personal physician, Rear
Admiral Cary Grayson, who arrived by car at about 9 a.m., one
hour after the blood vessel in the president's brain had exploded.[2]

Grayson confirmed to Edith that her husband, the chief executive of the United States, was paralyzed.

This presented a problem for Edith
—and for America. According to the
Constitution,** "In the Case of the Re-

** Article Two, Section 1,
Clause 6, if you're keeping score.

moval of the President from Office, or of his Death, Resignation,
or Inability to discharge the Powers and Duties of the said Office,"
his powers "shall devolve on the Vice President."

Sounds reasonably straightforward, no? The president of the
United States, paralyzed and close to death, lying in a pool of his
own blood. Check. Inability. Check.

But not to Edith Wilson. There was no way she was going to
allow a Hoosier hick named Thomas Marshall to take over.

And so, for eighteen months, Edith Wilson, Admiral Grayson,
and the president's private secretary, Joseph Tumulty, ran the show.

Vice President Marshall never got to see the president until the end of his term in 1921.[3]

Tumulty came along with a *Baltimore Sun* reporter, J. Fred Essary, to inform Marshall that the president could buy the farm at any moment, but apart from that, everything was A-OK. That was the extent of the communications from the White House.[4]

Later Marshall asked Agriculture Secretary David Houston for the lowdown, which wasn't terribly helpful. Houston observed that Marshall was close to panic. Marshall told Houston that it might be "a tragedy for him to assume the duties of President," personally and "for the people." Marshall added that it would be "especially trying" if he was forced "to assume the duty without warning."[5]

Historians have been hard on Marshall, writing him off as a ditherer with Jell-O for a spine. But that seems unfair. Most people, given the possibility that he had been given, would have started building themselves up for taking over; Marshall's self-assessment was not self-serving or flattering in the least. That has to count for something.

It may have been the case that he wasn't prepared for the presidency. Normally, presidents have ample experience running for office or leading large numbers of men, but not Marshall. He was a small-town lawyer from Columbia City, Indiana, who had run for office only two times before 1912.

In 1880 he ran for county prosecutor and lost. In 1908 he ran for governor of Indiana and won. Wilson, the brainy and bossy academic who thought the world of his own abilities, never liked him and never respected him.

HOOSIER DADDY?

The choice of Marshall had been a fluke of geography. The Republicans had put a Hoosier on the ticket, so the Democrats wanted one on Wilson's ticket. Wilson reluctantly agreed. Teddy Roosevelt's Bull Moose candidacy wiped out William Howard Taft, and Marshall found himself veep.

Marshall loved booze and cigars, though he gave up the bottle at the urging of his wife when he was forty-four. He continued to puff up a storm, however, and unlike many recovering alcoholics, he didn't lose his sense of humor.

True, his most famous witticism—"What this country needs is a good five-cent cigar"—was stolen from an Indiana comic strip, as historian John E. Brown has proved.[6] But Marshall came up with a lot of good lines.

Once, a tour guide who was bringing a group through the Senate pointed at the vice president's small office and made a small joke about it. Marshall heard the dig, opened the door and returned fire, saying, "If you look upon me as a wild animal, be kind enough to throw peanuts at me."[7]

There was honesty in that barb. Marshall found the job of vice president dispiriting, demeaning, and depressing. And the pay was lousy, too: $12,000 a year, compared to the president's $75,000. His final consideration of his office was a sad one: "I do not blame proud parents for wishing that their sons might be President of the United States. But if I sought a blessing for a boy I would not pray that he become Vice President."[8]

Wilson broke precedent by inviting Marshall to a cabinet meeting. He went once and never again. Why? Because, Marshall explained, "[I] would not be listened to."[9] In 1918, when Wilson was off in Europe making the world safe for democracy, he designated Marshall to preside over the cabinet. Marshall bowed out after a few meetings.

Wilson had wanted to drop him from the ticket in 1916, but the Indiana vote was considered too important. Marshall's stock, already low, sank lower when Republicans under Charles Evans Hughes took Indiana but lost the election.

Secretary of State Robert Lansing was the man who decided that it was probably a good thing for America to have a functioning government. He convened cabinet meetings during Wilson's "incapacity." His reward was to be sacked by Edith in 1920 for the offense of taking the Constitution seriously and arguing that Marshall should replace Wilson.

After his term of vice president was up, Marshall didn't seek any further office. He died in Washington in 1925, the same year his *Recollections* were published. In those, he reported that while presiding over a conference at the Smithsonian Institution, he had suggested archeologists dig under the surface of the capital, the better to find evidence of the existence of cavemen.[10]

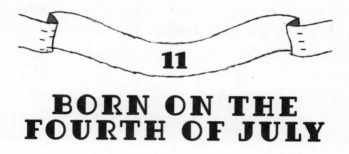

11

BORN ON THE FOURTH OF JULY

• • •

—CALVIN COOLIDGE

The quietude of our thirtieth president is the stuff of jokes. The most widely circulated is the one about the woman who was poking around the White House as part of a guided tour. She bumped into President Calvin Coolidge and told him several of her girlfriends had bet that she couldn't get him to say more than three words. "You lose," he replied.

But as I picked through the life of "Silent Cal," I began to wonder if that silence was caused by shyness or sorrow. His was a life of accomplishment, but it was also filled with tears. Even the manliest of men will have a hard time getting through some of the particulars without having to brush something out of their eyes.

It's never easy to lose a parent, harder still if it happens when you're young. Victoria Coolidge died when Calvin was twelve. She already suffered from tuberculosis; being struck by a runaway horse finished off what was left of her health. She was buried on the family estate in Plymouth Notch, Vermont. Her death was followed by the death of Calvin's sister Abigail when he was eighteen.

He never spoke about their deaths in public, but his private conversations and his writings revealed that he mourned them for a long time—perhaps for the rest of his life. He always carried with him a locket that contained a picture of his mother and a lock of her hair.

At the apex of his political career, it got worse. On the Fourth of July, 1924, Calvin Coolidge should have been celebrating with fireworks and a marching band. It was his birthday, and his political fortunes were fortunate indeed. He was only the second vice president after Theodore Roosevelt to (1) become president when his predecessor died and (2) clinch the nomination of his own party for the next election. He was broadly popular and looked like a lock for the fall election.

Instead, the White House was quiet. Four days before, the president's two sons, John and Calvin Jr., had been playing tennis on the White House lawn. Calvin Jr. had played sockless, and the shoe rubbed against the middle toe of his right foot, which blistered. The blister attracted an infection, and the boy began to feel weak and tired. White House physicians had a look.

It was a staph infection. Today it would be no big thing to treat it, but then, it was life-threatening. Doctors tried a few different treatments, including one mercury-based injection. Nothing took. The sixteen-year-old developed a fever, swollen glands, and red streaks. The president, looking to do something to bring some relief to his son, hunted around the White House grounds, caught a brown rabbit, and gave it to him as a present.

On July 5, Calvin Jr. was taken to Walter Reed Army Hospital for emergency surgery. There was a moment of false hope, but the boy only got worse. Mentally, he shifted between sleep and delirium, including nightmares.

President Coolidge stayed by the bedside. According to historian David Greenberg's vivid rendering of June 7, "the president passed into his son's hand his treasured gold locket containing a photo of Victoria Coolidge and a lock of her gold hair. But the boy, who was lapsing into a coma, kept dropping it. Repeatedly, the locket would fall to the floor and the president would pick it up and hand it to his son. . . . By nightfall, Calvin Jr. was unaware of his surroundings. At 10:20 p.m. he died."[1]

Coolidge's eulogy for his son takes up a little more than a page in his *Autobiography*. Calvin Jr., "a boy of much promise, proficient of his studies, with a scholarly mind, who had just turned sixteen" had had "a remarkable insight into things," and might have made something of himself, had he been given the chance.

The president believed in a good God, and he had a hard time squaring that with his son's awful death. He attempted to fob it off on mystery ("the ways of providence," "beyond our understanding," etc.) but ultimately ended up blaming himself for what happened.

Logically, if Coolidge had "not been President [his son] would not have raised a blister on his toe, which resulted in blood poisoning." He also looked upon the death as a curse. "I do not know why such a price was exacted for occupying the White House," he lamented. What he did know was this: "When he went the power and the glory of the Presidency went with him."[2]

SUFFER THE LITTLE CHILDREN

It's said that outliving your children is the loneliest curse, but it was a loss felt by the nation. When the Democratic convention learned of the death of Calvin Jr., the body immediately recessed. Letters of consolation flooded in from all parts of the country.

The president's bodyguard, Edmond Starling, found a child outside the White House who wanted to tell Coolidge "how sorry I am that his little boy died." When Starling asked his boss what he should do with such unexpected visitors, Coolidge replied, emotionally, "Whenever a boy wants to see me, always bring him in. Never turn one away or make him wait."[3]

He saw more young visitors than he did campaign rallies that year. Coolidge had a few previous obligations that he absolutely could not shirk, but for the most part he avoided the stump and mourned instead. Plenty of Republicans, including his ambitious and opinionated vice-presidential nominee, Charles Dawes, could campaign on his behalf.

The result was a landslide for Coolidge. He received 384 votes in the electoral college against 136 for the Democrats and 13 for the splinter Progressive Party.

Why? Coolidge benefited from a divided and dispirited opposition. There was also the mass media bump: he came to the White House during the rise of radio. His short, direct sentences translated well to that medium, and the inferior recording technology took some of the edge off his slightly reedy speaking voice.

Voters felt as if they had connected with this president more than any of his predecessors, and he was usually willing to go along with it. When he visited the family home in Vermont, he would pose for the cameras as he was chopping wood or doing other rugged "farm-y" things.

Coolidge's silent grief only added to that connection. Here was a man who had climbed to the highest summit of American power. Yet even he couldn't prevent the thing that every parent dreads might happen. If that didn't create a sympathy vote, nothing could.

RETURNS ON NORMALCY

All of these explanations add something to our understanding of Coolidge's success, but let's not forget the fact that his tenure in office was marked by peace and prosperity. Warren Harding and Coolidge had run after the global train wreck that was World War I—the Great War and, many hoped, the Last War.

When they took office in 1921, taxes were high, wartime measures were still in place, and wartime protestors sat rotting in jails. The Republicans had promised to return the country to "normalcy,"* which sounded okay to voters.

> * "Normalcy" was a word that Harding coined. Some of his opponents thought him a buffoon, but it turns out they misunderstood him.

They kept that promise. The government under Harding, and then Coolidge, let dissenters out of prison, scaled back or scrapped wartime restrictions, froze federal spending, and reduced the national debt.[4] Taxes were cut four times during Coolidge's six years in office. With wartime surtaxes still in place, the top tax rate was about 70 percent when he became president, and 20 percent when he contemplated running for reelection in 1928.

He unexpectedly decided against running for reelection and left office an immensely popular president. Today historians, claiming the benefit of the long view, don't tend to think very highly of his presidency. They look to the Great Depression that came after Coolidge and blame his generally small government, probusiness instincts for the stock market crash of 1929, and some critics add that he didn't manage to stop Germany from rearming for good measure.*

* He also failed to prevent bell-bottoms.

Rutgers historian Greenberg lays out the surprisingly weak case for the prosecution in his otherwise fine survey of Coolidge's life. The president cut the taxes of rich and poor, and some people used that money to buy stock, which in Greenberg's book was a bad thing.

How come? Because those cuts gave "investors more dollars to feed the market, helping to push the healthy investment of the mid-1920s into the gambling that followed." Some bought stocks on credit, which Greenberg regards as self-evidently nuts and obvious cause for regulation. It's one of five things that he fingers for causes of the Depression.

As for the economic gains made during the Roaring Twenties, Greenberg admits that they are real: "From 1923 to 1929, wages rose; inflation, unemployment, and interest rates fell." However, to call these gains the "Coolidge Prosperity," as many of the president's supporters did at the time, strikes him as a bit much.

"How much any president should receive credit or blame for the course of the economy on his watch is impossible to determine," he explains, but then turns around and argues that Coolidge shouldn't get much credit. Greenberg fingers several

other "causes" for economic growth: the wartime buildup, auto-
mobiles, the spread of electricity. I was half-surprised he didn't add
the spread of indoor plumbing to the list. All of these things contributed to economic growth; so did Coolidge's tax cuts.[5]

In their judgments about Coolidge, historians are only about
forty years behind the economic curve. The late Nobel Prize–
winning economist Milton Friedman proved that what caused
the Depression was largely a monetary problem. It was the
Federal Reserve's contracting of the money supply that really
scotched things—beginning about seven months after Coolidge
had left office.

It's not even a terribly controversial assertion among econo-
mists. At Friedman's ninetieth birthday, current Fed chairman
Ben Bernanke told the honoree he was right: "We did it. We're
very sorry. But thanks to you, we won't do it again."[6]

LAISSEZ FAIRY TALES

The arguments over the effects of Coolidge's allegedly laissez faire
policies could go on forever, but after a point they feel like debates
among cartoon characters, so tenuous is their connection to anything resembling political reality. Coolidge had been added to the
Republican ticket in the first place not because of airy-fairy support for unfettered capitalism or because big business *really wanted*
their guy on the ticket, but because of voter concerns over the
growing power of unions.

The concerns were grounded in real events. To wit, in
September 1919, Boston policemen went on strike over the right
to unionize. More than eleven hundred of the city's fifteen-hundred-

plus cops left their beats, which led to looting and deadly riots in South Boston, the North End, and the West End. The state militia and the full state guard had to be brought in to restore peace.

The police commissioner fired the striking cops and hired replacements. American Federation of Labor president Samuel Gompers protested by sending a telegram to Massachusetts's then Governor Coolidge. The governor's response had been simple and forceful: "There is no right to strike against the public safety by anybody, anywhere, anytime."

Coolidge was a small-town lawyer and Vermont transplant who rose to the top by slowly climbing the greasy pole of Massachusetts politics: city council, state house, mayor, state senator, president of the senate, lieutenant governor, and two-term governor. For much of his career, he had been considered a moderately progressive Republican. He favored female suffrage and better pay for teachers and other public employees, to take two hot issues of the day.

Coolidge drew the line at supporting Theodore Roosevelt in the former president's unsuccessful third-party run in 1912. The Republicans should have won the election, but Roosevelt's campaign gave the Democrats one of those rare openings. The result had been particularly galling—eight years of Democratic rule in a country that normally gave the GOP a lock on national elections.

The split between Republicans and progressives had long-term consequences for what Coolidge chose to emphasize. He had worked to settle strikes with more sympathy for the workers in the past. Even in the case of the police strike, he didn't think their concerns were without merit.

He believed police pay was too low and working conditions

cramped and wanted to gradually improve those things; the thing he is remembered for is supporting the police commissioner when he barred the strikers from further service in the Boston police department.

SWINGING IT

That was certainly one thing that stuck in the minds of the delegates to the national Republican convention the next year. Three heavy-hitting candidates had created a deadlocked convention. So Republican Party bosses who engineered the nomination of fifth place also ran candidate Ohio senator Warren Harding.

According to Coolidge biographer Robert Sobel, the delegates believed that they'd been manipulated into choosing Harding, and they were none too happy about that. When renegade Oregon judge Wallace McCamant made an unexpected speech endorsing Coolidge, it set off a wave of seconding speeches to stick it to the ringleaders.

Party bosses wanted Wisconsin senator Irvine Lenroot, but this time the delegates were determined that the bosses wouldn't get their way. Lenroot lost to Coolidge on the first ballot—146 to 674 votes.*

* Technically it was 146½ to 674½ votes, but I've no idea how you get a fractional vote.

People from all over the country wired Governor Coolidge with congratulations. Wilson's vice president Thomas Marshall wired him as well, with a different sort of message: "Please accept my sincere sympathy."

After a long call on that newfangled contraption the telephone, Coolidge told his wife that he'd been nominated for vice president.

"You aren't going to take it, are you?" Grace Coolidge asked.

"Well—I suppose I'll have to," he replied.[7]

That might-as-well-do ethos pervaded most of what Silent Cal did. It's one reason I can't help but like the man.

He was visiting his father in Vermont on August 2, 1923, when he learned President Harding had died suddenly of a massive heart attack. Coolidge's first coherent thought, he admitted later, was, *I believe I can swing it.* John Coolidge, a notary public, administered the oath of office on the spot.[8]

When the new president arrived in D.C., he had his work cut out for him. He wanted to continue the legacy of President Harding, but that was a mixed bag, to say the least.

Most famously, there was the Teapot Dome bribes-for-oil-contracts scandal, which eventually led to the imprisonment of the aptly named Secretary of the Interior Albert Fall, as well as the ousting of several Harding men, including Navy secretary Edwin Denby and Postmaster Will Hayes. Separate but related scandals would finish off Attorney General Harry Daugherty and veterans bureau chief Charles Forbes.

In one of those made-for-the-movies moments, Coolidge invited both Daugherty and his chief critic, Idaho senator William Borah, to the White House and puffed on a cigar at his desk while the two got into a shouting match over the attorney general's alleged crimes and ethical lapses. Daugherty stormed out in a huff but refused to quit; Coolidge eventually fired him.

A HIGH-RANKING WHITE HOUSE OFFICIAL

Coolidge's thinking in recent years had been heading in what we might call a more conservative direction, and his belief in federalism only added to his caution. He agreed to continue the twice-a-week press briefings that President Harding had set up with journalists but insisted that these be off the record.

Newspaper reporters attributed his words to a "White House spokesman" or what became a perpetual euphemism for the president, "a high-ranking White House official."

The president's insistence on anonymity was something of a departure. Teddy Roosevelt had pioneered the "bully pulpit," using the office of the presidency to campaign for his own favored initiatives. Coolidge understood the potential for a popular president to impose his will on the American electorate. He recoiled from that possibility.

On several significant issues, Coolidge had the chance to put his case to the American people but refused to do so, thereby dooming his own cause.

He thought that the U.S. government should pay for medical care for World War I veterans who suffered injuries but not grant them pensions. Congress disagreed and overrode his veto.

Again, with the Great Mississippi Flood of 1927, the president thought that the relief Congress was providing would really be a payout to profiteering businesses. He fought it, but he did not throw the full weight of his office against it. A compromise bill passed, and he reluctantly signed it.

On most other issues, his views were conventionally Republican. He wanted to hold spending down and cut taxes, and managed to do both. Coolidge was in favor of tariffs to raise necessary government revenues but kept them higher then necessary to shelter American industry. He quibbled with some of the finer points of the immigration restriction legislation and then signed off on it.

Two of the contradictory charges lobbed at Coolidge were (1) that he was stuck in the past, and (2) that he was too much in the thrall of free-market enthusiasms. A look at his farming policy should put the lie to both notions.

Coolidge vetoed farming bills that he insisted would help only the middleman and explained the dance that the administration would have to pull off to his advisors. The United States was urbanizing fast. There was little government could do to stop the shift from rural to urban. However, initiatives or fig-leaf legislation would be necessary to demonstrate the government's concern for this great, unprecedented demographic shift.

As for foreign policy, Coolidge proved himself to be the farthest possible thing from an adventurous, Theodore Roosevelt-style Republican. His "only instructions" to ambassador Dwight Morrow, who had been tasked with trying to deal with a revolutionary situation in Mexico, were "keep us out of war."[9]

American oil companies had wanted war as a way to recover some of their seized assets. But it turned out Calvin Coolidge, that alleged stooge of big business and the man wrongly credited with saying "the business of America is business," had other ideas.[10]

12

MY THREE VEEPS

*There is not anybody crazy enough
to shoot a vice president.*

—John Nance Garner

No compromise with Satan is possible.

—Henry Wallace

*The only thing new in life is
the history you don't know.*

—Harry Truman

The thing about Franklin Delano Roosevelt was, he didn't like confrontation. He expected to get his own way, and he usually did, but he had neither the inclination nor the temperament to be a bully. As a patrician born and bred, he took the attitude that opposition to his will was unreasonable; simply not the thing to be done.

Despite being the most controversial president in a good long time, FDR acted as if he was entirely above the fray. Drawing on his cigarette holder, his face fixed with a seemingly disinterested look, his authoritative drawl seemed to say, "Why cahnt we awl get ahlawng?"

Consider his radio broadcasts to the nation. Others might consider them an unparalleled and demagogic attempt to appeal over the heads of the elected representatives of the people. Other famous orators of the period used the radio to diabolize their opponents and encourage violence.

But to FDR they were homely "fireside chats." Why, he even began them with the harmless (and presumptuous) words "my friends" or "good evening, friends."

Yes, the man was a political genius.

He had three vice presidents. The first gave this book its title; the second was a little kooky; and the third was Harry Truman.

It's hard to say for certain, but I think FDR revolutionized the vice presidency. Before Roosevelt, the vice president might think he was the party's man, his nation's man, or even—hee hee—his own man.

Roosevelt tried to change that, with some success. Nowadays the vice president is the nominee's man, first, last, and always. It took some time to take, but Roosevelt gave us the new mold.

WORKING OUT HIS DESTINY

John Nance Garner, FDR's first vice president, was the last of the unambiguously old-school veeps. Garner refused to campaign, he refused to make ceremonial appearances, and he even refused Secret Service protection. "There is not anybody crazy enough to shoot a vice-president," he explained.[1]

Nicknamed "Cactus Jack," after a failed bid to make the prickly bush the state flower of Texas, Garner was secure enough in his person that he once went home fishing after FDR announced his plan to pack the Supreme Court.

Garner was an old-fashioned conservative Democrat. "My belief has always been in executive leadership, not executive rulership,"[2] he once said. His view of government was simple and modest. The words carved on his tombstone read: "There are just two things to this government as I see it. The first is to safeguard the lives and properties of our people. The second is to ensure that each of us has a chance to work out his destiny according to his talents."[3]

Garner was born in rural Texas a few years after the Civil War ended. His father, a cotton farmer and politician from Tennessee, served in the Confederate army. Garner later said much of his upbringing was in a log cabin, but he was exaggerating. Growing up, his family was never poor.

He attended the University of Tennessee, left without a degree, then returned to Texas and passed the bar in 1890. That same year he ran and lost the race for city attorney of Clarksville.

Undeterred, Garner then ran for county judge, won, and served until 1896. His candidacy for judge had attracted the opposition of Mariette "Ettie" Rheiner, who was scandalized by Garner's love of alcohol and cards. They were married two years later, and she became his permanent secretary.

The next stop was the Texas State Legislature. Garner was elected in 1898 and became chairman of the redistricting committee. He reapportioned a district for the House of Representatives to his liking, contested, and won it in 1902.

BUREAU OF EDUCATION

Garner served in the House for thirty years. His rise was slow, steady, and unstoppable. He was never interested in garnering headlines or attaching his name to the title pages of bills.

James Byrnes, who served with Garner for fourteen years in the House, said of him, "It was his policy, whenever he had an idea . . . to induce a prospective opponent or a doubtful supporter to sponsor the legislation. When he achieved that, he knew his purpose was accomplished."[4]

In 1910, Garner was elected the House Democratic whip. A decade later, he became the ranking Democrat on the Ways and Means Committee. He became House minority leader in 1929; and two years later, after the postcrash rout of Herbert Hoover's Republicans, Speaker.

Garner had a warm relationship with Republican speaker Nicholas Longworth (son-in-law of Theodore Roosevelt). Together they convened the "Bureau of Education," an illegal speakeasy in the deepest recesses of the Capitol.[5]

He had a neat trick for putting off politicians who wanted something he didn't want to give. He'd have a drink, and then tell the congressman that he'd have to have one too, lest he have the advantage. Supplicants typically left so drunk they had no idea what they'd gone to see him about.

With Garner's strong opinions on the strict separation of powers, he was not likely to get along with FDR. But party loyalty, along with a pinch of personal ambition, led him to accept the vice presidency.

Garner was championed for president by William Randolph

Hearst, but he was barely interested. However, a large group of delegates at the 1932 convention were interested in him and kept voting for him through a few rounds of ballots.

At that time, Democratic Party candidates needed two-thirds of the vote to be nominated. Roosevelt's men, terrified of a brokered convention, persuaded him to move his delegates to FDR in exchange for the number-two spot.

DEAL OR NEW DEAL

The vice president was a very reluctant supporter of the New Deal, and he detested Roosevelt's "Brains Trust." But he shepherded the Roosevelt legislation through Congress anyway, reasoning that the Depression required some kind of extraordinary action and that party allegiance demanded it.

Garner had made known his opposition to several of Roosevelt's policies, including the National Recovery Act and diplomatic recognition of the Soviet Union. Given his druthers, Roosevelt would have preferred a true believer as vice president, and in 1936 had the opportunity to replace Garner. Roosevelt insisted upon and got the two-thirds rule repealed, but Roosevelt knew Garner's continuing presence was a comfort to those Democrats who believed the president needed restraining.

Garner broke decisively with Roosevelt after the 1936 election. He strongly resisted antibusiness labor legislation, FDR's failed scheme to appoint six new pliant Supreme Court justices in order to get the court to stop declaring his programs unconstitutional, and Roosevelt's campaign in 1938 against recalcitrant Democratic incumbents.

In words that sound awfully quaint today, Garner said, "Party policy is not made by one man without consultation with elected officials from another branch of government."[6] Garner's rebellion marked the last time in Congressional history the president was seen as merely primus inter pares, instead of pope of his party.

Garner was appalled by Roosevelt's decision to run for a third term in 1940. He said privately that he wouldn't vote a third term for his own brother.

Breaking with tradition himself, he ran against his president, but his was a passive campaign swept away by the domestic repercussions of Hitler's triumphs in Europe.

ON THE GRAPEVINE

FDR was willing to forgive Garner's transgressions, but this New Deal "Brains Trust" was not. They thought him a traitor. To another president this would have been a big problem. But not to Roosevelt. As Jonathan Daniels, press secretary to both FDR and Truman, recalled, "Roosevelt never fired anybody." Instead, "he just left them on the vine."[7]

The New Dealers wanted Secretary of Agriculture Henry Wallace, and they got him. By election day, Garner was so alienated from FDR that he didn't even vote. After attending Roosevelt's third inauguration, he returned home to hunt and fish and tend his real-estate interests. He never saw Washington again.[8]

Garner may have been bitter, but at least he never lost his sense of humor. Theo Lippman Jr. reported in the *San Francisco Chronicle* that Garner "was walking down the halls of the Capitol when the circus was in Washington. A fellow came up to him and introduced himself, 'I am the head clown in the circus,' he said. Very solemnly, Garner replied, 'And I am the Vice President of the United States. You'd better stick around here a while. You might pick up some new ideas.'"[9]

And of course Garner made a famous plea to Lyndon Johnson not to do what he had done. After Johnson was offered the vice presidency by Kennedy in 1960, Johnson called Garner on the phone and asked his advice.

Garner said, "You shouldn't take it. It's not worth a bucket of warm piss."[10] Johnson didn't listen, but Garner's anger was reserved for the press, who bowdlerized "piss" as "spit." As quotable as ever, Garner railed against "those pantywaist writers."[11]

FATHER OF FOOD STAMPS

Henry Wallace, FDR's second vice president, was a man of considerable accomplishment. He was also a dupe who ended his political career as a pawn of the Communist Party USA.

Allen Drury, the reporter-turned-best-selling-political-novelist, said of him, "He looks like a hayseed, talks like a prophet, and acts like an embarrassed schoolboy."[12]

Wallace came from a family of Iowa farmers in which the boys were called Henry. His grandfather was a Presbyterian preacher-turned-farmer and founder of *Wallace's Farmer*. His son took over the family magazine and was also professor of dairy science at Iowa State University, president of the Cornbelt Meat Producers Association, and secretary of agriculture under Republican President Warren Harding from 1921 until his death in 1924.

Henry Wallace would reject his father's party, just as he would reject his Presbyterian church. He was New Age before his time, flirting with (in alphabetical order) Buddhism, Catholicism, Christian Science, Islam, Judaism, Zoroastrianism, finally adopting Episcopalianism, but always leaving space for Nicholas Roerich and other theosophist quacks. In 1910, he graduated from Iowa State and went to work for *Wallace's*, which he would edit from 1924 to 1929.

Wallace was a pioneer of scientific agriculture, especially in the development of plant genetic crossbreeding. In 1924, he invented and patented the first high-yield, disease-resistant seed corn, the profits from which resulted in the founding two years later of the Hi-Bred Corn Company, which became Pioneer Hi-Bred in 1935. Pioneer, now owned by DuPont, is one of the world's most profitable agribusinesses.

The Depression transformed Henry Wallace's ideas of federal power and made him something of a socialist. FDR rewarded his support in 1932 by appointing him the second Wallace to serve as secretary of agriculture. Unlike Garner, Wallace was as happy with the New Deal as a hog in slop.

It is to Henry Wallace that we owe food stamps, the school-lunch program, and agricultural price supports.

COMMON MANNERISMS

FDR rewarded Wallace again in 1940 when he made him his vice-presidential candidate. Wallace was an ideologically radical candidate and represented a serious departure. He balanced the ticket in no way except geographically.

Wallace was more liberal than Roosevelt and would have

been the last choice of conservative Democrats. But Roosevelt made it clear he would not run if he didn't get his own pick of nominee. The party acquiesced after so much booing by the anti-Wallace faction that the vice-presidential nominee didn't dare give an acceptance speech.

Republicans had come across copies of Wallace's embarrassing correspondence with guru Roerich, but the Democrats black-mailed them into not using it by threatening to release the details of an affair by Republican candidate Wendell Willkie. FDR and his new number two then won easily in November, which gave them a chance to try something new.

As early as 1920, Roosevelt had written that the vice president should be "a kind of roving commission" and a "super handy man."[13] This is what Roosevelt got, to the anger of Roosevelt's cabinet and later to the anger of Roosevelt himself.

Wallace became the most powerful vice president to that point. By December 1941, America was at war, and Wallace was appointed to the War Cabinet. He was made chairman of both the Board of Economic Warfare and the Supply Priorities and Allocations Board—positions which he used as a platform to con-test the power of Secretary of State Cordell Hull and Secretary of Commerce Jesse Jones.

The vice president was everywhere, using his own bully pulpit to argue for a sort of new New Deal, for America and for the rest of the world. In South America, he attempted to impose American working conditions on native workers. He was the first vice president to fly the flag abroad.

On May 8, 1942, he gave the famous "century of the common man" speech in New York City. Speaking of the Second World

War, he said, "No compromise with Satan is possible . . . The people's revolution is on the march, and the devil and all his angels can not prevail against it. They can not prevail, for on the side of the people is the Lord."[14] Wallace's detractors (including Winston Churchill) seized on the "people's revolution" line and insisted that it was more than a mere rhetorical flourish.

A year earlier, Roosevelt had given the Board of Economic Warfare the power to sign contracts with foreign powers. In February 1943, he attempted to seize control of the Reconstruction Finance Commission. This was too much for Commerce Secretary Jones, who protested to the president. Wallace responded by publicly accusing Jones of delaying critical medical supplies to soldiers.

With the feud out in the open, FDR didn't have much of a choice but to act. He brought the conflict to an end by abolishing the Board of Economic Warfare.

WE WANT WALLACE

Rather than telling Wallace that he didn't want him for a running mate for his fourth term, Roosevelt simply left him out on the vine. The vice president was sent on a long visit to China and the Soviet Union, where he formed positive impressions. When he returned, he was informed by reporters that he was through.[15]

It was a close-run thing. By 1944, Wallace had amassed a devoted following of more populist Democrats who saw his removal as a slight. This time Wallace did speak to the convention, and the Democratic leadership adjourned rather than let the vote for the vice-presidential nomination proceed.

Overnight, a letter from Roosevelt damning Wallace with

faint praise was released, and Wallace's candidacy fizzled. Even so, he was ahead on both the first and second ballots. Finally, the momentum shifted behind a "nobody" the president and the party could trust: Senator Harry Truman.

Roosevelt gave Wallace the consolation prize of Jesse Jones's old job, secretary of commerce. He took office in March 1945, but Roosevelt died a month later, and Truman succeeded him.

Wallace seemingly operated under the impression that he was secretary of commerce for the whole world. In September 1946, he gave an anti-anti-Communist speech at Madison Square Garden, in effect predicting that his own administration's newfound anti-Sovietism would drag America into another world war. Truman fired him days later.

Wallace went off to edit the *New Republic*, and in 1948, ran for president at the head of the Progressive Party, a Communist front. He received 2.4 percent of the vote, eighteen thousand fewer than Strom Thurmond's Dixiecrats. Despite these defections from the left and the right, Truman won an upset victory over Thomas Dewey.

Like Garner, Wallace eventually gave up on politics. Unlike Garner, fishing wasn't enough. He returned to agriculture and continued to make significant advances in genetics.

S IS FOR SOMETHING

FDR had looked like death warmed over for many months before he died in 1945. Even so, the nation was shocked. But not as shocked as Harry Truman was when he learned how little he knew about what Roosevelt had been up to.

Journalist Malcolm Muggeridge was mightily amused when he

discovered that Truman's middle initial S "stands for nothing." Truman was born "Harry Truman" and added the S for effect. Fortunately for America and the world, Truman was an accidental president—as are many veeps who become president—but he was hardly a nothing.

Truman's father was a Missouri farmer and unsuccessful speculator in Independence, Missouri. Harry Truman was only a high school graduate, but he was an autodidact. He once said, "The only thing new in life is the history you don't know."

After high school, he returned to work on the farm and stayed there until the onset of World War I, whereupon he enlisted at age thirty-three in the Missouri National Guard. His terrible eyesight should have kept him out of the service (he had earlier been

Courtesy of the White House

Truman: Figured it out

rejected for West Point), but he cheated on his eye test. He rose
to the rank of captain, serving mostly in France.

After demobilization, Truman returned to Independence,
where, except for his time in Washington, he would live for the
rest of his life. He set up as a haberdasher. He went bankrupt in
1922, but after years of effort, paid his non-legally-binding debts
in full.

With the support of the formidable party boss Tom Pendergast,
Truman was elected a county judge three times. Pendergast supported Truman for the Democratic nomination for the Senate in
1934, and he won the general election. In 1939, Pendergast pleaded
guilty to massive corruption and was sentenced to fifteen months
imprisonment and a whopping fine. Truman later confessed he
had played along with Pendergast schemes but insisted he had
always avoided the worst of them.[16]

Truman was reelected in 1940 with the support of St. Louis
party boss Robert Hannegan. His work on a Senate committee
investigating military procurement fraud earned him praise and
the cover of *Time* in 1943. After Henry Wallace had proved an
embarrassment and a possible rival to President Roosevelt,
Democratic Party leaders, including Hannegan, brokered the deal
to put Truman on the ticket.

Roosevelt was clearly grievously ill, but the press downplayed it, and he was easily reelected yet again. Unlike Roosevelt,
Truman relished conflict and didn't give a
damn what others thought of him.* He
shocked many just after his inauguration
when he attended his old mentor Pendergast's
funeral.[17]

* But woe betide any man
who dared criticize his
mother, wife, or daughter.

THE MARSHALL PLAN

By the time Roosevelt and Truman were inaugurated in March 1945, Roosevelt was so far gone he practically needed a cattle prod to keep him moving. But Roosevelt's daughter, Anna, was perfectly happy for America to have a zombie president, just as Edith Wilson had been.

What really happened was revealed only decades later by Jonathan Daniels. Daniels confessed in a 1963 interview: "I was first shocked and disturbed and greatly worried after Yalta when Anna Roosevelt took me aside and expressed her fears, not of the president's death but of his increasing incapacity. And there was a certain suggestion of something in the nature of a regency in which she and her husband John Boettiger would hold what would be dynastic positions."[18]

According to Daniels, Anna Roosevelt had tapped him to be "a sort of front." This "never would have worked," Daniels concluded, "because people not only want to go directly to the president . . . but it was essential to their prestige that they see not an assistant, but Mr. Big himself. This couldn't have worked without unhappiness, confusion, and danger."[19]

Luckily for America, FDR's head exploded. As Daniels put it, "I've often said that Roosevelt was blessed and the country was blessed, by the fact that when he got a cerebral hemorrhage, it was massive." Nearly twenty years after the fact, Daniels was still aghast at Anna Roosevelt's plot. "It scared the pants off of me at the time," he admitted, "and it scares me in history."[20]

Interviewed for this book, Paul Kengor—Grove City College political-science professor, who is probably the world's foremost expert on the subject of vice presidents and foreign policy—describes FDR's treatment of his eighty-two-day vice president as "both disappointing and even disturbing."[21]

FDR, Kengor explains, "kept Truman completely in the dark on the most vital national-security issues of the day, from FDR's often private discussions with Churchill and Stalin at Yalta to the Manhattan Project. When Truman became president, he had no information on these extremely important issues. What FDR did in that regard was irresponsible, especially given that he knew that his health was in serious decline."

As president, Truman made sure no one would ever have to go through what he had suffered at FDR's feeble hands. Kengor says, "Truman took immediate steps to rectify the situation once he became president. Through the National Security Act of 1947, to which Truman had input, President Truman ensured that the vice president would be a statutory member of the newly created National Security Council. Also, Truman saw to it that his vice president would receive copies of all crucial national-security memoranda that the president saw, and that the vice president would sit in on all NSC briefings. Truman vowed that no vice president should ever again be as misinformed and out-of-the-loop as was he under Roosevelt."[22]

FDR's vision of the vice president as administrative agent combined with Truman's strange new statutory respect gave us a new kind of vice president. Truman's veep Alben Barkley was a throwback—a Senate leader who had missed out on a chance at the number-two slot because he defied Roosevelt over a tax bill. But pretty soon an ambitious young man would come along and change everything.

NIXON'S THE ONE?

You are afraid of the truth.

—RICHARD NIXON

Vice President Richard Nixon had faced plenty of angry South American protestors during his tour of the region in 1958, but from the moment his party arrived at the airport in Caracas, Venezuela, it was clear these mobs were different. As they took part in the normal public diplomatic niceties, including the vice president and Second Lady, Pat Nixon, standing for their host country's national anthem, a hostile crowd spat at the Americans and threw garbage.

They might have been wise to reboard the plane and fly back to the United States, but Nixon was determined to send a message: America wanted to engage its southern neighbors and would not back down in the face of Communist and leftist intimidation.

He had already been forced to cancel a lecture at San Marcos University in Lima, Peru, by rock-throwing protestors. Nixon, ever the fan of parting shots, stood up in the rear seat of the car as it retreated. He yelled at them, "You are cowards, you are afraid of the truth! You are the worst kind of cowards!" and his translator repeated the taunts in Spanish.[1]

The Secret Service managed to clear a path to the cars in Venezuela, and the Americans had a go at it. They passed locals with placards, including several that read "Go Home Nixon" and "Death to Nixon."

About four blocks from their planned destination, the motorcade was slowed to a halt, and everything went pear-shaped. According to Nixon's own account, the first rock to hit the front window lodged itself in the glass, "spraying us with tiny slivers." One sliver found its way into the eye of the Venezuelan foreign minister, who bled all over the place. He struggled to staunch the flow, "moaning over and over, 'this is terrible.'"[2]

Then the vice president saw "a thug with an iron pipe work his way up to the car." The pipe wielder went to work on the window. Thankfully "the glass held," but the passengers had to fend off more jagged slivers.

The car started to move, which gave Nixon some relief until he realized that it wasn't moving *forward*. The crowd was rocking it "back and forth, slower and higher each time," to turn it over. "[A]t that moment, for the first time, each of us in the car realized we might actually be killed," he later recounted.[3]

Secret Service man Jack Sherwood drew his gun and yelled, "Let's get some of these sons of bitches!" but Nixon ordered him to stand down. He thought, "[O]nce a gun went off the crowd would go berserk and that would be the end of us."[4] Besides, the car hadn't capsized. Yet.

The press truck in front of the vice president's vehicle managed to clear a path, which the driver powered through, breaking away from the mob. Nixon then made a snap decision that probably saved the lives of everybody in his entourage. He ordered the car to make a sharp right turn. They cancelled plans to go to a planned wreath-laying event and instead blazed a path to the American embassy.

Venezuelan police would later shake down local Communists and fellow travelers and discover what Nixon had guessed when he ordered the car off of its planned route. The first crowd wasn't spontaneous; it was supposed to soften up the target, for another assault just down the road.

There, another mob would attack the car with rocks and fruit and immobilize it. A second wave would come in with homemade bombs to finish them off. Police found one cache of nearly four hundred Molotov cocktails that might have been used in that second attack.[5]

Holed up in the American embassy, the Americans tried to figure out how to get out of this one. In the White House, President Dwight Eisenhower had one idea of how to do it. He ordered thousands of U.S. troops relocated to Guantánamo Bay and Puerto Rico to ready for an invasion of the country, and even joked to Mamie   * It's true, I swear. Eisenhower that he would try his old uniform to see if he could lead the charge himself. The marines and air force prepared for "Operation Poor Richard."[6]*

The Venezuelan government got wind of the buildup and

didn't want to risk an invasion. It now took no chances with the vice president's security. Police cleared the route for his return trip to the airport with tear gas. Luckily, protestors didn't have a stash of gas masks.

GIVE ME A WEAK

Vice-presidential expert Paul Kengor likes to trot out that story when people charge that Eisenhower had not had much use for Nixon.

The charge usually comes from a comment that Eisenhower made when journalists were peppering him with questions about his vice president during a press conference in August 1960. A newsman asked the president to give "one major idea of [Nixon's] that you had adopted." He replied, "If you give me a week I might think of one."[7]

There's no question that remark hurt Nixon in the 1960 election with Kennedy. According to Kengor, however, it was "totally misunderstood. Eisenhower made the comment out of frustration with a nagging press that quite literally hated Nixon and quite literally fawned over JFK. For the rest of his life, Ike apologized to Nixon for the comment, knowing from the outset that it did not reflect any disappointment in Nixon's striking service to Ike. He had easily been the most active vice president up to that point in history, and Ike knew that and valued him greatly."

So what about the comment? I asked Kengor how that could be understood as anything other than a slap at Nixon. "Ike actually meant that he wanted some time to think about his response to the question, which was typical of Ike," he explained. My sense is that Kengor has a point, but he overplays it. When Eisenhower was fishing for a vice president, he wanted someone who hit hard but played fair—qualities that he thought Nixon had demonstrated.

After all, Senator Nixon had beat two incumbents in California: Representative Jerry Voorhis and Senator Helen Douglas. He was fervently, even viscerally, anti-Communist. You could even call him a red baiter. But as far as Eisenhower was concerned, there was a world of difference between his could-be vice president and the drunken paranoid theatrics of Senator Joe McCarthy.

The crucial difference in Eisenhower's estimation was this: McCarthy made charges; Nixon made them stick. Nixon alleged that former State Department official Alger Hiss was a Soviet agent. The allegations stuck, albeit in a roundabout fashion. Hiss eventually went to jail because he had perjured himself in his testimony before Congress.

The Hiss case is where Nixon, an otherwise moderate-to-liberal congressman, first attracted a large conservative following and plenty of liberal antipathy. The character witness list for Hiss reads like a *Who's Who* of famous liberal Democrats of the time. And a key witness against Hiss was everyone's favorite spy who came in from the cold, Whittaker Chambers, a famous contributor to the conservative anti-Communist magazine *National Review*.

"Belief in the guilt or innocence of Alger Hiss," explained the late senator Daniel Patrick Moynihan, "became a defining issue in American intellectual life."[8] Nixon later admitted that he would not have become vice president without the Hiss trial, and also that he would have far fewer enemies if the Hiss trial had never happened.

CHINESE CHECKERS

Eisenhower was on the Hiss-is-guilty-as-sin end of the spectrum.
The former general looked at the former naval supply officer
who had brought Hiss down and saw in him a political soldier—
someone who was willing to use every legitimate line of attack,
as well as some iffier tactics, to triumph mightily over his ever-
multiplying list of enemies.

Ike's attitude toward Nixon as a vice-presidential candidate
was similar to his approach to the men under his command during World War II: respectful but calculated. It's popular these days
for politicians to pledge their unflagging "support for the troops,"
but generals don't have that luxury and never did. They have to
criticize and even court-martial troops that don't come through
and reluctantly send others to their deaths in the service of the
greater objective.

Which is precisely where Nixon came in. The former general
needed him to help accomplish key political objectives:

- Eisenhower was sixty-two when he ran for office in 1952
  and looked older. He needed a younger man for vice
  president to lower the actuary average of the Republican
  ticket.
- The primaries that year had been a long, hard slog, with
  conservative favorite Senator Robert Taft dogging him
  every inch of the way. If Ike was going to win, he needed
  to pick someone who was acceptable to the right.
- He needed help in California; Nixon had already carried
  a statewide election there.

But then an unexpected problem cropped up. A campaign slush fund was made public, and the California senator was accused of feathering his own nest with campaign contributions.

Some of Eisenhower's men approached Nixon and pressured him to drop out, but Nixon wasn't about to give up the biggest prize of his life that easily. As he would explain shortly, "I don't believe that I ought to quit, because I'm not a quitter."[9]

Instead, the candidate delivered a live half-hour speech on television in which he maintained he had not profited unfairly from politics. He listed his own family's meager assets and said that his wife, Pat, owned no decadent fur coats. He promised to "campaign up and down in America until we drive the crooks and the Communists and those that defend them out of Washington."[10]

Nixon admitted to only one possibly improper gift. A supporter had given the family a cocker spaniel named Checkers. Nixon said that his daughters, "like all kids, love the dog and I just want to say this right now, that regardless of what they say about it, we're gonna keep [the dog]." At his request, thousands of irrational dog lovers flooded Republican campaign headquarters with orders to keep this man on the ticket.

Courtesy of the White House

Nixon: Kept the dog

Again in 1956, there was pressure to drop Nixon from the ticket. Ike put it to his vice president directly: if he would bow out and let the Party pick another nominee, Nixon could have his pick of the cabinet departments.

It's impossible to know Eisenhower's exact motive for encouraging Nixon to step aside. The pro-Nixon interpretation is that the president knew how hard it had been for sitting vice presidents to be elected and wanted to give his vice president a better platform to run for president in 1960. The anti-Nixon interpretation is that the president was looking for some excuse to get a controversial veep off the ticket.

We know that Nixon considered the offer a demotion. He would be stepping down from a national constitutionally elected office into an appointed one, and if Ike kicked the bucket, someone else would get to be president. So he said that he'd rather remain vice president for the second term, thank you.

Given how the last attempt to drop him from the ticket had worked out, that was the end of the discussion.

NOT A NONENTITY

So the relationship between Eisenhower and Nixon was complicated, to say the least. Where Kengor really does have a point is his assessment of Nixon's expanded role as vice president.

The expansion of the vice presidency was Eisenhower's idea, from both inclination and necessity. His personal belief, all other things being equal, was that "the Vice President of the United States should never be a nonentity. I believe he should be used. I believe he should have a very useful job."[11]

The "useful job" Nixon thought he could do was in the area of foreign policy. He wanted to serve as a sort of super-ambassador to the world and a special advisor to the president. He also attended all National Security Council and cabinet meetings and ran them in the president's absence.

Nixon got his first experience as an American goodwill ambassador in 1953 when he went on a seventy-two-day world tour that concentrated on the Near East. But the bulk of his foreign-policy contributions came during the second term of the Eisenhower administration.

In 1958, Nixon went on his infamous South American tour. That same year, he was also tasked with meeting new Cuban leader Fidel Castro when he visited the United States and giving Eisenhower a thumbs-up or thumbs-down assessment. After meeting with Castro, he pushed for a more hard-line position.

The next year Nixon was sent to the USSR, where he sparred with Soviet ruler Nikita Khrushchev over what on the surface was the most mundane of topics: whether American kitchens really were as awesome as the floor displays.[*]

In response to his slowly failing health, Eisenhower developed a set of precedents for how, if, and when the office of the presidency would

> [*] Answer: Not quite, but American floor displays were a lot closer to the mean than their Soviet counterparts. Take that, central planning!

be passed to the vice president during the president's "incapacity." Kengor views these guidelines as a feather in Nixon's cap, and he's probably right.

Edith Wilson's puppetry, as well as FDR's family's foiled regency plot, demonstrated nothing but contempt for the sitting vice presidents; Eisenhower's actions demonstrated hard-won trust and respect.

KINDER-GENTLER NIXON

Having gained Eisenhower's respect, Nixon had to try to make the sale to the nation. He was popular among the Republican rank and file, but he couldn't close the deal. Conservatives were divided over him, liberals hated him, and independents broke for Kennedy.

The nation decided for the John Kennedy–Lyndon Johnson ticket over Nixon and former senator Henry Cabot Lodge Jr. by a narrow margin. The final was 303 to 219 in the electoral college and a whopping .2 percent win—note the decimal—in the popular vote.

Nixon's loss was actually much worse than it looked. The Eisenhower-Nixon tickets had won 442 electoral votes in 1952 and 457 in 1956. On his own, Nixon garnered only 219 electoral votes. If you throw in the disputed states of Illinois and Texas, he would have received 270, a 187-vote drop from 1956.

Some of the drop-off could be blamed on a long recession. The 1958 midterm election had been a bloodbath for the GOP. It's also true that Nixon had what modern pollsters refer to as "high negatives," which is an all-too-polite way of saying that plenty of people hate your guts and aren't likely to change their minds.

And his political judgment proved to be awful, awful, awful. Nixon had made his name as an effective hatchet man but sounded during the debates as if he was kissing up to his opponent. A kinder-gentler Nixon the nation wasn't ready for. Worse, as candidate for his vice president, Nixon picked former senator Lodge. This was the man who had lost the reelection bid for his Senate seat in 1953 *to John Kennedy.*

To get an idea of how dumb that was, imagine if the Democrats had nominated former Texas governor Ann Richards for vice president in 2000 or 2004. The Republican Party would have had to surrender its long-standing Stupid Party nickname at gunpoint.

Nixon tried to make a comeback in 1962 by challenging popular Democratic governor Pat Brown. When he lost, he called a press conference, telling reporters, "You won't have Dick Nixon to kick around anymore." The outburst was so bitter and so revealing that we can only conclude he meant it, but eventually he shook it off. The former vice president would come back for more abuse and even manage to get himself elected president, but we'll take that up in another chapter.

14

PANSIES! COWS! GLADIOLAS!

*The most important thing a man has
to tell you is what he's not telling you.*

—LYNDON JOHNSON

According to Tony Montana, in the United States, "first you get the money, then you get the power, then you get the woman."[1] Lyndon Baines Johnson did it a little differently. First he got the power, then he got the money, then he got more power. He got the woman, too.

Then he got the vice presidency. There's a great scene in the movie version of *The Right Stuff* that shows just how frustrating he found that. In January 1962, John Glenn, Mercury astronaut superstar, had his history-making flight on *Friendship 7* postponed because of bad weather.

LBJ, the chairman of the Space Council and the man who brought NASA flight control to Houston, figured this was a great opportunity to grab some good publicity by consoling Glenn's wife, Annie.

What Johnson didn't know was that Annie Glenn had a jackhammer stutter and was painfully shy. She wanted Johnson's faux consolation like she wanted a case of the clap, but Johnson's people were pressing the case—hard. In a panic, Annie Glenn called her husband at work. He told his wife that if she didn't want Johnson in the house, he wasn't getting in, and that was that.

In response, Johnson goes nuts. Is there no one on his staff who can browbeat a *woman*? He pounds the upholstery in his limousine and shouts, "Pansies! Cows! Gladiolas!"[2] This wasn't the last time Johnson would learn that in this country, celebrity beats a full house.

Within two years he would be president, but his administration was hostage to the celebrity of the martyred President Kennedy. All the good stuff he inherited—like the Great Society—was credited to Saint Jack. All the bad stuff he inherited—like the slow build-up in Vietnam that he would escalate into a full-blown war, was blamed on him.

Unlike Glenn and Kennedy, Johnson was not what you would call telegenic. With his sad eyes, his supersized ears and nose, his jowls, and thinning hair combed straight back, he looked like a B-movie villain, a caricature of the corrupt Southern pol.

But back when LBJ got into politics, back in those pre-TV days, looks weren't that important. Personal relationships were important, and LBJ was better at kissing butts and twisting arms than anyone Washington had ever seen.

GO EAST, YOUNG MAN

Lyndon Johnson was born in Stonewall, almost smack-dab in the middle of Texas. He had three sisters and a brother, Sam, who in the great tradition of presidential siblings became infamous for being "colorful."

Although LBJ liked to boast about his humble origins in the Hill Country, they weren't all *that* humble. Johnson City was named after his father's cousin. His great-grandfather was president of Baylor University. His father served five terms in the Texas House of Representatives and became chummy with future House Speaker Sam Rayburn. Johnson's father also farmed and traded in cattle and real estate, none too successfully.

When he graduated from Johnson City High School in 1924, Johnson would not have impressed many as someone cut out for great things. He was smart, but not scholarship smart. His two great attributes were his size and his tongue. He was six foot three inches tall, rail thin but powerful. And, my, how he loved to talk.

After graduation, Johnson headed west to California in search of work. He finally found a job as an elevator operator in San Bernardino—pretty much the only private-sector job he ever held. He returned in 1925 and enrolled at Southwest Texas State Teacher's College, but couldn't afford it.

Johnson was forced to leave after a year and then spent a year teaching destitute Mexican Americans in Cotulla. With some money in his pockets, finally, he completed his degree and briefly taught high school in Houston.

Teaching was an odd choice for a man as ambitious as LBJ, but he was determined not to end up like his father, smothered by an avalanche of bills. A government paycheck is a government paycheck.

In 1930, after a candidate for governor no-showed for a speech, Johnson was deputized. Welly Hopkins, a state senate candidate, was so pleased that he made Johnson the manager of his successful campaign. Hopkins told Congressman Richard Kleberg about this forceful young man, and Kleberg hired Johnson as his secretary.[3]

So Johnson headed east to the nation's capital. He was a quick study. When he became "Speaker" of the "Little Congress," an association of D.C. aides, he also learned that many congressmen are too bored, lazy, incompetent, or drunk to care much about their duties, and so aides who master their bosses' briefs are influential way beyond their job titles.

Johnson learned the power of quid pro quo. Most important, he learned the secret to success in Washington: suck up shamelessly to those who are more powerful than you, and bully those who are not.

BRIGHTEST BULB

Having established himself in Washington, Johnson worked to shore himself up on the Texas front. He married Claudia Alta Taylor, a woman who passed his two tests for a wife; she had to be from a good family that was also a rich family.

Since childhood, Claudia had been known as "Lady Bird," so upon her marriage she became another LBJ. The Johnsons became obsessed with these initials. They had two LBJ daughters: Lynda

Bird and Lucy Baines. There was even an LBJ doggie: Little Beagle Johnson.

Lady Bird Johnson was the perfect political wife. Johnson repaid her loyalty with numerous affairs, including one with Senator Helen Douglas, the famous "Pink Lady" that Richard Nixon knocked off.[4]

In 1935, Johnson, having ingratiated himself with the New Dealers, was appointed head of the Texas section of the National Youth Administration. The NYA,* which was part of the WPA (Work Progress Administration) doled out federal money to students.

> * Not to be confused with the NWA.

Two years later, Johnson was ready to move on up—to the House of Representatives. His wife provided ten thousand dollars from her mother's estate to pay for his first campaign in a special election for Texas's tenth congressional district. LBJ's winning slogan was "Franklin D. and Lyndon B."

In Texas, as in everywhere else in America, the reaction to the New Deal was binary. To the poor, it was manna from heaven. To the better off, it was unconstitutional and downright Communist. The well-heeled FDR was sometimes spoken of as a traitor to his class. Even Johnson's fiercest critic, biographer Robert Caro, acknowledges that Congressman Johnson was beloved by his poor constituents.

Caro reflected on the times when he was "interviewing in the Hill Country." "No matter what I was talking to people about," said Caro, "I found that one phrase was repeated over and over again: 'He brought the lights. No matter what Lyndon was like, we loved him because he brought the lights.'

"They were talking about the fact that when Johnson became

congressman from the Hill Country in 1937, at the age of twenty-eight, there was no electricity there. And by 1948, when he was elected to the Senate, most of the district had electricity," wrote Caro.[5]

That goes a long way toward explaining why the voters kept returning him to office. Just try arguing with electricity.

FROM THE THRONE

Not even Johnson's fiercest critics could deny that he was a fero-cious taskmaster. We all know the cliché about a hard-driving boss who asked no more from his underlings than he was willing to give himself. In Johnson's case, it was actually true. There was nobody in Washington who worked harder than LBJ. His famous "double days" day began at 6:30 a.m. and, after lunch and a siesta, contin-ued until 1 or 2 a.m.[6]

Lady Bird said that "Lyndon acts as if there is never going to be a tomorrow."[7] He treated his body as if there wasn't, until his heart attack in the midfifties. He smoked three packs a day and wolfed down enormous quantities of down-home cookin' in record time. When he had finished his own plate, he regularly stole food off the plates of others.

Johnson's intensity made it possible for him to give people what came to be known as "the treatment." This was equal parts oral and physical intimidation, gamesmanship, and outright bad manners. He was lewd, crude, and obnoxious. In search of favors, he would talk congressmen to sleep and jolt them awake. He would grab them by the knee or the shoulder or press his face so close to theirs they could hardly breathe.

In the 1960s, LBJ bullied his staffers into swimming nude with him in the White House pool.[8] He subjected aides and others to conferences in the "skunk works"—pants down around his ankles, he would issue orders from his toilet throne. He was quite fond of his penis—which he called "Jumbo"[9]—and wasn't shy about whipping it out, as he once did to a group of reporters when trying to justify the Vietnam War.

Those same reporters would profess to be scandalized when Johnson pulled his beagle up by its ears or when he pulled down his pants to reveal his appendectomy scar. But they were more "shocked—shocked!" than actually surprised. Everyone in Washington knew well Johnson's "comfort with every aspect of the human body"—as LBJ knockoff Buck Strickland's wife on *King of the Hill* described her husband. And they all knew how much pleasure LBJ took in discomfiting others.

LBJ told Doris Kearns Goodwin that "one of the delicate Kennedyites" had come "into the bathroom with me and then found it utterly impossible to look at me while I sat there on the toilet. You'd think he had never seen those parts of the body before."

This "Kennedyite," Johnson complained, stood "as far away from me as he possibly could, keeping his back toward me the whole time, trying to carry on a conversation." This created a problem because "I could barely hear a word he said." Finally, Johnson asked him to come closer, which precipitated "the most ludicrous scene I had ever witnessed.

"Instead of simply turning around and walking over to me, he kept his face away from me and walked backwards, one rickety step at a time. For a moment there I thought he was going to run right into me. It certainly made me wonder how that man had made it so far in the world," Johnson said.[10]

That's one way of looking at it. Goodwin had a different view: "In renouncing his civility he stripped them of theirs; he reduced them to his own ignominy."[11]

HOW TO WIN

But Johnson was ever so civil to those men he needed to culti-vate, who included FDR, his Texan vice president John Nance Garner, Speaker of the House Texan Sam Rayburn, and Senate Armed Services Committee Chairman Richard Russell, a Georgian. There was nothing he wouldn't do for them, even unto becoming a surrogate son to both Rayburn and Russell, lonely bachelors who both delighted in the attention Lyndon and Lady Bird showered on them.

However, after LBJ had stabbed Garner, Rayburn, and Russell in the back, they all learned that Johnson's only loyalty was to power.

Despite his unfailing kindness to Garner, Johnson abandoned him when he fell out with FDR. He was determined to push aside his only rival to determining most of the government jobs that were dished out in Texas. Despite Rayburn getting Johnson his NYA gig and Rayburn's stalwart service on behalf of the New Deal, Johnson made up and sold to FDR the story that Rayburn was a traitor to the president. Russell hung on the longest but was tossed aside after LBJ's supposedly Damascene conversion to the cause of civil rights in 1957.[12]

One of the great false truths is that bullies are cowards. LBJ was a bully through and through, but he was no coward. Bullies usually get what they want simply because they have the guts to do what other men are too cowardly to try.

Nobody would have guessed that a one-term congressman could bump off John Nance Garner and Sam Rayburn; but then no one other than LBJ would have had the cojones to even try, let alone the confidence to know he would succeed.

Johnson succeeded in business as well. His success was the telecommunications business, which depends on government licensing. In 1942, he spent $17,500 of his wife's money to buy KTBC (now KLBJ), a no-account radio station in Austin. The station was a perennial money loser, but after LBJ bought it in his wife's name, it started making a tidy profit, especially after those who wanted to do federal business in Texas were persuaded to advertise on it. LBJ needed FCC approval for this takeover, but FDR fixer Tommy Corcoran handled it.[13]

It was convenient for LBJ to pretend that the radio station was his wife's business. This became more convenient when, in 1952, he got the first TV station in Austin, KTBC-TV, and persuaded all the competing networks to give him exclusive local-programming rights.[14] The Johnsons' media empire was sold in early 1973 for $25 million—about $116 million today.

Johnson: The face of a winner

Courtesy of the White House

Johnson suffered his first of only two political defeats in 1941 when he ran for the Senate in a special election. Both sides engaged in massive election fraud, but the sitting governor, Wilbert "Pappy" O'Daniel, proved to be better at it and won by just over 1,300 votes. After that defeat, LBJ learned the great lesson of crooked politics: he who counts last, laughs best.

A, B, C, D, ELECTED

On December 7 of that year, Japan attacked Pearl Harbor, and America was at war. Congressman Johnson weathered it better than most. He entered the Naval Reserve as a lieutenant commander and was awarded the Silver Star, which is bestowed for "gallantry in action against an enemy of the United States." The gallantry that LBJ displayed was in being a passenger in a plane that was probably not fired upon by the Japanese.

FDR sent LBJ on a three-man fact-finding mission to the Pacific. In Australia, he tagged along on a dangerous bombing route to New Guinea. One of the bombers was destroyed by Japanese fighter planes. The bomber that held Johnson, however, blew a generator and had to return to base. Johnson maintained that it was fired upon during the return, but in 2001, the only surviving member of the plane's crew said that was not the case.[15]

Whether or not Johnson's plane saw action, it was a useful story. General Douglas MacArthur presented him with America's fourth-highest medal for valor—either unwittingly or because he wanted the congressman's cooperation. It worked, in any event. Johnson's mission to Asia made a big impact in Washington and led to greater resources and better matériel for the Pacific theatre.

Nineteen forty-eight was the year of the veteran in the congressional elections, and Johnson's "good war" was a boon to him, just as it was to first-timers John Kennedy and Richard Nixon. More important were further cartloads of stolen votes, which in Johnson's case included 202 that had somehow been cast in alphabetical order. In his primary runoff against former governor Coke Stevenson, a multitude of dead rose from the grave to support LBJ, who voted last and best this time, and won by eighty-seven votes.

There was some unpleasantness in the courts over "Landslide" Lyndon's phantom army, but LBJ lawyer Abe Fortas managed to fend off the legal challenges, and Johnson won the general election in a walk.* Just about the first thing Johnson did as senator was to meet Senate page Bobby Baker. Johnson asked him if he "knew where the bodies are buried." Baker said he did, and they got along like a house being burgled. He eventually became LBJ's chief of staff.

* After Johnson was president, he persuaded Justice Arthur Goldberg to leave the Supreme Court to make room for Abe, and in 1968, he nominated his old lawyer as chief justice. The Senate suffered one of its periodic spasms of morality, and Fortas was forced to withdraw.

It's not hard to see why. Baker was the kind of man who can get anything: votes, money, pliable women. He provided the latter to any who asked, including John and Robert Kennedy. He was one of the sleaziest politicos in American history, but just as LBJ was surrogate son to Rayburn and Russell—men of unimpeachable personal morals—Baker became a surrogate son to LBJ.

Baker named one of his children Lynda and another Lyndon John, and Baker became known as "Little Lyndon."[16] He told Big

Lyndon exactly what he wanted to hear: that he was the greatest thing since rural electrification.

Big Lyndon imparted to him, as reported by Caro, his credo: "Watch their hands, watch their eyes. Read eyes. No matter what a man is saying to you, it's not as important as what you can read in his eyes. The most important thing a man has to tell you is what he's not telling you. The most important thing he has to say is what he's trying not to say."[17]

The most important thing Democratic senators didn't want to impart to LBJ was that they were afraid of him. This, and the support of Richard Russell, was how in 1952—after a mere four years—he managed to become minority leader. When the Democrats took control of the Senate in 1954, he became majority leader and the second most powerful man in the country.

Johnson's greatest legislative achievement as majority leader was the 1957 Civil Rights Act, the first since Reconstruction. It was a very modest civil rights act, but it allowed him to lay down a marker as a progressive Southern Democrat at a time when that electoral mix was a winner.

MEET THE NEW FRONTIER

With his rapid rise and his impressive record, LBJ must have thought that he'd have the 1960 Democratic nomination in the bag. He believed he could secure it the same way he secured his other triumphs—with fraud and backroom pressure—but that turned out to be the wrong bet.

Johnson avoided the early primary contests, allowing Kennedy to become the popular choice after he finished off Hubert Humphrey, the Minnesota senator who would become Johnson's vice president, in West Virginia with charges he had been a "slacker" during World War II.[18]

Kennedy never liked Johnson much, and the Kennedyites liked to call him "Uncle Cornpone." But 1960 was expected to be a close election, and Kennedy needed his support to carry cornpone America. So he offered Johnson the veep slot, then changed his mind after Johnson had accepted and the announcement had been made.

JFK sent his brother to do his dirty business and persuade LBJ to drop himself from the ticket. This was a serious error, as LBJ hated RFK. Perhaps if a more suitable messenger boy had been found, our history would have turned out a lot differently, but there was no way a man as proud as Johnson was going to give way to a wet-behind-the-ears snot like Bobby Kennedy.

This would have serious consequences for Johnson later on. Bobby Kennedy was not a man to forget an insult, even one he deserved. He became Johnson's enemy. Once he became attorney general, RFK went after Bobby Baker, which was risky, given that one of Baker's lady friends had been involved sexually with both Jack and Bobby.

In the meantime, there was the matter of winning an election. Jack Kennedy wowed Americans in the nation's first televised debates, but two men did more than anyone else to put him over the top: Chicago mayor Richard Daley and Johnson, who knew how to win close Texas elections.

Sore loser Nixon would concede and then grouse about the results in his *Six Crises* and *Memoirs*, but that didn't mean that he was wrong necessarily. As *New York Times* reporter Tom Wicker, no friend of Nixon, later wrote, "Nobody knows to this day, or ever will, whom the American people really elected President in 1960. Under the prevailing system, John F. Kennedy was inaugurated, but it is not clear that this was really the will of the people."[19]

MAH FELLOW AHMURICANS

For the man who had been a major power broker in U.S. politics, the vice presidency was torture for Johnson. Senators were no longer afraid of him. They rejected his request to remain chairman of the Democratic Conference, and Kennedy rejected William Fulbright, his suggestion for secretary of state.

Johnson's ultimate humiliation occurred when his pick for a federal judgeship—Sarah Hughes, the woman who would later swear him in as president—was rejected by Bobby. In the end, Rayburn had to intervene to secure Hughes's appointment. About the only bone that President Kennedy was willing to throw Johnson was the head of the space council, and even in that he couldn't get any respect.

Johnson's term as vice president was not only agonizing for him, but it was also increasingly hazardous, as Bobby Kennedy's noose became tighter around Baker's neck. The exposure of Baker's kickbacks and shady connections threatened to expose LBJ's own corruption, and raised the question of how much scrutiny the aide and the vice president were willing to take before they started excavating the Kennedy family graveyard.

A Senate committee was having so much fun shining a light on Baker on November 22, 1963, that they decided to skip lunch. When they emerged, they discovered that Kennedy was dead.[20] In the interest of national unity, the Baker scandal died, and Johnson no longer had to worry about being dropped from the ticket.

Johnson made mincemeat of Barry Goldwater in the 1964 election—a forty-four-state rout. The Republicans were in a state of undeclared civil war, while the Democrats successfully painted Goldwater as a dangerous, unstable warmonger who would blow up little girls playing with daisies. Johnson won more than 61 percent of the popular vote, but the victory seemed more like Kennedy's than his own.

Out of loyalty to Kennedy's memory, Johnson kept on the cabinet, including super-duper dud Robert McNamara. He also continued Kennedy's policies, including the Cold War gamesmanship. LBJ was only following JFK's script in Vietnam, but as thousands of kids began chanting, "Hey, hey, LBJ, how many kids did you kill today?" the late president who had attacked Richard Nixon (and Eisenhower) as soft on Communism was recast as Mr. Sunshine, Lollipops, and Rainbows.

The person who benefited from this was Bobby Kennedy. He had been so anti-Communist he'd actually worked for Joe McCarthy, but he bailed on LBJ the first chance he got, and waited for an opening to strike.

In terms of legislation, the Great Society, the War on Poverty, and the Civil Rights Act should have cemented LBJ's reputation as the greatest liberal reformer in American history. But he wasn't then, and he isn't now.

Back then he was the most hated president ever—the man who died a little more each time he interrupted TV shows with a baleful "Mah fellow Ahmuricans" and laid a little more buzz kill on the happiness explosion that was the 1960s.

Above all, he was a usurper. Today, for all his accomplishments, he is regarded as an embarrassment. Thankfully for Johnson's party, he was succeeded by a man, Richard Nixon, who became even more hated.

History credits Senator Eugene McCarthy with knocking Lyndon Johnson out of the box in 1968, with his surprisingly strong showing in the New Hampshire primary. Afterward, Johnson took the rebuke, withdrew from the primaries, and returned to his Texas ranch to die; his health slowly faded, and he expired in January of 1973. But the real knife in the back was wielded by Bobby Kennedy, who entered the race four days after McCarthy proved Johnson was vulnerable.

Johnson lived by the motto "What have you done for me lately?" and he died from it. Even Machiavelli might have admitted that Johnson would have been better served if he had been feared a little less and loved a little more.

15

COLD, COLD, COLD

*Lyndon Johnson's going to be
sore as hell about this.*

—HUBERT HUMPHREY

In 1969, the year Hubert Humphrey finished his term as vice president, he was asked by the *Minneapolis Tribune* to sum up his experience as veep. His answer wins the prize for the bleakest assessment of the office ever: "It's like being naked in the middle of a blizzard with no one to even offer you a match to keep you warm . . . You are trapped, vulnerable and alone, and it does not matter who happens to be president."[1]

The last part was a bit of an overstatement. It was Humphrey's great misfortune that the man who happened to be president when he was vice president was Mr. Charm himself, Lyndon Johnson.

Humphrey was extremely loyal to Johnson. He worked hard to get Johnson's Great Society programs passed by Congress, and he orated endlessly across America and the world in favor of the president's Vietnam policy, even though he didn't agree with it. Despite the heavy cost of this to Humphrey's reputation as the liberal's liberal, Johnson's repayment to Humphrey was to browbeat him like a rented mule.

Johnson thought anyone stupid enough to accept the vice presidency deserved exactly what he got—that is, exactly what Johnson got from Kennedy.

"You know Jack Kennedy made the greatest mistake of his presidency when he took me out of the Senate and had me run as his vice president . . . He has cut off my balls, and I am just sitting around with nothing to do," Johnson told William Welsh, Humphrey's chief aide, in 1962.[2]

Like Johnson, Humphrey was first elected to the Senate in 1948, from Minnesota, and like Johnson, Humphrey rose high in the Senate leadership, becoming majority whip in 1961. Just as Kennedy had tried to soundly humiliate Johnson over the vice-presidential nomination, Johnson humiliated Humphrey, making him jump through hoops and wait until the last minute.[3]

As Welsh dryly noted, "However much his treatment by Kennedy may have rankled, this did not cause Johnson to treat his own vice president much differently."[4]

Johnson subjected Humphrey to one indignity after another. He led his veep to believe that he was getting the same intelligence briefings as the president. By statute, he should have been, but Johnson ordered the National Security Agency to withhold some information. This led to considerable embarrassment for Humphrey during his failed presidential campaign.

Humphrey was kept out of the loop about the current status of the Paris peace talks. If he had known how badly the efforts to get them off the ground were going, he would never have suggested ending the bombing of North Vietnam, as he did in a speech in Salt Lake City. Nixon staffers charged that he was giving aid and comfort to the enemy; Johnson refused to come to Humphrey's defense.[5]

UNHAPPY WARRIOR

Johnson loved to toy with Humphrey. After Humphrey gave a pro-Vietnam speech to a hostile audience of protestant divines and received a standing ovation, Johnson called him over to his private quarters in the White House and lamented, "Hubert, I hear you gave a great speech to those preachers. Why can't I get standing ovations? Let me hear what you said."[6]

Humphrey gave him the gist, and then Johnson clarified his demand: "No Hubert, don't tell me about it. Stand over there, and give me that damn speech. I want to hear it from you just as you gave it this afternoon." Hubert did as he was told, giving the speech meant for hundreds to a smirking audience of one.

He never learned loyalty was a one-way street to LBJ: you gave; he took. One day in October 1968, LBJ asked fellow Texan and longtime Washington power-broker Robert Strauss, "Bob, what do you think of my Asia policy?" Strauss admitted: "[I] told him everything I thought he wanted to hear, not one word of which did I really believe."[7]

Strauss knew that the right answer for any query from LBJ was "yes sir, no sir, three bags full, sir." Humphrey, on the other hand, figured he'd earned the right to tell LBJ that only two of the bags were full. It didn't go over well.

In his memoirs, *Caveat*, former White House chief of staff Alexander Haig tells a story that would be preposterous if told about any other president than Lyndon Johnson.

"In at least one White House meeting that I attended, with members of the NSC and Congressional leaders present," Haig wrote, "President Johnson allotted the loquacious Hubert Humphrey five minutes in which to speak ('Five minutes, Hubert!'); then Johnson stood by, eyes fixed on the sweep-second hand of his watch, while Humphrey spoke, and when the vice president went over the limit, pushed him, still talking, out of the room."[8]

Johnson was so infuriated by candidate Humphrey's baby steps away from the president's Vietnam policy that he gave every indication he was rooting for Nixon to win. And three days after the 1968 election, three days after Humphrey had come agonizingly close to overcoming Nixon's seemingly insurmountable lead, Johnson twisted the knife one last time.

As paraphrased by Welsh, LBJ had these words of comfort for Humphrey and his running mate, Senator Edmund Muskie: "You boys should have listened to me and not tried to second guess my efforts to get this damn war over. You lost this election, I didn't. That platform fiasco at Chicago would never have happened if you hadn't given your liberal friends and the anti-war freaks a goddamn opening when you tried to negotiate with them."[9]

Hubert Humphrey was known as the "Happy Warrior." "Battered Wife" would have been a better metaphor. He was terrified of LBJ even after death.

In 1977, racked with the cancer that would kill him a year later, Humphrey got some unexpected news. A survey of one thousand D.C. politicos ranked him the best senator of the century. He responded, "Jesus Christ, Lyndon Johnson's going to be sore as hell about this."[10]

16

THAT SEVENTIES DECADE

*The president of the United States
has a right to communicate directly
with the people who elected him.*
—Spiro Agnew

I can't explain.
—Gerald Ford

I go to funerals.
—Nelson Rockefeller

The seventies were the most vice-presidential decade ever. Every time you cocked your head, you saw a different veep out of the corner of your eye: first Spiro Agnew, then Gerald Ford, then Nelson Rockefeller, and then, finally, Walter Mondale (who, by virtue of being alive, gets his own chapter). The '20s, '40s and '60s had four vice presidents; the '70s had four in four years.

If the 1970s as a cultural epoch began in 1974, when Nixon resigned, the man who best sums up its "vibe" was Gerald Ford—

either him or Chevy Chase playing him as a bumbling idiot on *Saturday Night Live*, but after all these years it's hard to tell the difference.

He held national office for only three years, but Ford was the man who told America that "our long national nightmare is over."[1] He put Nixon behind us and made it possible for Americans to "do a little dance, make a little love, get down tonight."

Or so the obituary writers emoted when Ford died at the age of ninety-three in 2006. Ford, they explained, was bereft of ambition, a humble man with much to be humble about, an All-American "nice guy [who] played too much football with his helmet off"[2]—as that not-nice guy Lyndon Johnson had put it. The "nice guy" part I won't dispute, but the rest is pure hokum.

Ford's genius was in knowing that Americans will take people by their own account. In his vice-presidential confirmation hearings, the Michigan congressman promised to be "a ready concilia-

Courtesy of the White House

Ford: Also not a Lincoln

tor and calm communicator between the White House and Capitol Hill."[3] He called himself a moderate, a fiscal conservative, and an internationalist to anybody who would listen.

He was also for ice cream and against mean people.

Beneath the lazy talk, the goofy grin, and the polka-dot ties worn with plaid suits beat the heart of a relentless Republican with ambition to burn. Ford is said to have been humble because he had the presidency thrust upon him.

His wife, the inimitable Betty, let it be known that she didn't want him to take it. She wanted him to run for one more term in his district, his thirteenth, then retire. Ford's ability to laugh at himself is thrown in as the clincher: didn't he claim to be "a Ford, not a Lincoln" in his acceptance speech?

Yes he did. So what? Self-deprecating humor is always the least risky kind. Speechwriters routinely put a few zingers into politicians' mouths in order to take the sting out of more serious criticisms and to demonstrate that their guy has the common touch. But if Ford was humble, he was humble like a fox.

It is possible that Mrs. Ford would have prevailed on her husband to retire, but (1) that's not what happened, and (2) one does not rise to the post of minority leader—let alone president—through self-renunciation.

Finally, there is one huge problem with the "reluctant president" riff: Ford ran for reelection in 1976.

FARTING AND CHEWING GUM

Political conservatives tend to view 1976 through the lens of the 1980s' "Morning in America" and Ford's bizarre brain lock during the second presidential debate. "I don't believe the Poles consider themselves dominated by the Soviet Union," he said.[4]

They see Ford as the last gasp of the old Republican establishment, a man so clueless he picked Nelson Rockefeller as his vice president; so hapless he was beaten by a peanut farmer from the Deep South; so stubborn he wouldn't bow out of the race when confronted by a superior and vastly more popular rival, Ronald Reagan.

But it is a mistake to read the past by the standards of the present. Yes, Ford was a dealmaker; he was also a partisan. He led the doomed fight against LBJ's Great Society programs and was detested by LBJ in turn. Johnson said that Ford was so dumb he couldn't "fart and chew gum at the same time."[5]

As for Ford's moderation, it's almost forgotten today that he led the effort to impeach—for being a supposed pornography lover, among other crimes—Supreme Court Justice William Douglas, the archliberal conservatives loved to loathe.[6]

Ford was a man who knew his own mind, even when it was wrong. He didn't think it was right to bail out the bankrupt New York City, and he resisted attempts to do so with such force and for so long that the *New York Daily News* ran the infamous headline: "Ford to City: Drop Dead."

He thought that Alexander Solzhenitsyn was trying to kill détente with the Soviet Union, so he refused to invite him to the White House. The president groused privately that the Nobel laureate and hero was "a godd—ed horse's ass."[7]

Ford was nowhere near as dumb as LBJ and the writers of *Saturday Night Live* believed, however. After graduating from the University of Michigan with a bachelor's in political science and economics, he was accepted into Yale Law School, from which he graduated in the top third.

Years later, when asked to explain this seeming anomaly, he replied, "I can't explain."[8] Actually, it's fairly easy to explain. He had ambition, a strong work ethic, and above-average intelligence.

He was no stumblebum either. He was one of the greatest

players in the history of one of America's greatest college football teams: the University of Michigan Wolverines, who retired his uniform number 48 in 1994. He was offered professional contracts by both the Green Bay Packers and the Detroit Lions.

BAD TO BE KING

Ford's childhood has much in common with Bill Clinton's. He was not born Gerald Rudolf Ford Jr., but rather Leslie Lynch King Jr.

King Sr. beat his wife, Dorothy, and threatened worse, so she left him soon after young Leslie's birth. Dorothy moved to Grand Rapids, Michigan, to enlist the help of her parents to raise the boy. There she met and married Gerald Ford Sr. Her son eventually changed his name to mirror his stepfather's.

Ford met his biological father only once. King introduced himself to Ford at the hamburger joint where Ford worked part-time during high school, and invited him to lunch. According to biographer Douglas Brinkley, "although Jerry accepted King's invitation . . . the encounter left him bitter at his birth father's long absence and resentful of his apparent wealth."[9]

Why was King in Michigan? He had come to Detroit "to pick up a new Lincoln."

So, a Ford, not a Lincoln, but also a Ford, not a King. Ford, like Clinton, had "father issues" and was just as determined.

In 1948, he managed to depose a sitting Republican congressman, Bartel Jonkman, by arguing that Jonkman was an "avowed, dedicated isolationist."[10] Just before the election, Ford was confident enough to marry an unlikely political wife, a divorced model and dancer named Betty Warren.

Ford rose to minority leader in the House of Representatives because he backed a successful coup against the incumbent, Charles Halleck. He never planned on national office, but when Richard Nixon came calling for the second time, he didn't say no.

Nixon and Ford, both members of the House's class of 1948, were old friends, and Ford cemented the ties when he sent Nixon a rousing telegraph after the Checkers speech. Nixon had considered Ford for vice president in 1960 and, more seriously in 1968, even though he had already decided on Spiro Agnew.[11]

Ford told Nixon the job he really wanted anyway was Speaker of the House.

That dream died in 1972. Despite Nixon's runaway victory, the Republicans were still in the minority in Congress. Ford asked his wife, "If we can't get a majority against McGovern, with a Republican winning virtually every state, when can we?"[12]

NUMBER FOUR TO NUMBER TWO

Fortune favors the brave, but it favors the lucky even more. The next year Agnew was caught with his hand in the cookie jar, and the Twenty-fifth Amendment kicked in for the first time. Nixon wanted John Connally, former Navy secretary, Treasury secretary, and former Texas governor, as his second VP.

However, Connally was a turncoat Democrat, and the Democrats in Congress didn't look kindly on his party-switching ways. Nixon's second and third choices were Reagan and Rockefeller. Reagan was too right-wing for the Democrats; Rockefeller was too left-wing for the Republicans. That left one name on the list.

Watergate had weakened Nixon by that point. He wasn't calling the shots, and he knew it. The Democrats, and especially Speaker of the House Carl Albert, were. Albert was blunt afterward: "We gave Nixon no choice but Ford."[13]

When Ford was sworn in on December 6, 1973, Nixon's chief of staff, Alexander Haig, saw the writing on the wall. He complained, "Ford was treated throughout the ceremony and afterwards as a president-in-waiting, especially by Republicans, and there can be little question that Richard Nixon's presidency was over, in their minds, from the moment his successor took the oath."[14]

As vice president, Gerald Ford crisscrossed the country, making speeches trying to keep up Republican spirits. But his optimism had its limits. When Arizona senator Barry Goldwater turned on Nixon, Ford knew that he was soon to inherit a job rather more powerful than Speaker.

Al Haig told Ford as much shortly before Nixon's resignation in August 1974. He also mentioned that the new president would be so powerful he could even pardon the old president.[15] Hint, hint.

Ford took the hint, but he always denied there was any deal. Supposedly, the pardon killed Ford's chance of reelection, but this ignores two important considerations. First, Ford came very close to winning anyway. Second, it's hard to see how the pardon could have been any worse for the Republicans than a prospective Trial of the Century.

As expected, the Republicans were crushed in the 1974 midterms, which ushered in arguably the most radical Congress since the Radical Republican Congresses of Reconstruction. The Democrats enjoyed commanding majorities in both houses.

In response, Ford became "President No." In eight years, President Reagan would rack up seventy-eight vetoes; Ford managed to send sixty-six bills back to Congress in just two and a half years, and cobbled together a large enough coalition to uphold most of those vetoes.

GREAT GREEK HOPE

The 1970s were the great "what if?" decade of politics. What if the Twenty-fifth Amendment hadn't been ratified in 1967? House Speaker Carl Albert would have become president in 1974. What if Spiro Agnew hadn't been caught with his fingers in the cookie jar? He might have become the great realigning president of the Republican Party.

Like Ford and Clinton, Agnew shrugged off his birth name: Spiros Theodore Anagnostopoulos. As a child, he grew tired of enduring all the vicious vowel-based abuse, so he shortened it when he could.

Ted Agnew, as he became known, was the son of a Greek immigrant and restaurateur who longed to become an unhyphenated American. He became an Episcopalian, a professional man and, finally, a Republican.

After some study at Johns Hopkins, Agnew sold insurance and groceries and got a law degree at the University of Baltimore. He first became involved in politics by working on the campaigns of James Devereux in several successful bids for the House of Representatives and one disastrous run at the governor's office.

Agnew was appointed to the Baltimore County Board of Appeals in 1957. His first race for elected office as circuit court judge in 1960 was a debacle and a learning experience. He placed fifth in a field of five candidates.

His subsequent electoral triumphs derived from his exploitation of divisions in the Democratic Party: first as Baltimore County executive in 1962; then succeeding where his mentor had failed, as governor of Maryland in 1966.

Agnew's opponent, George Mahoney, was an unrepentant segregationist, while Agnew had ordered Baltimore dances desegregated. It was as a "new style" Southern politician that Agnew first came to national attention, though he famously gathered Baltimore's African-American leaders into a room and bawled them out over a race riot that had occurred in the city.[16]

Although the Maryland governor placed Richard Nixon's name in nomination at the Republican convention in 1968, he was not considered vice-presidential material. His selection was met with media consternation and a revolt on the convention floor, which Nixon's forces ruthlessly quashed.

After the uproar, it turned out that Nixon knew what he was doing. He had three criteria for his choice: (1) the nominee must come from outside the Republican establishment, (2) he must have experience in urban development, and (3) he must carry a few border states for the GOP.[17]

Nixon's campaign started with an enormous lead over Democratic candidate Hubert Humphrey, and then the campaign hit a rocky patch. Nixon won the popular vote by only 500,000 votes, though his electoral college victory was a comfortable 301 to 191.

According to LBJ, by way of Nixon, Agnew could "take credit or at least a great deal of the credit" for carrying South Carolina,

* And, with only four
electoral votes, nobody
cares about Maine.
North Carolina, Virginia, Tennessee, Kentucky, and Maryland, as opposed to Democratic VP nominee Edmund Muskie, who could take credit only for carrying his home state of Maine.[18*]

SILENT SCREAM

Agnew proved a natural campaigner, despite such early stumbles as calling Humphrey "soft on Communism" and referring to an Asian-American reporter, jokingly, as a "fat Jap." He was mocked as "Spiro the Zero," "Spiro T. Eggplant," and Nixon's Nixon, but it was all water off a Greek's back.

Many reporters mocked Agnew in 1968. By 1970 they feared him. Agnew had become "Spiro Our Hero" to adoring Republicans, one of the most loved and hated men in America. There was even a short-lived craze for Spiro Agnew watches.

On November 3, 1969, Nixon gave a televised speech appealing to the "silent majority" to support his policy on Vietnam. Nixon had tapped into Main Street America's resentment of elite opinion and countercultural chaos.

The nation rallied behind him. His approval rating reached a record 68 percent a week later, but Nixon was enraged by the "biased and distorted 'instant analysis'" of the speech by the commentators of the television networks.[19]

So when speechwriter and aide Pat Buchanan suggested that Agnew act as the point man for an attack on the legitimacy of television punditry, Nixon was easily persuaded. Agnew then lambasted Nixon's enemies as "radiclibs," "nattering nabobs of negativism," "pusillanimous pussyfoots," an "effete corps of impudent snobs," and the "4-H club: hopeless, hysterical hypochondriacs of history."[20]

This was a hard act to follow, but the thirty-minute speech Buchanan drafted for Agnew to deliver in Des Moines on November 13, 1969, marked a turning point in American political history. Speaking live on all three networks, Agnew accused TV news of being as powerful as the president, but unlike him of being unelected and unaccountable.

"A small group of men, numbering perhaps no more than a dozen anchormen, commentators, and executive producers, settle upon the twenty minutes or so of film and commentary that's to reach the public. . . . They decide what forty- to fifty million Americans will learn of the day's events in the nation and in the world," Agnew said.[21]

He accused the networks of willful, aggressive, and partisan distortion. While he agreed that "every American has a right to disagree with the president of the United States and to express publicly that disagreement," he also insisted that the president "has a right to communicate directly with the people who elected him."[22]

And those voters "have the right to make up their own minds and form their own opinions about a presidential address without having a president's words and thoughts characterized through the prejudices of hostile critics before they can even be digested."[23]

The networks reacted like scalded cats. Frank Stanton, president of CBS, spoke of "an unprecedented attempt by the vice president of the United States to intimidate a news medium which depends for its existence upon government licenses."[24]

AGNEW'S THE HUN

Buchanan and Agnew had invented the conservative strategy of running against the media. Agnew became the leading edge of the great Republican realignment. The party of the North became the party of the South, and the party of the rich became the party of the working class.

For the 1970 midterm elections, Nixon designated Agnew as "the perfect spokesman to reach the silent majority on the Social Issue."[25] The term was invented by Democrats Richard Scammon and Ben Wattenberg to describe the fear of and alienation from the craziness of the 1960s as experienced by "the average American voter," who back then was described as "a 47-year-old housewife from Dayton, Ohio, whose husband was a machinist."[26]

What we now know as social conservatism starts here. This was a new kind of populism, one based not on the rich–poor class division but on the hip–square class division. It was a lifestyle conservatism that led to Republican presidential victories in 1980, 1984, 1988, and beyond.

Back in the 1960s, we were all "liberals." After Agnew's offensive, the term was a swear word.

Nearing the end of his first term, Agnew wanted out. He had tired of his office, as most vice presidents do, and was suffering from "money problems."[27] Nixon wanted him out too; he wanted Connally as his VP in 1972, just as he did in 1973.

Unfortunately for Nixon and for Agnew, Agnew was too popular with the Republican rank and file—arguably more so than Nixon himself. There was little choice but to keep him on the ticket.

However, by April 1973, Agnew was being investigated by the

U.S. Attorney in Baltimore. He steadfastly denied all allegations to Nixon and to the public. By September, the Justice Department had collected irrefutable evidence that Agnew had collected bribes as Maryland governor and vice president and had laundered money in order to evade taxes.[28]

On October 10 of that year, he became only the second VP to resign.* He pleaded no contest to reduced charges, paid a $10,000 fine, and was placed on probation for three years. In 1974, he was disbarred in Maryland, and in 1983 a civil suit forced him to repay $268,482 received in bribes.[29]

> * John Calhoun jumped ship early to take a Senate seat.

Agnew published an autobiographical novel in 1976 and his memoirs in 1980. The latter expressed great bitterness at what he considered grossly unfair treatment for common political corruption. He also hinted that Al Haig had threatened him with dire shame-if-something-were-to-happen-to-you–style consequences if he didn't resign.[30]

NOT FOR SALE

Nixon favorite John Connally finally did run for president in 1980. He spent $11 million and won precisely one delegate. Connally learned one of the great political lessons: you can't buy the presidency.

Which brings us to the most important thing to know about Nelson "Rocky" Rockefeller: he was born rich. How rich was he? As governor of New York, when asked his opinion on a change to pension rules that would increase worker take-home pay, he asked without a hint of guile, "What is take-home pay?"[31]

He was one of five sons born to John D. Rockefeller Jr., who was the only son of oil titan John D. Rockefeller Sr. Today, when politicians rail against Big Oil, they rail against Amoco, Atlantic Richfield, Chevron, ConocoPhillips, ExxonMobil, Marathon, and Sohio. Until the trust was busted by the Supreme Court in 1911, all of these companies used to be one company: Standard Oil, co-founded and run by John D. Rockefeller Sr.

Nelson Rockefeller's grandfather was one of the richest men of all time. His father was a little less rich, and Nelson was a little less rich still. But he was still stupendously wealthy. Why did he want to become president of the United States?

Rocky explained his Sisyphean goal like so: "When you think of what I had, what else was there to aspire to?"[32]

He managed to come off as a real "man of the people," though this was probably an accidental by-product of a learning disability. Rockefeller was left-handed. At the time, this was thought to be a sign that something was seriously wrong with you.

John Jr. attempted to cure him of this fault by attaching a string to his left hand and yanking it whenever he used the wrong hand. It messed up his son's right–left brain divide, with the result that he always found studying a trial. He had great difficulty in remembering people's names, so he hailed them all with the same greeting, "Hiya, fella!"[33]

An army of tutors managed to get him through Dartmouth. Afterward, he joined the family business.

Like many in his social circles, he professed a great love of art, though this sometimes proved embarrassing. He commissioned the Communist Mexican artist Diego Rivera to paint a gigantic mural for the RCA building in Rockefeller Center. Rivera delivered an anti-American work that glorified Lenin and refused to alter it. Rocky had it smashed to bits.[34]

HIYA, ROCKY!

He entered government service in 1940 under FDR, specializing in Latin America and rising to assistant secretary of state. Truman disliked him and got rid of him, but Rockefeller returned with a vengeance under Eisenhower. He became an undersecretary at Health and Welfare and served on a secret committee that monitored the CIA.

In 1958, Rockefeller defeated Averill Harriman for governor of New York and was thrice reelected. His motto was the same as his state's: *Excelsior!* It means "ever upward," which is exactly what happened to state spending under his watch. The splurge funded many worthwhile things, I'm sure, along with thousands of hideous public monuments.

Rocky was popular statewide, but many Republican activists couldn't stand him. The New York Conservative Party was launched in large part to be a countervailing influence to his socially liberal, free-spending ways.

Nationwide, his runs for president became a marker for the ideological makeup of the national party. In 1960, he dropped out of the primaries after poor early showings and supported Nixon, so long as the vice president agreed not to be overly right-wing.[35]

In 1964, conservative firebrand Arizona senator Barry Goldwater's campaign was defined almost entirely in opposition to Rockefeller, the politician *and* the man. Rockefeller had recently divorced his wife, Mary, with whom he'd had five children, and convinced Margaretta ("Happy") Murphy to leave her husband and four children.

Only days before the crucial California primary in June 1964, Happy brought her fifth child into the world. To Mr. and Mrs. Average Republican Voter, that seemed like deliberate provocation. Rockefeller lost and was booed when he was scheduled to speak at the convention and then sulked, sitting out the election.

After his second loss to Nixon in 1968, it was clear that the only way Rockefeller was going to succeed to higher office was to be appointed to it, which is what happened in 1974. He had the résumé for it, and as a three-time loser, was hardly a political threat.

Rockefeller began his term with high hopes but should have known better. After all, he admitted, "I've known all the vice presidents since Henry Wallace. They were all frustrated and some were pretty bitter."[36]

He thought he was going to be a kind of czar of domestic policy. Rockefeller had Ford's promise he would be a "full partner." They even pinky swore on it. But the vice president hadn't counted on White House Chief of Staff Donald Rumsfeld, who crushed his ambitions and practically elbowed him out the door.

Rockefeller gave up and devoted himself to designing a new vice-presidential seal. He gave his job description as: "I go to funerals."[37] In 1976, to placate conservatives, President Ford replaced him with Kansas senator Bob Dole, who didn't even get to go to funerals.

The former vice president lasted only two years after leaving office. It was initially reported that he'd bought the farm at work, but that story quickly collapsed.

What did happen, according to Texas A&M professor Leroy Dorsey, was that "Nelson Rockefeller died of a heart attack on January 26, 1979, while in the much-publicized company of a young female 'research assistant.'"[38]

17

THE YOUTH AND INEXPERIENCE OF WALTER MONDALE

He was kind of a mean old man.

—WALTER MONDALE

Before an event on the office of the vice president at the Wilson Center auditorium, people exchanged political chitchat as they made their way to their seats. Someone mentioned Senator Ted Kennedy; a lady behind me replied, "I remember when he was cute." Former ABC news anchor Sam Donaldson slid into his seat in the second row just under the wire. The center's president and retired Indiana congressman Lee Hamilton called the event to order.

The first speaker at this April 2007 symposium was Walter Mondale. He gave a clue into the audience's . . . distinguished demographic makeup. "The room is full of people that I've worked with," the near-octogenarian former vice president said. They had come out either because public service binds people together "in a remarkable relationship that lasts a lifetime" or because there was free food and booze after.

In his short talk, Mondale played the grand old man and the clever partisan. Often, one shifted effortlessly into the other. For all the failures of the Carter administration, he said that no one could deny these propositions: "We told the truth, we obeyed the law, and we kept the peace."

He offered a sketch of the evolution of the vice presidency that I'll simplify only a little by saying that there were Before Mondale, After Mondale, and, finally, the Years of Our Cheney.

Before Mondale: He opened with a John Adams quote: "I have no desire ever to open my mouth again, on any question," followed by a dig at Spiro Agnew, who was a member of two branches of government but "neither branch wanted to see him." Vice presidents were powerless and something of a joke, and he didn't want that for himself.

After Mondale: "But [pregnant pause] it changed." When Carter approached him about the possibility of taking the number-two spot on the ticket, Mondale accepted only on the condition that he be given a larger role. Carter agreed and, as president, made good on his word. The veep had an office in the West Wing, was able to insert several of his own staffers into important agencies, and was consulted on all matters that the executive took up. Mondale "often met two, three, four hours a day with the president when events were intense."

The Years of Our Cheney: This expanded role of vice president is called the Mondale Precedent, and he's mighty proud of it, as I would find out. But the first question from the audience was, in light of the Cheney vice presidency, did he help to create a monster? "I've thought about that," said Mondale, and he went on to give the reasons why the current vice president has plowed what he takes to be new and dangerous ground.

In Mondale's telling, the "Carter-Mondale" administration wasn't a "co-presidency." Mondale was powerful only as someone who had the president's ear. He was not a prime minister or an operator with an independent base of power.

Plus, Cheney is a meanie: "If something can be said that's really mean, sooner or later he'll say it."

MOURNING IN AMERICA

Mondale's mentor, senator, and former veep, Hubert Humphrey, was known as the Happy Warrior, but the tag is more appropriate for Mondale. He was also a *successful* warrior, right up until the 1980 Carter-Mondale reelection campaign, which was a disaster. Mondale had run several important campaigns for giants of Minnesota politics before being appointed and reelected as the state's attorney general, and appointed and twice reelected as a U.S. senator.

Then 1980 happened. The Democrats lost in all but six states, and D.C. victories in the candidates' home states of Georgia and Minnesota accounted for nearly half of their pathetic electoral college showing of forty-nine votes. Democrats were mourning in America.

It would be hard to do worse than that, but somehow Mondale managed. He faced President Ronald Reagan in 1984, which was right about the height of the conservative president's popularity. In his acceptance speech to the Democratic Convention,

Mondale promised, "Mr. Reagan will raise taxes, and so will I. He won't tell you. I just did."

Duly noted, said American voters. The ticket of Walter Mondale and New York Congress*woman*(!) Geraldine Ferarro lost forty-nine states and only squeaked by in Minnesota. Afterwards, Reagan's people were kicking themselves for not putting a little more effort into Minnesota. A few thousand more votes would have given them a fifty-state rout. Only the "I'd rather be dead than Republican" voters in the district would have kept them from an achievement that equaled George Washington's.

That was quite enough for Mondale, at least for a while. He retired from the Senate and went back to practicing law in Minnesota.

President Bill Clinton appointed him ambassador to Japan and then special envoy to Indonesia. For the most part, however, Mondale spent his later years doing the post–vice-presidential equivalent of putting around the garage: he taught and organized events at the University of Minnesota, served on the boards of about a dozen nonprofits and corporations, and served on a bipartisan commission to study campaign-finance reform.

And then, in 2002, he did something that I believe to be truly awe inspiring. Liberal Minnesota senator Paul Wellstone had been campaigning for reelection when he died in a plane crash just eleven days before voters cast their ballots. Local Democrats had to find a candidate quick in what was shaping up to be a decidedly non-Democrat-friendly cycle. Barely a year had passed since the terrorist attacks of September 11, and President George W. Bush still enjoyed Sun God–sized approval ratings.

Mondale agreed to run for the suddenly open seat. His candidacy was billed as a continuation of Senator Wellstone's legacy. Mondale demonstrated his fighting spirit by again promising to raise taxes. He ran hard for eleven days, attacking his opponent, Norm Coleman, as a shape-shifter and a party changer. Polls showed the candidates neck and neck. And after returns came in on election night, Mondale learned that he had lost by about 50,000 votes.

It was a feat perversely more impressive than Ronald Reagan's: he had run for and lost an election in all fifty states.

SPANKED FOR BRAGGING

I had heard through the grapevine that Mondale did not want to talk about the 2002 election, so when I spoke with him a few weeks after the symposium, I didn't bring it up. Afterward, that seemed like a mistake. He certainly treated every other subject as fair game, even when the questions were impertinent. To wit:

YOURS TRULY: Did you always want to be president?
WALTER MONDALE: Uh, not always. When I was in the first grade, I didn't give it much thought. But you know, as I—
YT: How about the second?
WM: I was still unsure of it. I would say that, you know, probably midthirties or something like that.

and

YT: How many funerals did you have to attend?
WM: Only one. I didn't want to get on the croak list.

and

YT: Please confirm or deny that you are an avid fan of the British comedy troupe Monty Python.
WM: Yes I am. Good stuff.

Mondale: Super veep

Unlike a lot of politicians, Mondale really does have a decent sense of humor. In the 1984 election, the chief voter concern about Reagan was that he was getting too old. When the age issue was put to the president in a debate, he settled the issue once and for all. Reagan said that he wouldn't allow his opponent's youth and inexperience to be used against him. It was a great line that ended Mondale's one outside shot at election. But there was no one who laughed harder at the joke than Walter Mondale.

In the forum and the interview, he exhibited not so much a false modesty as a calculated modesty. When I asked if he thought he played some role—any role—in Carter's close 1976 victory over Gerald Ford, he cautioned, "You get spanked for bragging out here." Then he laid out the case for where he very well might have helped Carter and said he'd "rather others conclude what effect that had. You know, I think it was effective, but I don't know."

When I pushed him on things that he was really invested in, however, he got very assertive very fast. I pointed out that Alben Barkley was the first vice president who was a statutory member of the National Security Council and who received the same national security briefings as the president, and that Vice President Richard Nixon served as a sort of superambassador for the Eisenhower administration.

YT: So could you say that the Mondale Precedent
      built on the Barkley and Nixon precedents?
WM: I wouldn't want to say that, no.

He explained that while the permanent National Security Council position for the veep "was clearly a step forward," unless "the president wanted to bring a vice president really along," the vice presidency was "still a marginal, nominal presence. You weren't in the White House. You weren't in the loop."

Wait, a card-carrying member of the National Security Council is not in the "loop"? There are loops within loops, it turns out, because, Mondale told me, "the president often brings things to the Security Council after he's decided or close to having decided."

Whether or not he's right about that, it's hard to deny that if you have an office in the West Wing of the White House, as Mondale did, as well as dozens of your own men strategically inserted into the federal bureaucracy, you're likely to have a bit more influence.

SIXTY SECONDS

Of course, there is a downside for vice presidents who are very invested in their president's administration. Their successes are your successes, true. And their failures are your failures. The closeness can lead to a lack of perspective about why you lost and make it that much harder to mount a comeback.

In Mondale's estimation, the Democrats weren't reelected in 1980 because "the ball kept bouncing against us." They were unlucky, cursed with "very high inflation . . . high interest rates . . . the capture of our hostages in Iran . . . the invasion of Afghanistan by the Soviets. . . . And then we had a Democratic challenge and a third-party challenge." It all made for a "very tough year." And four years later, voters already had fixed in their minds about what a Mondale administration might look like.

But was it a wrong impression? I pressed Mondale on the Iran question because he is willing to admit something extraordinary but then deny what most people would take to be its plain meaning. In November 1979, Iranian militants seized fifty-two Americans in the U.S. embassy in Tehran, and the new Islamic government then took custody of the Americans. The Carter administration negotiated for the release of the hostages for more than a year and failed.

Then Reagan was elected. Carter had said during the debates that the world's biggest problem was nuclear proliferation.* Reagan argued instead that the two largest problems were Soviet ambition and American weakness, and he seemed to show real willingness to use force.

* His daughter told him so.

Here is the thing that the former vice president will admit: "[Grand Ayatollah Ruhollah] Khomeini, sweet guy, released our hostages the minute Reagan was sworn in."

The.

Minute.

The normal interpretation of these events would be that Khomeini feared what Reagan might do about the hostage situation and decided not to take any chances. Now check out Mondale's interpretation: "I think if we had been reelected, he might have released them earlier. I don't know. He was kind of a mean old man and I think was playing cat and mouse with those people."

18

THAT VOODOO
THAT YOU DO

Why was he so admired? Why was he so beloved?
—George H. W. Bush

You can't win! Or at least I couldn't.
—Dan Quayle

What matters is that we find one of those precious few moments in all of human history when we have a chance to cause the change we wish to see in the world—by seeking a common agreement to openly recognize a powerful new truth that has been growing just beneath the surface of every human heart: It is time to change the nature of the way we live together on this planet.
—Al Gore

Washington D.C., with its museums, its monuments, and its history, is the mother of all tourist traps. Every spring and early summer, the masses descend like a loud, credit card-wielding horde of locusts. They fill up the Mall, double or triple restaurant waits, and pack into Metro cars like sardines.

The city needs a place to put all of these visitors, which means lots of hotels. Several chains have more than one hotel in the city, and it can be difficult to keep them straight. To make it easier, locals come up with nicknames.

For instance, take the Washington Hilton on Connecticut Avenue, north of Dupont Circle. If you stop an old-timer and ask for directions, odds are he'll distinguish that one from the one on Capitol Hill by calling it the Hinckley Hilton.

That nickname can shock visitors who followed the news even casually in the early 1980s. To outsiders it seems so casually callous.

The date was March 3, 1981. President Ronald Reagan had addressed an audience of union members of an AFL-CIO-affiliated convention. He was trying to drum up support for tax cuts and budget reductions.

It was a tough crowd, but Reagan tried his best. When the president and his people were outside the building, heading for the cars, six shots were fired.

A failed and crazed songwriter named John Hinckley unloaded the contents of his Röhm RG-14 revolver into Reagan, White House press secretary Jim Brady, policeman Thomas Delehanty, and Secret Service agent Tim McCarthy.

Thus, the Hinckley Hilton.

CONTROL ISSUES

Most of the events of that day have been widely reported. A few of the more memorable details were the heroics of agent McCarthy, who jumped into the line of fire; Reagan's insistence on walking into the George Washington University Hospital rather than being carried in on a stretcher; his dramatic collapse inside the building; the bullet exploding in the laboratory after the doctors dug it out of him; and, of course, the theatrics of Secretary of State Al Haig.[1]

Haig's claim that "I am in control here" probably was not meant in the spirit in which it was received. It was a qualified answer in response to a journalist's query about who, if anyone, was in charge now. Haig only claimed that he was running things "in the White House" until the vice president returned, and he promised that he "would check with" Vice President George H. W. Bush if "something came up."[2]

That would have been innocuous on its own. Unfortunately, Haig was genuinely confused about the line of succession, and he made the mistake of broadcasting his ignorance. Haig believed

Photograph from Architect of the Capitol, AOC no. 73009-24

Bush: Got to be president; Quayle not so much

he was third in line for the presidency and told this to reporters. This was interpreted as a power play at the worst possible moment. It wasn't feasible for Reagan to fire him at the time, but Haig was forced out the next year.

Where was Bush during all of this? He had been dedicating a historic site in Fort Worth, Texas. He was returning by plane to D.C. when a confusing message came in over the transom. Network broadcasts clarified things for the passengers of *Air Force Two*: the president had been shot.

The plane touched down at Andrews Air Force Base in Maryland. From there, his advisors wanted to deliver Bush to the seat of power via the fastest possible route. It was proposed that a helicopter deliver him directly to the White House's South Lawn. Bush said no.

In the most inspiring words of his vice presidency—perhaps the most inspiring words he ever spoke—Bush explained: "[O]nly the president lands on the South Lawn."[3]

ACCEPTING APPLICATIONS

That restraint was as commendable as it was hard to explain, except as an outgrowth of Bush's character. Bush had been twice considered for vice president—in 1968 and 1974—but he was passed over in favor of Spiro Agnew and Nelson Rockefeller. He had been far from Reagan's first choice in 1980, and the two were never what you would describe as "close."

Bush ran against Reagan in 1980, and there were a number of memorable primary scrapes between the two. "Voodoo economics" was how Bush described Reagan's proposal for tax cuts that would be at least partially paid for by increased economic growth. Reagan's "I am paying for this microphone!" riposte was in response to Bush ordering the moderator to cut his opponent off. After being mocked by Reagan as a "Brooks Brothers Republican," Bush thought he could score points by opening his jacket to reveal the label of J. Press. And another preppie bit the dust.

By the end of the primary campaign season, Reagan wanted nothing to do with "Mr. Résumé." But what a résumé it was: Phillips Andover Academy; youngest pilot in the history of the navy; a service record that included a Distinguished Flying Cross and three Air Medals; Yale; Skull & Bones;* founder of Zapata Oil; three-term congress- man from Houston, Texas; ambassador to the United Nations; head of the Republican National Committee; liaison to the People's Republic of China; director of the CIA; chairman of the First National Bank.

* Don't tell anyone.

The man most responsible for Bush becoming Reagan's run- ning mate was Gerald Ford. Reagan wanted Ford for vice presi- dent, but Ford had already been vice president and wasn't wild about the job, especially under a man he had decided against for vice president and running mate in 1974 and 1976.

Amid all the talk of Vice President Walter Mondale's expanded role as veep, Ford asked for more, both in private and in public. Ford wanted a large say in foreign policy. He even wanted some control over cabinet appointments. The usual chorus of television talking heads started to get excited about the possibility of a "co-presidency."

Reagan told him *nyet*, as he would tell Gorbachev several years later. It was probably the right call politically, but it created a problem. The former governor of California was conservative and stubborn, but he knew that without Ford he still needed a Republican who could convince (1) moderate Republicans that they would have a place at the table and (2) D.C.-establishment types that they could work with a man that many thought crankishly right-wing.

The Reagan team eventually decided in favor of the man whose campaign had boasted of "the best résumé in America." In the general election, they made short work of President Jimmy Carter and VP Mondale, crushing them 489 to 49 in the electoral college.

STRONG AND GENTLE

At Ronald Reagan's funeral on June 11, 2004, George H. W. Bush gave an eloquent tribute. He posed the questions, "Why was he so admired? Why was he so beloved?"

Bush's answer: "He was beloved, first, because of what he was. Politics can be cruel, uncivil. Our friend was strong and gentle. Once he called America hopeful, big-hearted, idealistic, daring, decent, and fair. That was America and, yes, our friend. And next, Ronald Reagan was beloved because of what he believed. He believed in America, so he made it his shining city on a hill."

On a personal note, Bush added, "As his vice president for eight years, I learned more from Ronald Reagan than from anyone I encountered in all my years of public life. I learned kindness; we all did."

Public eulogies are normally jam-packed with fulsome in-sincerity, but there is no reason to doubt that Bush was speaking anything other than what he knew to be the truth. Bush was a loyal servant of Reagan; Reagan repaid him with a serious effort to make Bush his successor.

The two didn't see eye to eye on a lot of things, but Bush had come Reagan's way on the ones that mattered. He switched from a terse pro-choicer to awkward pro-lifer, supported Reagan's defense buildup and the outlines of his economic plan. "Read my lips, no new taxes," Bush promised.

Some conservatives were shocked and upset with Reagan for supporting Bush, but they shouldn't have been. Before the down-to-the-wire 1976 Republican convention, Reagan had announced that the moderate-to-liberal Pennsylvania senator Richard Schweiker would be his vice president.

In a private audience, several Reagan supporters urged their candidate to dump Schweiker and announce a new number two. They argued it was necessary—the only way to secure the nomination. Reagan rejected their proposal and shamed them for making it. He later named Schweiker to head the Department of Health and Human Services.

Reagan was a conservative, sure, but he was also a partisan Republican who was capable of great loyalty. His track record of loyalty made the notion that he wouldn't support Bush absurd.

He did, and Bush won, beating Massachusetts governor Michael Dukakis handily,* albeit not by the forty-nine-state rout that the "Morning in America" campaign managed to roll up in 1984.

* 426 to 111

The victory was so much sweeter for Bush because the man the Democrats nominated for vice president, Lloyd Bentsen, had beat out Bush for a Senate seat in 1973. "Senator" was one of the few jobs that Bush was never allowed to add to his résumé. He had to settle for "president" instead.

NAME, RANK, AND SERIAL NUMBER

Many of the low points of the 1988 campaign concerned Bush's pick of vice president. As I was reminded on my trip to the Vice Presidential Museum, the choice of Indiana senator Dan Quayle wasn't absurd on its face. Quayle had been an ambitious and popular senator, and his status as a social conservative and a man of faith helped to hold together an important part of the Reagan coalition.

Then again, it sure seemed like a disaster at the time. I say this not based on any bias or animosity toward the man but on his own assessment.

In his 1994 autobiography *Standing Firm*,* which is remarkably candid for a book published while the writer was considering whether or not to run for president in 1996, he writes that after his candidacy was announced at the Republican convention, "the media were out for blood—mine. I was reduced to a defensive crouch."

> * Based on the dust jacket image, you half expect the book to be titled *Standing Firm in an Ugly Sweater.*

Quayle admits that he didn't handle the controversy well. At one point, to try to diffuse the scandal of his service in the National Guard,** he even took one unnamed "TV comic's recommendation that I try a little humor."

Dumb. Dumb. Dumb. "I recited my name, rank, and serial number—

> ** Here's the scandal in a nutshell: My God, he served in the National Guard during Vietnam and didn't ever set foot in a single jungle.

a joke that fell absolutely flat," Quayle writes. The problems, for those who've seen the attempt, were (1) that he had no comic timing, and (2) that he looked slightly crazed. The vice-presidential nominee recognized, "I was no Johnny Carson, and I dropped the act."

The press takes on an almost diabolical role in the story. He constantly complains about the unfair treatment, and how close it came to convincing him to step down:

- "The press and I were at war and as the weekend wore on they came close to winning."
- "This day wasn't just the worst day of the whole campaign; it was one of the worst days of my life."
- "You can't win! Or at least I couldn't."
- Reporters follow his son, Ben, as the boy is walking the neighbor's Rottweiler. Ben tells them that if they get any closer, he'll sic the dog on them. Quayle's response: "Smart kid."
- "I was exhausted and my pinched nerve was killing me, and I wanted to stop the free fall. I thought there was only one sure way to do that and that was to get off the ticket."

Finally his wife, Marilyn, has to step in for one of those moments of clarity. "Is anything that they're saying, is one single allegation, true?" she asked. Well, no, he replied. "If you get out now, everyone for the rest of your life will believe that it is true," she argued. Her bottom line: "You have to stay . . . and you have to fight."[4]

CROUCHING QUAYLE, HIDDEN DRAGON

The national press looked at Dan Quayle and saw the second coming of Spiro Agnew. In the famous "battle of Huntington," at Quayle's first rally in his hometown after he had been nominated for vice president, his campaign team "decided to crank up the microphones so the crowd would hear all of the give-and-take" between Quayle and the press, in order to create "a little healthy antagonism." The crowd vigorously booed the journalists' questions.

Quayle's reaction was that he "loved every minute of it." He explains: "For three days I'd been a punching bag, and suddenly I had twelve thousand troops punching back on my behalf."[5]

During his campaign and the vice presidency, Quayle took the kind of media criticism that had been pioneered by Agnew and extended it, adding a generational twist. Quayle speculates that he was hated because he was not only a conservative but a conservative Baby Boomer.

Ronald Reagan's social conservatism reporters could contextualize by telling themselves, "That's what Dad believed." It was a little harder to make that exception for a young senator with movie-star good looks* and the possibility of succeeding George H. W. Bush as president.

If Quayle had downplayed his critique during his time in office, he might have been able to establish something like a truce with the press. Instead, he continued to push the wrong buttons. After the Rodney King-inspired Los Angeles riots, he gave a speech on the importance of intact fami-

* We can quibble about any other judgment in this book, but Dan Quayle was a good-looking man. In the interest of bipartisanship, Al Gore used to look like a Roman senator.

lies to keeping social peace in which he shamed "prime-time TV" for its malignant neglect of the importance of marriage. Exhibit A was the Candice Bergen sitcom character, Murphy Brown, an "intelligent, highly paid, professional woman" who'd decided to conceive and raise a child without a father.

"I know it is not fashionable to talk about moral values, but we need to do it. Even though our cultural leaders in Hollywood, network TV, the national newspapers routinely jeer at them, I think that most of us in this room know that some things are good, and other things are wrong. Now it's time to make the discussion public," Quayle said.[6]

Since it was an election year, you can guess the outrage the speech provoked. Plenty of reporters, news anchors, pundits, network execs, and civil libertarians complained that he was calling for censorship. Which wasn't true exactly. He was doing something much more offensive. Quayle was suggesting that the kind of folks who would normally raise the censorship objection were *bad people*.

LIGHTNING ROD OR HUMAN SHIELD

One advantage Quayle enjoyed during all of this over Agnew was the unflagging support of his president. Bush called Quayle up after the disastrous you're-no-Jack-Kennedy debate with Lloyd Bentsen and said he thought he'd done a fine job. He resisted calls to drop Quayle in both 1988 and 1992, and he gave his vice president some important responsibilities. Quayle was given a huge role in selling the Iraq war.

Was Bush's support for Quayle worth it? Hard to say. Bush didn't win a second term, but the evidence for that being Quayle's fault is skimpy, at best. One of the metrics that Quayle used during the media firestorm of the 1988 election was the campaign's poll numbers. If they dropped, he writes that he would have dropped off the ticket voluntarily.

But they didn't. Bush continued to gain against Dukakis. Two possible, not mutually exclusive, explanations were (1) that very few people were deciding how to vote based on who was the number two on the ticket, or (2) that Quayle was acting as a sort of "lightning rod," attracting most of the negative coverage. That is, Bush looked better because reporters and opponents were wasting time attacking his vice president.

If Dan Quayle was the "Vice President as Lightning Rod," then I propose that Al Gore was the first "Vice President as Human Shield." On the eve of President Bill Clinton's impeachment trial before the Senate, that grand old man of the right, William F. Buckley Jr., argued against the president's removal. All things being equal, Buckley might have allowed that Clinton should be removed from office, but he didn't want the nation to be saddled with President Gore.[7]

Gore's sensibilities weren't offensive to the press, as Quayle's had been, but they worried conservatives. It wasn't just Gore's politics. It was the seeming intensity of his belief in those politics.

The most obvious example of this is Gore's environmentalism. Most senators either believe or profess to believe that environmental concerns are paramount, but they balk at the costs of environmentalism. They prefer speechifying or halfway measures to tougher measures. When President Clinton promised to sign the Kyoto climate treaty, the Senate passed a resolution refusing to ratify Kyoto unless certain well-nigh-impossible conditions were met.

Clinton signed the agreement at Gore's urging. Since the publication of his book *Earth in the Balance*, Gore has been identified as one of the neon-greenest politicians in the country. He advocates tough medicine to what he thinks of as a dying planet. In it he explained why he thought that his overheated rhetoric really wasn't overheated: "It is not merely in the service of analogy that I have referred so often to the struggles against Nazi and communist totalitarianism, because I believe the emerging effort to save the environment is a continuation of these struggles."[8]

Critics attacked his first book from about every possible angle for several years. The most effective was to set passages from *Earth in the Balance* alongside paragraphs from the Unabomber's *Manifesto*, or to read them out loud on the radio, and ask people to identify the author. Gore's grandiose, run-on prose, such as the quote at the head of this chapter,* was ripe for such mockery.[9]

And it was ultimately effective. What the impeachment and the removal trial came down to for

* From Gore's new book: *The Assault on Reason*, or *Why I Still Can't Believe I Lost to George W. Bush: What the Hell is Wrong with You People?*

many Republicans was, who do you want in the White House, Bill Clinton or the guy who sounds like the Unabomber?

YOU COMPLETE ME

Unfair? Yes. Absolutely. But while politicians often claim that they got into the thick of it to make things more fair, the nature of their business is anything but.

Many progressives believe that the ads that highlighted a brutal murder by Willie Horton were the height of ugly, racist campaigning. Horton was a black man from Massachusetts, who had already been convicted of first-degree murder and who was out on weekend release, which Governor Michael Dukakis had refused to abolish. The Bush campaign and independent groups picked the case up as a weapon to bludgeon the Dukakis campaign.

And who brought the Horton case to the Republicans' attention? Tennessee senator Al Gore, looking for some issue that would give him traction in the primaries, had first used the case publicly against Governor Dukakis.

The point here is not to get caught up in the partisan foofaraw, but to show that it matters. Sometimes it breaks against you; sometimes everything lines up just right. Normally Clinton wouldn't even have considered Gore for vice president, but he needed to do something to send a message that he had seen the light and would change the error of his ways.

The charismatic Southern governor had a zipper problem, a draft-dodging problem, zero foreign policy experience, and wanted to forever banish his party's reputation for being soft on crime. Here was a noncharismatic senator, one of only ten Democrats who'd voted for the first Gulf War; a family man; a veteran of Vietnam; and the guy who'd helped to send death-penalty opponent Michael Dukakis packing. As Jerry Maguire would say, "You complete me."

Electorally, the two had an easy run of it. In 1992, they benefited from a divided Republican Party and the third-party candidacy of eccentric billionaire Ross Perot.* In 1996, they ran against Senator Bob "Spirit of 76" Dole, a future Viagra spokesman, and Jack Kemp, an android that had a feedback mechanism problem. It kept going on about "hope, growth, and oppor-

* Their electoral college majorities were 370 to 168 and 379 to 159.

tunity" during the vice-presidential debates, even in response to a question about a Major League second baseman spitting on an umpire.

Vice President Gore enjoyed great influence initially and was allowed to oversee much of the administration's foreign policy. He met frequently with foreign leaders, both here and around the world. He signed several agreements with the Russian government on behalf of the U.S. government—an unprecedented and bold move for a vice president.

However, as Clinton's second term began to go badly, so, apparently, did the relationship between president and veep. One of the problems with their relationship was that old classic: not enough time. Both men had to fend off accusations of fund-raising irregularities. Clinton had an impeachment to fend off and a legacy to establish; Gore had an election to prepare for.

Gore reluctantly stood by Clinton during the impeachment mess. By the time of the 2000 elections, he campaigned very much as his own man. He won the popular vote narrowly and lost by the narrowest of narrow margins in the electoral college. It all hinged, or dangled, on how the recount of the very close Florida election came out.

The vice president dragged the recount out for nearly a month, but two Supreme Court rulings finally forced him to throw in the towel. He retired to private life and dabbled in several different ventures, including documentary filmmaking, experiments in citizen journalism, and polemics against the Bush administration. He's never written any memoirs but, judging by the tone and tenor of his latest best seller, he may well be the most frustrated man in America.

THE UNDISCLOSED
VICE PRESIDENCY

*I can tell you the government had
absolutely nothing to do with it.*

—DICK CHENEY

In 1962, Dick Cheney was flunking out of Yale University. The future vice president did what many directionless twenty-one-year-olds do when facing that predicament: he came running home.[1] He could do that without hanging his head too low, because his parents didn't pay for those wasted years. Cheney had gone to Yale on a scholarship arranged by a local oilman.[2]

Small blessings, I guess. It was far from a triumphant return to Casper, Wyoming, for the former high school class president/captain of the football team, who had dated the baton-twirling homecoming queen. Content to coast for a while on his high-school glory days, Cheney took a union job as lineman for a power company and worked at it for two years.

During those years, he racked up a couple of DUIs before he

straightened himself out. He got himself back into school to win back the love and respect of the homecoming queen, Lynne Ann Vincent—now known from China to Chattanooga as Second Lady Lynne Cheney.

You could probably extract some kind of character-building lesson from this blue-collar interlude. He falls from grace; he stumbles; he picks himself up. Or you might deduce that he is a Man of the People. Throughout his political career, friends would say of Cheney that he worked hard* and partied hard—traits not uncommon to blue-collar workers.

> * Though not at Yale, apparently.

But it's easier to just turn it into a metaphor: Richard Bruce "Dick" Cheney—the vice president who built and repaired power lines.

The metaphorical power lines Vice President Cheney believes he is repairing run to the office of the president. These are based on legal and constitutional arguments about executive power and congressional overreach.

To help repair what he sees as a dangerously hobbled executive, Cheney has taken on extraordinary powers for a vice president. He thinks that those powers are attached to him, personally, as he works to restore what was knocked down in the storms over Watergate and Vietnam.

In fact, the personal connections Cheney has amassed have enabled him to carve out a niche that make him arguably—no, scratch that, objectively—the most powerful vice president in the history of the United States; he's a prime minister to Bush's faux monarchical self.

Someone once made that comparison to President Bush

directly. He corrected it, saying the two were like the top brass of a big company, with Bush as the CEO and Cheney the COO. Cheney enjoys that special status because of his connections that were built over a long career in Washington as an advisor to four different administrations.

STAPLE THAT RÉSUMÉ

At the age of twenty-eight, Cheney landed a job in 1969 as a White House intern through the influence of Republican congressman William Steiger from Wisconsin. By then he had married Lynne and had two young daughters, Elizabeth and Mary.

Cheney admits that his wife got him out of his blue-collar slump. "She made it clear that she wasn't interested in marrying a lineman for the county. That was really when I went back to school," he once said. He headed to Washington with a master's in political science under his belt from the University of Wyoming.

It was during his studies at Wyoming that he read intensely the works of Winston Churchill and began mulling over the use of executive power during a time of crisis. During his sophomore year of college, in 1965, Cheney would have witnessed in newspapers and on television the spectacle of Churchill's state funeral—the first of a British statesman in the twentieth century—as the wartime prime minister's oversized legacy was hashed out.

Cheney has been called a "master bureaucrat." He's got the résumé for it, having learned the ins and outs of Washington power politics from both government service and what passes for the private sector here.

In 1969, intern Cheney quickly moved over to join the staff

of Donald Rumsfeld, then director of the Office of Economic Opportunity. He weathered the Watergate years as assistant director of the Cost of Living Council and then spent the next year in the private sector as the vice president of an investment firm.

When Gerald Ford assumed the presidency after Nixon's resignation, Cheney returned to the White House as an assistant to the president and then as chief of staff. There he lobbied along with Secretary of Defense Rumsfeld to convince Ford to replace CIA director William Colby with George H. W. Bush. The move would pay dividends to Cheney down the road.

Cheney ran for and won a congressional seat in Wyoming in 1978 and was reelected five times. He chaired the Republican Policy Committee during most of the '80s and in 1988 was elected House minority whip. "Staunch" is the word writers love to stick beside the word "conservative" when describing guys like Cheney: anti-abortion, anti-gun control, pro-military. He was a strong supporter of Reagan's "Star Wars" SDI missile defense shield.

In 1989, George H. W. Bush named him Secretary of Defense, a post he held through the administration. He oversaw two major operations, Operation Just Cause in Panama and Operation Desert Storm in Kuwait and Iraq. After Republicans lost the White House to Bill Clinton in 1993, Cheney became a fellow at the conservative think tank, the American Enterprise Institute. Then, in 1995, he took the job of CEO of Halliburton, a Texas oilfield company with a variety of subsidiaries and . . . interests.

Up until the years in the Clinton wilderness, Cheney led a pretty public life. But before that public life began, there is one gaping hole in his résumé worth thinking about: his lack of military service. It became a minor issue during President George W.

Bush's reelection campaign in 2004, when the country was at war and the Democrats had selected Senator John "Reporting for Duty" Kerry as their candidate.

Here's the score: Cheney received three student draft defer-ments, the first in 1963 due to his enrollment in Casper Community College, during his lineman years. In 1966, married and with a pregnant wife, he applied for and received 3-A status. Twenty-three years later he would become Secretary of Defense.

TRUTH ON THE BOILERPLATE

On July 25, 2000, at a rally at the University of Texas, Governor George Bush announced that his running mate would be Dick Cheney. It wasn't for Wyoming's three electoral votes that he had picked Cheney, Bush declared, but because Cheney was "fully capable of being president."[3]

This is political boilerplate, of course, but just because it's boilerplate doesn't mean it's wrong. For much of Bush's time in office, no one charged that Cheney was incapable of being presi-dent. The charge was quite the opposite. Opponents accused Cheney of being more capable than the president, the power behind the throne.

The line that Democrats fed to their supporters about the Bush-Cheney pairing was the old Reagan–Bush Sr. formulation; the president is stupid, and the vice president is clever but wicked. With Cheney this was easy to apply because of the Left's suspicion of big business and big oil. Through his leadership of Halliburton, Cheney embodied both.

The future VP demonstrated his cleverness and dispelled any

* Twenty-two million new jobs, millions of new businesses, blah, blah, blah.

notion of him being a dull, humorless bureaucrat in the vice-presidential debate a month ahead of the vote, by brutally body checking his opponent.

Al Gore's running mate, Senator Joseph Lieberman, was deflecting criticism from Cheney that little had been accomplished during the Clinton years. After rattling off stats,* Lieberman took a shot at Cheney's personal fortune, estimated in the media at that time at $50 million,[4]** and . . .

** A total ballpark figure. In 2002, his total assets were estimated to fall somewhere between $19 and $86 million. Bottom line: He's rolling in it.

LIEBERMAN: I think you ask most people in America that famous question that Ronald Reagan asked, "Are you better off today than you were eight years ago?" most people would say yes. I'm pleased to see that you're better off than you were eight years ago, too. [*laughter*]

CHENEY: I can tell you the government had absolutely nothing to do with it. [*laughter*] [*applause*] [*blown kisses*]

MODERATOR: The question to you . . .

LIEBERMAN: I can see my wife and I think she is saying, "I think he should go out into the private sector."

CHENEY: Well, I'm going to try to help you do that, Joe.

Cheney's claim that the government "had absolutely nothing to do with it" was stretching the truth. While Cheney was CEO of Halliburton, the company doubled the amount it made on government contracts, bringing in $2.3 billion from public-service work. During his tenure, Halliburton also doubled its lobbying expenses. Apparently, the system works.

The connection to Halliburton would continue to dog Cheney throughout his tenure as vice president, particularly because of the large, untendered contracts awarded to Halliburton subsidiary Kellogg Brown and Root (KBR) for military support services in Iraq, building housing for soldiers, repairing oilfield services, and constructing enemy prisoner-of-war camps.

Cheney was secretary of defense back in 1992 when his department commissioned a study from KBR predecessor Brown and Root on outsourcing some aspects of military engineering and construction. The study looked at how to best downsize following the Gulf War and the end of the Cold War. The company was awarded the first contract that resulted from its recommendations in 1992 but lost it five years later, incidentally while Cheney was Halliburton CEO.

The Senate would determine there was nothing untoward in KBR's Iraq contracts, but public suspicion remained high. It was the Bush administration's shaky case for war in Iraq that fed the suspicion.

WELL, SHOOT

On the morning of September 11, from a bunker below the White House, Dick Cheney uttered the words that hatched the one conspiracy theory about that day that I still am not convinced is completely bogus.

What did he say? Cheney informed Secretary of Defense Donald Rumsfeld via video conference that he had given the order for fighter jets over Washington to shoot down any approaching aircraft.[5]

That was at 10:39 a.m., slightly less than an hour after American Airlines Flight 77 crashed into the side of the Pentagon, and almost exactly an hour after the FAA had halted all U.S. flights. President Bush was already in the air, having left from Sarasota, Florida, where he had been visiting a school, promoting his "No Child Left Behind" education boondoggle.

Cheney and Bush spoke four times by phone before Cheney had his conversation with Rumsfeld. The first, at 9:15, was while Bush was still at the school. They spoke a half hour later while Bush was on the tarmac with *Air Force One*. *Air Force One* phone logs, as well as those in the White House bunker, show two other calls between the two, at 10:18 and 10:20.

Both Cheney and Bush told the 9-11 Commission that it was during one of the latter two conversations that the president okayed the order to shoot. Nevertheless, the commission concluded there was no documentary evidence to support this. In other words, there were no recordings of the calls, nor did anybody near either man make notes of what was said.

In its inability to wholly accept the word of the president and the vice president, the commission fueled suspicion that Cheney had given the order to shoot without consulting the president first.

For a few months, for instance, your humble correspondent

was absolutely convinced that Cheney had issued the order without so much as by-your-leave, and I regret to report that I was rather obnoxious about it.

Fools are known by their many words. This fool, for instance, was at a lounge one night, laying out the case against the Prince of Darkness, our Imperial Vice President, when one guy a few barstools down had had enough. He did the verbal equivalent of smashing an empty glass bottle over my head:

YOURS TRULY: We have a vice president who ordered planes shot down *over American soil* and didn't even clear it with the president. Can you believe that? I mean, what a—

THAT GUY: Let's assume that everything you say is true, okay. You're the vice president. It's September 11. The Pentagon and the World Trade Center have been bombed, and there are reports of more trouble on the way. The president is out of pocket. You think more planes are going to crash into Congress, the White House, whatever. You can do something about it, whether or not you technically have the "authority." What would you do?

YOURS TRULY: Uh . . .

THAT GUY: What would you do?

YOURS TRULY: I . . .

THAT GUY: Well?

YOURS TRULY: I'd order them to shoot down anything that twitches.

The truth is that we'll never know what was said between Bush and Cheney that day. It's not out of the realm of possibility that the vice president raised the issue of more attacks, and the president said, "Shoot 'em down." The more important point is that Bush and Cheney had a relationship where that sort of thing was even conceivable.

At any rate, Cheney's order to shoot was without consequences. It was never passed on to the fighter pilots by either the mission commander or the weapons director, unsure of how the pilots would proceed with the order.

Cheney managed to relay/give the order to shoot without having another heart attack, which probably surprised some people, so convinced were they that his health was eggshell fragile due to his ongoing heart problems.

Formerly a heavy smoker, he had the first of four heart attacks when he was thirty-seven. He was in the hospital, undergoing a coronary artery stenting while the Florida recount dragged on in November 2000. CNN's Larry King, no slouch in the heart-attack department, called Cheney up in his hospital bed at George Washington University Hospital and asked him about stress, with his future hanging from a chad or two down in the land of the gator.

Cheney was calm. "Well, I . . . frankly, it may sound hard to believe, but I have not found this last couple of weeks as stressful, for example, as, say, the Gulf War. Really comparing the relative stress in different situations, my time in the Pentagon during the Gulf War was far more stressful," he said.[6]

In March the next year, he underwent urgent coronary balloon angioplasty. That was five months before September 11. Considering the magnitude of the attacks, and the uncertainty and fear they created, and the particular responsibility Cheney bore, it can be safely said that his doctors know what they're doing.

MANHATTAN TO THE MIDDLE EAST

After the invasion of Afghanistan to rout the Taliban, the Bush administration quickly set its sights on Iraq. Hold on a second; that might be mixing up the order. Iraq and Saddam Hussein were in the sights of a lot of American superhawks long before September 11, and we can count Cheney among them.

They believed, and apparently still believe, that taking out the Hussein regime and replacing it with a democratic government is but the first step in restructuring and stabilizing the Middle East. That view was promoted by longtime Cheney acquaintance, Paul Wolfowitz, who had worried about the rise of Iraq since the 1970s.[7] Wolfowitz was undersecretary of defense for policy under Cheney in the administration of George H. W. Bush. Under the younger Bush, Wolfowitz served as deputy defense secretary from 2001 until he left in 2005 to take on the presidency of the World Bank.[*]

*Which didn't work out so well.

The public and political climate following September 11 allowed them to put the replacement plan into practice. But first they had to sell the war.

The selling of the Iraq invasion would lead a few quixotic House Democrats to propose articles of impeachment against Cheney for high crimes and misdemeanors—specifically that he "purposely manipulated the intelligence process to deceive Congress and the citizens of the United States by fabricating a threat of Iraqi weapons of mass destruction to justify the use of the United States Armed Forces against the nation of Iraq in a manner damaging to our national security interests."[8]

Certainly Cheney was on the record saying numerous times that

Hussein was pursuing nuclear weapons. He did liaise with the CIA in the run-up to the March 2003 invasion and question their findings on Iraq's weapons program and its links to al-Qaeda. Ultimately, the 2002 National Intelligence Estimate, which Congress considered prior to its vote to authorize force, did flirt with the opinion shared by Cheney and others that Saddam was an imminent threat.

How much of the NIE's findings were due to pressure from Cheney is a matter of interpretation. Defenders minimize his involvement and point out that a lot of people were concerned about Hussein, thinking he was up to all kinds of no good. They could also add that a few congressmen relied on the ambiguous findings to vote *against* the resolution. Detractors point out that Cheney wanted the war and tried to influence the outcome of the report.

Both charges aren't terribly disputable, but these were secondary considerations to Cheney, who believed that many of the steps taken to sell the war in Iraq, including making the case to the United Nations, should not have been necessary. He firmly believed it was the president's constitutional duty as commander in chief of the military to protect the United States, and the president's call on matters of war.

TAKE THAT, CONGRESS

"I am one of those who believe that was an infringement on the authority of the president," Cheney said about the War Powers Act of 1973.[9] He made that statement following the revelation that the president had permitted domestic wiretaps on international calls without warrants, despite a law requiring one, in the wake of September 11.

The vice president defended that decision to reporters on a trip to Oman in December 2005. "I believe in a strong, robust executive authority, and I think that the world we live in demands it," Cheney said. It was then that he described the Nixon-era Watergate scandal as "the nadir of the modern presidency in terms of authority and legitimacy."[10]

The scandals and the congressional response constrained the chief executive's leadership at a difficult time for the nation. The Nixon administration was trying to extricate American forces from Vietnam while maintaining some sort of minimal support for the South Vietnamese. Congress responded by cutting off all funds and passing the War Powers Act, which forces the president to consult Congress before he enters into potentially long-term hostilities.

Cheney also pointed out that his opinion on this matter was on the public record. He had written, he said, minority views in 1987 on the Iran-Contra affair while in Congress. "Nobody's ever read them, but . . . I think [they] are very good in laying out a robust view of the president's prerogatives with respect to the conduct of especially foreign policy and national security matters," Cheney told reporters.[11] It was a nice way of saying, "Here, let me help you with your homework."

Those who bothered to dust off that minority report will read Cheney asserting that "throughout the Nation's history, Congress has accepted substantial exercises of Presidential power—in the conduct of diplomacy, the use of force and covert action—which had no basis in statute and only a general basis in the Constitution itself."

Having established the "general basis" standard, Cheney argued that "much of what President Reagan did in his actions toward Nicaragua and Iran were constitutionally protected exercises of inherent Presidential powers." So Congress should bugger off.

As for the power of the purse, he reminded that it "is not and was never intended to be a license for Congress to usurp Presidential powers and functions." Throughout American history "Presidents exercised a broad range of foreign policy powers for which they neither sought nor received Congressional sanction through statute," and rightly so.

Their past actions spoke "volumes about the Constitution's allocation of powers between the branches," leaving "little, if any, doubt that the President was expected to have the primary role of conducting" the country's foreign policy.[12]

In the 1980s, Cheney counseled "a considerable degree of skepticism" toward congressional actions to handicap the president's foreign-policy powers. Those interferences with the president's "core . . . foreign policy functions" should be "struck down," and in all events, "doubtful cases should be decided in favor of the President."[13]

It was a stated Cheney objective to restore the power of the presidency. Some have called it his personal theory of presidential power, but it's gone from theory to practice, and he admits as much. Cheney bragged, "To some extent now we've been able to restore the legitimate authority of the presidency."

LIKE A VETO

In order to keep an eye on Congress, Cheney hired lawyer David Addington as legal adviser in 2001. When chief of staff I. Lewis

"Scooter" Libby resigned after he was indicted on a perjury charge in October 2005, Cheney appointed Addington to replace him.

Cheney's acquaintance with Addington went back to the time of Iran-Contra when Addington was a Republican staffer. That Cheney would turn to this particular person should not surprise. When Cheney became secretary of defense, Addington was hired as counsel for the Pentagon.

Addington's main role in the Bush administration has been to read through legislation and sniff out any clause or provision that might limit the power of the president. If such a clause was found, the administration would issue a "signing statement."

Presidential signing statements can be issued to serve five different purposes. The first, mostly benign, is to simply explain what the president believes the likely effects of a piece of legislation might be. The second is to give directions to officials on how to interpret legislation it accompanies.

The third, more controversial purpose is to give the president's opinion that while a bill might be constitutional on its face, in certain circumstances it might not be. A fourth purpose is to declare that in the president's opinion, a piece of legislation is flatly unconstitutional. In effect, the president can maintain the right to ignore or enforce a law because of his interpretation of the Constitution. That opinion can be tested in court, but until it is, the president can act accordingly.

All previous presidents combined have issued fewer signing statements—approximately six hundred—than President Bush in five years, who has signed more than 750 of them. Two of the most controversial uses of these statements were on the oversight provisions of the PATRIOT Act and on legislation to ban torture.

The practice of issuing signing statements was rare until President Reagan began employing them with some frequency. Reagan was writing them for an entirely different purpose from the four just listed. His purpose was to create executive history; he would explain his understanding of a bill that he signed in order that at some future date, if necessary, the Supreme Court might reference it and give it weight.

In attacking Cheney and his legislative gatekeeper Addington, some have advanced the argument that a president should just veto a bill he believes is unconstitutional.* If Cheney wants to publicly defend the Bush administration over its use of signing statements, I predict he will dust off another largely unread government document, a Department of Justice memo titled "The Legal Significance of Signing Statements," prepared for President Clinton's counsel, Bernard Nussbaum.

* The argument goes back to 1791, when Thomas Jefferson advised President Washington not to sign a "Bill for Establishing a National Bank." Washington signed it anyway.

"In light of our constitutional history," the DOJ legal beagles wrote, "we do not believe that the President is under any duty to veto legislation containing a constitutionally infirm provision, although of course it is entirely appropriate for the President to do so."[14]

So far, Cheney has kept his powder dry on that front.

DUCK, DUCK, BANG

You didn't think I could get through a whole book on the vice presidents without writing about the Cheney hunting accident, did you?

It became a punch line that comics could fit in anywhere. Iraq war? "Good news, ladies and gentlemen, we have finally located weapons of mass destruction: it's Dick Cheney," quipped late-night talk show host David Letterman. Old-age pensions? "Dick Cheney said he felt terrible about shooting a seventy-eight-year-old man, but on the bright side, it did give him a great idea about how to fix Social Security," said Bill Maher, one of Letterman's low-rent competitors.

NBC's non-funny Brian Williams gave the event a little historical context. "It's believed to be the first time since Aaron Burr that a sitting vice president has shot another man. That shooting was intentional; this incident was not."

What he said just before that, however, put it in its comedic context: "Many have called it a plot line right out of *Saturday Night Live*. The truth is it's a serious matter, and there is still a lot of information we still don't know about what happened on a private Texas ranch on Saturday when Vice President Dick Cheney accidentally shot a member of his hunting party."[15]

When all the information about what happened on Saturday, February 11, 2006, did come out, the comparisons with Burr would be sidelined; the jokes would remain.

Roughly what happened was this: Cheney, an avid hunter,* was part of a hunting party out for quail on a ranch

> * And lifelong fisherman; Cheney never travels in Wyoming without his fly-fishing gear.

owned by Katherine Armstrong. A guest of Armstrong's, seventy-eight-year-old lawyer Harry Whittington from Austin, broke away from the group to retrieve a downed bird.

Without announcing his return, Whittington joined up with the group just as Cheney was preparing to shoot. The old man stepped into the line of fire and was peppered with buckshot on the face and neck.

In his two terms as vice president—with the country at war—the shooting incident would be the one event that would stick in just about everybody's mind when they thought of Dick Cheney. Either that or the fact that his younger daughter, Mary, who served as his aide for a few years, is a lesbian.

Mary's sexual orientation actually allowed the Democrats, who had long been willing to condemn Republicans—especially religious ones—as "homophobic," to start gay bashing again. In fact, some found ways to combine the shooting, Cheney's drinking, and Mary's lesbianism into one.

Maher said that there was some "discrepancy about what happened on this hunt, because Ann Armstrong, the woman who has this ranch, said there was no alcohol involved, and Dick Cheney said he had one beer." The punch line: "So, apparently, Dick Cheney can't keep his rifle, his story, or his daughter straight."

ACCIDENTS OF HISTORY

Cheney has had no difficulties, however, keeping straight his role in the Bush administration: to reestablish the president's "lost" powers.

New Yorker scribe Seymour Hersh described second-hand a meeting on national security at the Executive Office Building a month prior to the November midterm election.[16] Cheney was there, and Iran's steady progression toward becoming a nuclear power was on the table.

The conversation turned to speculation on what would happen if the Democrats won the House and the Senate. How would that constrain the Bush administration from dealing with a hostile Iran?

According to Hersh's source, Cheney started reminiscing about his time as a lineman in Wyoming. Because of the high cost of copper wire, the company ordered its lineman to return all unused pieces longer than three feet. They were also required to fill out paperwork on the returns.

That was too much of a pain in the neck at the end of day, so the lineman just chopped up any long wire into pieces shorter than three feet and chucked it away; they called this little act of time-saving sabotage putting "shorteners" on the wire.

If the Dems won the Senate and the House—as they did—the president would not be constrained from using a military option on Iran if he believed it was necessary. They would just put "shorteners" on any congressional bill attempting to restrict executive power, and the otherwise cumbersome War Powers Act does allow the president to undertake limited engagements without the consent of Congress.

"Yikes!" said critics, including former vice president Walter Mondale, who have consistently charged that Cheney is far too powerful. It's hard to deny that they have a point. The Constitution didn't envision a large role for the vice president until his boss kicks the (warm) bucket.

On the other hand, the role of the vice president is so vague that it's almost as if the Constitution was asking for trouble. By most accounts, Dick Cheney believes that his actions have all been in the service of restoring the power of the *presidency*, not his own inferior office.

Whether you believe that or not, it's true that Cheney has

never sought the presidency. His own influence as vice president is based on his relationship with President Bush as well as the role that he's carved out for himself: he who repairs the lines controls the juice.

Logically, future vice presidents *could* have less power. I suspect, however, that Cheney will not be unique in his Godzilla-sized influence. In the ongoing story of the vice presidency, accidents of history are the rule, not the exception.

APPENDIX: THE CHECKERS SPEECH

This speech was delivered on September 23, 1952. Republican candidate for vice president Richard Nixon had come under fire for allegedly pocketing $18,000 worth of illegal campaign contributions to a special "slush fund." Presidential nominee Dwight Eisenhower's men pressured Nixon to drop off the ticket. Instead, Senator Nixon addressed the nation in this half-hour live broadcast. From the El Capitan Theatre in Hollywood, he made the case for his own integrity to a truly massive national audience.

I include it here as more than a novelty. It was a significant event in the history of the vice presidency—in part because it saved Nixon's political career. It was filmed during television's infancy, and yet Nixon "got" television in a way that few politicians since have managed, and even Nixon never managed to top it.

The modern pol might deny that the money in a campaign slush fund was improperly used, as Nixon did, but Nixon went much further. He bared his soul.

Nixon promised the audience "a complete financial history, everything I've earned, everything I've spent, everything I own," and a detailed outline of the family's debts, holdings, and earnings, including what they paid for houses in D.C. and in Whittier, California, the amounts they still owed on the loans, and the interest rates on those loans.

It came to be known as the "Checkers speech" because Nixon did confess to one possible illegal donation. He said that an unidentified "man down in Texas" had caught a radio broadcast in which Pat Nixon mentioned "that our two youngsters would like to have a dog." In short order, a black-and-white cocker spaniel arrived at a train stop in Baltimore. Daughter Tricia Nixon named it "Checkers," and Nixon told the audience "I just want to say this, right now, that regardless of what they say about it, we're gonna keep [the dog]."

The knowing laugh that the Checkers line is likely to provoke in the modern reader should be set aside for a moment. After the speech, the Republican National Committee was carpet-bombed with cards and letters saying, "Keep this man on the ticket." The viewers did that not because Dick Nixon was keeping the dog but because they thought the man was worth keeping. He had done something so gutsy, so audacious, that they almost didn't have a choice in the matter. With that said, here it is . . .

My Fellow Americans,

I come before you tonight as a candidate for the Vice Presidency and as a man whose honesty and integrity has been questioned.

Now, the usual political thing to do when charges are made against you is to either ignore them or to deny them without giving details. I believe we've had enough of that in the United States, particularly with the present Administration in Washington D.C. To me the office of the Vice Presidency of the United States is a great office, and I feel that the people have got to have confidence in the integrity of the men who run for that office and who might obtain it.

I have a theory, too, that the best and only answer to a smear or to an honest misunderstanding of the facts is to tell the truth. And that's why I'm here tonight. I want to tell you my side of the case. I'm sure that you have read the charge, and you've heard it, that I, Senator Nixon, took 18,000 dollars from a group of my supporters.

Now, was that wrong? And let me say that it was wrong. I'm saying, incidentally, that it was wrong, not just illegal, because it isn't a question of whether it was legal or illegal, that isn't enough. The question is, was it morally wrong? I say that it was morally wrong—if any of that 18,000 dollars went to Senator Nixon, for my personal use. I say that it was morally wrong if it was secretly given and secretly handled. And I say that it was morally wrong if any of the contributors got special favors for the contributions that they made.

And now to answer those questions let me say this: Not one cent of the 18,000 dollars or any other money of that type ever went to me for my personal use. Every penny of it was used to pay for political expenses that I did not think should be charged to the taxpayers of the United States. It was not a secret fund. As a matter of fact, when I was on "Meet the Press"—some of you may have seen it last Sunday—Peter Edson came up to me after the program, and he said, "Dick, what about this 'fund' we hear about?" And I said, "Well, there's no secret about it. Go out and see Dana Smith who was the administrator of the fund." And I gave him [Edson] his [Smith's] address. And I said you will find that the purpose of the fund simply was to defray political expenses that I did not feel should be charged to the Government.

And third, let me point out—and I want to make this particularly clear—that no contributor to this fund, no contributor to any of my campaigns, has ever received any consideration that he would not have received as an ordinary constituent. I just don't believe in that, and I can say that never, while I have been in the Senate of the United States, as far as the people that contributed to this fund are concerned, have I made a telephone call for them to an agency, or have I gone down to an agency in their behalf. And the records will show that, the records which are in the hands of the administration.

Well, then, some of you will say, and rightly, "Well, what did you use the fund for, Senator?" "Why did you have to have it?" Let me tell you in just a word how a Senate office operates. First of all, a Senator gets 15,000 dollars a year in salary. He gets enough money to pay for one trip a year—a round trip, that is—for himself and his family between his home and Washington, D.C. And then he gets an allowance to handle the people that work in his office to handle his mail. And the allowance for my State of California is enough to hire 13 people. And let me say, incidentally, that that allowance is not paid to the Senator. It's paid directly to the individuals that the Senator puts on his pay roll. But all of these people and all of these allowances are for strictly official business; business, for example, when a constituent writes in and wants you to go down to the Veteran's Administration and get some information about his GI policy—items of that type, for example. But there are other expenses which are not covered by the Government. And I think I can best discuss those expenses by asking you some questions.

Do you think that when I or any other Senator makes a political speech, has it printed, should charge the printing of that speech and the mailing of that speech to the taxpayers? Do you think, for example, when I or any other Senator makes a trip to his home State to make a purely political speech that the cost of that trip should be charged to the taxpayers? Do you think when a Senator makes political broadcasts or political television broadcasts, radio or television, that the expense of those broadcasts should be charged to the taxpayers? Well I know what your answer is. It's the same answer that audiences give me whenever I discuss this particular problem: The answer is no. The taxpayers shouldn't be required to finance items which are not official business but which are primarily political business.

Well, then the question arises, you say, "Well, how do you pay for these and how can you do it legally?" And there are several ways that it can be done, incidentally, and that it is done legally in the United States Senate and in the Congress. The first way is to be a rich man. I don't happen to be a rich man, so I couldn't use that one. Another way that is used is to put your wife on the pay roll. Let me say, incidentally, that my opponent, my opposite number for the Vice Presidency on the Democratic ticket, does have his wife on the pay roll and has had it—her on his pay roll for the ten years—for the past ten years. Now just let me say this: That's his business, and I'm not critical of him for doing that. You will have to pass judgment on that particular point.

But I have never done that for this reason: I have found that there are so many deserving stenographers and secretaries in Washington that needed the work that I just didn't feel it was right to put my wife on the pay roll.

My wife's sitting over here. She's a wonderful stenographer. She used to teach stenography and she used to teach shorthand in high school. That was when I met her. And I can tell you folks that she's worked many hours at night and many hours on Saturdays and Sundays in my office, and she's done a fine job, and I am proud to say tonight that in the six years I've been in the House and the Senate of the United States, Pat Nixon has never been on the Government pay roll.

What are other ways that these finances can be taken care of? Some who are lawyers, and I happen to be a lawyer, continue to practice law, but I haven't been able to do that. I'm so far away from California that I've been so busy with my senatorial work that I have not engaged in any legal practice. And, also, as far as law practice is concerned, it seemed to me that the relationship between an attorney and the client was so personal that you couldn't possibly represent a man as an attorney and then have an unbiased view when he presented his case to you in the event that he had one before Government.

And so I felt that the best way to handle these necessary political expenses of getting my message to the American people and the speeches I made—the speeches that I had printed for the most part concerned this one message of exposing this Administration, the Communism in it, the corruption in it—the only way that I could do that was to accept the aid which people in my home State of California, who contributed to my campaign and who continued to make these contributions after I was elected, were glad to make.

And let me say I'm proud of the fact that not one of them has ever asked me for a special favor. I'm proud of the fact that not one of them has ever asked me to vote on a bill other than of my own conscience would dictate. And I am proud of the fact that the taxpayers, by subterfuge or otherwise, have never paid one dime for expenses which I thought were political and shouldn't be charged to the taxpayers.

Let me say, incidentally, that some of you may say, "Well, that's all right, Senator, that's your explanation, but have you got any proof?" And I'd like to tell you this evening that just an hour ago we received an independent audit of this entire fund. I suggested to Governor Sherman Adams, who is the Chief of Staff of the Dwight Eisenhower campaign, that an independent audit and legal report be obtained, and I have that audit here in my hands. It's an audit made by the Price Waterhouse & Company firm, and the legal opinion by Gibson, Dunn, & Crutcher, lawyers in Los Angeles, the biggest law firm, and incidentally, one of the best ones in Los Angeles.

I am proud to be able to report to you tonight that this audit and this legal opinion is being forwarded to General Eisenhower. And I'd like to read to you the opinion that was prepared by Gibson, Dunn, & Crutcher, and based on all the pertinent laws and statutes, together with the audit report prepared by the certified public accountants. Quote:

It is our conclusion that Senator Nixon did not obtain any financial gain from the collection and disbursement of the fund by Dana Smith; that Senator Nixon did not violate any federal or state law by reason of the operation of the fund; and that neither the portion of the fund paid by Dana Smith directly to third persons, nor the portion paid to Senator Nixon, to reimburse him for designated office expenses, constituted income to the Senator which was either reportable or taxable as income under applicable tax laws.

(signed)

Gibson, Dunn, & Crutcher,

by Elmo H. Conley

Now that, my friends, is not Nixon speaking, but that's an independent audit which was requested, because I want the American people to know all the facts, and I am not afraid of having independent people go in and check the facts, and that is exactly what they did. But then I realized that there are still some who may say, and rightfully so—and let me say that I recognize that some will continue to smear regardless of what the truth may be—but that there has been, understandably, some honest misunderstanding on this matter, and there are some that will say, "Well, maybe you were able, Senator, to fake this thing. How can we believe what you say? After all, is there a possibility that maybe you got some sums in cash? Is there a possibility that you may have feathered your own nest?" And so now, what I am going to do—and incidentally this is unprecedented in the history of American politics—I am going at this time to give to this television and radio audio—audience, a complete financial history, everything

I've earned, everything I've spent, everything I own. And I want you to know the facts.

I'll have to start early. I was born in 1913. Our family was one of modest circumstances, and most of my early life was spent in a store out in East Whittier. It was a grocery store, one of those family enterprises. The only reason we were able to make it go was because my mother and dad had five boys, and we all worked in the store. I worked my way through college, and, to a great extent, through law school. And then in 1940, probably the best thing that ever happened to me happened. I married Pat who's sitting over here. We had a rather difficult time after we were married, like so many of the young couples who may be listening to us. I practiced law. She continued to teach school.

Then, in 1942, I went into the service. Let me say that my service record was not a particularly unusual one. I went to the South Pacific. I guess I'm entitled to a couple of battle stars. I got a couple of letters of commendation. But I was just there when the bombs were falling. And then I returned—returned to the United States, and in 1946, I ran for the Congress. When we came out of the war—Pat and I—Pat during the war had worked as a stenographer, and in a bank, and as an economist for a Government agency—and when we came out, the total of our savings, from both my law practice, her teaching and all the time that I was in the war, the total for that entire period was just a little less than 10,000 dollars. Every cent of that, incidentally, was in Government bonds. Well that's where we start, when I go into politics.

Now, what have I earned since I went into politics? Well, here it is. I've jotted it down. Let me read the notes. First of all, I've had my salary as a Congressman and as a Senator. Second, I have received a total in this past six years of 1,600 dollars from estates which were in my law firm at the time that I severed my connection with it. And, incidentally, as I said before, I have not engaged in any legal practice and have not accepted any fees from business that came into the firm after I went into politics. I have made an average of approximately 1,500 dollars a year from nonpolitical speaking engagements and lectures.

And then, fortunately, we've inherited a little money. Pat sold her interest in her father's estate for 3,000 dollars, and I inherited 1500 dollars from my grandfather. We lived rather modestly. For four years we lived in an apartment in Parkfairfax, in Alexandria, Virginia. The rent was 80 dollars a month. And we saved for the time that we could buy a house. Now, that was what we took in. What did we do with this money? What do we have today to show for it? This will surprise you because it is so little, I suppose, as standards generally go of people in public life.

First of all, we've got a house in Washington, which cost 41,000 dollars and on which we owe 20,000 dollars. We have a house in Whittier, California, which cost 13,000 dollars and on which we owe 3,000 dollars. My folks are living there at the present time. I have just 4,000 dollars in life insurance, plus my GI policy which I've never been able to convert, and which will run out in two years. I have no life insurance whatever on Pat. I have no life insurance on our two youngsters, Tricia and Julie. I own a 1950 Oldsmobile car. We have our furniture. We have no stocks and bonds of any type. We have no interest of any kind, direct or indirect, in any business. Now, that's what we have. What do we owe?

Well in addition to the mortgage, the 20,000 dollar mortgage on the house in Washington, the 10,000 dollar one on the house in Whittier, I owe 4,500 dollars to the Riggs Bank in Washington D.C., with interest 4 and 1/2 percent. I owe 3,500 dollars to my parents, and the interest on that loan, which I pay regularly, because it's the part of the savings they made through the years they were working so hard—I pay regularly 4 percent interest. And then I have a 500 dollar loan, which I have on my life insurance.

Well, that's about it. That's what we have. And that's what we owe. It isn't very much. But Pat and I have the satisfaction that every dime that we've got is honestly ours. I should say this, that Pat doesn't have a mink coat. But she does have a respectable Republican cloth coat, and I always tell her she'd look good in anything.

One other thing I probably should tell you, because if I don't they'll probably be saying this about me, too. We did get something, a gift, after the election. A man down in Texas heard Pat on the radio mention the fact that our two youngsters would like to have a dog. And believe it or not, the day before we left on this campaign trip we got a message from Union Station in Baltimore, saying they had a package for us. We went down to get it. You know what it was? It was a little cocker spaniel dog in a crate that he'd sent all the way from Texas, black and white, spotted. And our little girl Tricia, the six year old, named it "Checkers." And you know, the kids, like all kids, love the dog, and I just want to say this, right now, that regardless of what they say about it, we're gonna keep it.

It isn't easy to come before a nationwide audience and bare your life, as I've done. But I want to say some things before I conclude that I think most of you will agree on. Mr. Mitchell, the Chairman of the Democratic National Committee, made this statement—that if a man couldn't afford to be in the United States Senate, he shouldn't run for the Senate. And I just want to make my position clear. I don't agree with Mr. Mitchell when he says that only a rich man should serve his Government in the United States Senate or in the Congress. I don't believe that represents the thinking of the Democratic Party, and I know that it doesn't represent the thinking of the Republican Party.

I believe that it's fine that a man like Governor Stevenson, who inherited a fortune from his father, can run for President. But I also feel that it's essential in this country of ours that a man of modest means can also run for President, because, you know, remember Abraham Lincoln, you remember what he said: "God must have loved the common people—he made so many of them."

And now I'm going to suggest some courses of conduct. First of all, you have read in the papers about other funds, now. Mr. Stevenson apparently had a couple—one of them in which a group of business people paid and helped to supplement the salaries of State employees. Here is where the money went directly into their pockets, and I think that what Mr. Stevenson should do should be to come before the American people, as I have, give the names of the people that contributed to that fund, give the names of the people who put this money into their pockets at the same time that they were receiving money from their State government and see what favors, if any, they gave out for that.

I don't condemn Mr. Stevenson for what he did, but until the facts are in there is a doubt that will be raised. And as far as Mr. Sparkman is concerned, I would suggest the same thing. He's had his wife on the payroll. I don't condemn him for that, but I think that he should come before the American people and indicate what outside sources of income he has had. I would suggest that under the circumstances both Mr. Sparkman and Mr. Stevenson should come before the American people, as I have, and make a complete financial statement as to their financial history, and if they don't it will be an admission that they have something to hide. And I think you will agree with me—because, folks, remember, a man that's to be President of the United States, a man that's to be Vice President of the United States, must have the confidence of all the people. And that's why I'm doing what I'm doing. And that's why I suggest that Mr. Stevenson and Mr. Sparkman, since they are under attack, should do what they're doing.

Now let me say this: I know that this is not the last of the smears. In spite of my explanation tonight, other smears will be made. Others have been made in the past. And the purpose of the smears, I know, is this: to silence me; to make me let up. Well, they just don't know who they're dealing with. I'm going to tell you this: I remember in the dark days of the Hiss case some of the same columnists, some of the same radio commentators who are attacking me now and misrepresenting my position, were violently opposing me at the time I was after Alger Hiss. But I continued to fight because I knew I was right, and I can say to this great television and radio audience that I have no apologies to the American people for my part in putting Alger Hiss where he is today. And as far as this is concerned, I intend to continue to fight.

Why do I feel so deeply? Why do I feel that in spite of the smears, the misunderstanding, the necessity for a man to come up here and bare his soul as I have—why is it necessary for me to continue this fight? And I want to tell you why. Because, you see, I love my country. And I think my country is in danger. And I think the

only man that can save America at this time is the man that's running for President, on my ticket—Dwight Eisenhower. You say,
"Why do I think it is in danger?" And I say, look at the record. Seven
years of the Truman-Acheson Administration, and what's happened?
Six hundred million people lost to the Communists. And a war in
Korea in which we have lost 117,000 American casualties, and I say
to all of you that a policy that results in the loss of 600 million people
to the Communists, and a war which cost us 117,000 American
casualties isn't good enough for America. And I say that those in the
State Department that made the mistakes which caused that war and
which resulted in those losses should be kicked out of the State
Department just as fast as we get them out of there.

And let me say that I know Mr. Stevenson won't do that
because he defends the Truman policy, and I know that Dwight
Eisenhower will do that, and that he will give America the leadership that it needs. Take the problem of corruption. You've read
about the mess in Washington. Mr. Stevenson can't clean it up
because he was picked by the man, Truman, under whose
Administration the mess was made. You wouldn't trust the man
who made the mess to clean it up. That's Truman. And by the
same token you can't trust the man who was picked by the man
that made the mess to clean it up—and that's Stevenson.

And so I say, Eisenhower, who owed nothing to Truman, nothing to the big city bosses—he is the man that can clean up the mess
in Washington. Take Communism. I say that as far as that subject
is concerned the danger is great to America. In the Hiss case they
got the secrets which enabled them to break the American secret
State Department code. They got secrets in the atomic bomb case
which enabled them to get the secret of the atomic bomb five years

before they would have gotten it by their own devices. And I say
that any man who called the Alger Hiss case a red herring isn't fit
to be President of the United States. I say that a man who, like Mr.
Stevenson, has pooh-poohed and ridiculed the Communist threat
in the United States—he said that they are phantoms among our-
selves. He has accused us that have attempted to expose the
Communists, of looking for Communists in the Bureau of Fisheries
and Wildlife. I say that a man who says *that* isn't qualified to be
President of the United States. And I say that the only man who
can lead us in this fight to rid the Government of both those who
are Communists and those who have corrupted this Government
is Eisenhower, because Eisenhower, you can be sure, recognizes the
problem, and he knows how to deal with it.

Now let me say finally, this evening, that I want to read to you,
just briefly, excerpts from a letter which I received, a letter which
after all this is over no one can take away from us. It reads as follows:

Dear Senator Nixon,

*Since I am only 19 years of age, I can't vote in this presi-
dential election, but believe me if I could you and General
Eisenhower would certainly get my vote. My husband is in the
Fleet Marines in Korea. He's a corpsman on the front lines
and we have a two month old son he's never seen. And I feel
confident that with great Americans like you and General
Eisenhower in the White House, lonely Americans like myself
will be united with their loved ones now in Korea. I only pray
to God that you won't be too late. Enclosed is a small check to
help you in your campaign. Living on $85 a month, it is all I
can afford at present, but let me know what else I can do.*

Folks, it's a check for 10 dollars, and it's one that I will never cash. And just let me say this: We hear a lot about prosperity these days, but I say why can't we have prosperity built on peace, rather than prosperity built on war? Why can't we have prosperity and an honest Government in Washington D.C., at the same time? Believe me, we can. And Eisenhower is the man that can lead this crusade to bring us that kind of prosperity.

And now, finally, I know that you wonder whether or not I am going to stay on the Republican ticket or resign. Let me say this: I don't believe that I ought to quit, because I am not a quitter. And, incidentally, Pat's not a quitter. After all, her name was Patricia Ryan and she was born on St. Patrick's day, and you know the Irish never quit.

But the decision, my friends, is not mine. I would do nothing that would harm the possibilities of Dwight Eisenhower to become President of the United States. And for that reason I am submitting to the Republican National Committee tonight through this television broadcast the decision which it is theirs to make. Let them decide whether my position on the ticket will help or hurt. And I am going to ask you to help them decide. Wire and write the Republican National Committee whether you think I should stay on or whether I should get off. And whatever their decision is, I will abide by it.

But just let me say this last word: Regardless of what happens, I'm going to continue this fight. I'm going to campaign up and down in America until we drive the crooks and the Communists and those that defend them out of Washington. And remember folks, Eisenhower is a great man, believe me. He's a great man. And a vote for Eisenhower is a vote for what's good for America.

THANKS

Thanks to Joel Miller for the indulgence, Alice Sullivan for cracking the whip, and Julie Foster for her fine edits. Several editors green-lighted pieces on vice presidents, which proved to be an invaluable way to move the project forward. They are: Carol Herman, Wlady Pleszczynski, and Sarah Courteau. Research assistants Kevin Steel and Kevin Michael Grace can now take a bow, and take some time off. This book was made possible in part by the Competitive Enterprise Institute. The good folks there awarded me the 2007 Warren T. Brookes Journalism Fellowship and offered invaluable support—including a salary, an office, and equipment—and feedback. Special thanks to CEIers Jody Clarke and Ivan Osorio. Thanks to Robert VerBruggen for the countless hours of head-clearing Mario Kart play, Jim Antle for holding down the fort at JeremyLott.net, and Shawn Macomber and Michael Brendan Dougherty for the Burr-Hamilton reenactment. Thanks, finally, to Jamie Dettmer. He knows why.

NOTES

INTRODUCTION

1. Richard H. Abbott, "Henry Wilson" in *Vice Presidents: A Biographical Dictionary* (Checkmark, 2001), 168.
2. David Greenberg, *Calvin Coolidge* (Times Books, 2006).
3. Katherine M. Skiba, "Ex-VP No Airport VIP," *Milwaukee Journal Sentinel*, June 14, 2002, http://www.jsonline.com/story/index.aspx?id=51090.
4. James Grant, *John Adams: Party of One* (Farrar, Straus and Giroux, 2005), 353.

CHAPTER 1

1. "Quayle Center and the United States Vice Presidential Museum," roadsideamerica.com, http://www.roadsideamerica.com/attract/INHUNquayle.html.

CHAPTER 2

1. Edmund S. Morgan, *The Meaning of Independence: John Adams, George Washington and Thomas Jefferson* (Norton, 1978), 19.
2. Mark O. Hatfield, with the Senate Historical Office, *Vice Presidents of the United States, 1789–1993* (Government Printing Office, 1997).
3. Ibid.
4. George Washington, Farewell Address, http://usinfo.state.gov/usa/infousa/facts/democrac/49.htm.
5. *Wait, Wait . . . Don't Tell Me*, National Public Radio, July 20, 2000, http://www.npr.org/programs/waitwait/archquiz/2001/010707.html.
6. Richard Norton, *Patriarch: George Washington and the New American Nation* (Houghton Mifflin, 1993).

7. Bernard Mayo, *Jefferson Himself: The Personal Narrative of a Many-Sided American* (University of Virginia Press, 1970).

8. David Meschutt, "The Adams-Jefferson Portrait Exchange," *American Art Journal* 14, no. 2 (Spring 1982).

9. "Alien and Sedition Acts," Library of Congress, http://www.loc.gov/rr/program/bib/ourdocs/Alien.html.

10. Paul Johnson, *A History of the American People* (Harper, 1999), 241.

11. Hatfield, *Vice Presidents*.

12. Richard Brookhiser, *Alexander Hamilton, American* (Free Press, 1999).

13. Lester J. Cappon, ed., *The Adams-Jefferson Letters: The Complete Correspondence Between Thomas Jefferson and Abigail and John Adams* (University of North Carolina Press, 1988).

CHAPTER 3

1. The Burr-Hamilton duel was reenacted in Weehawken on its 200th anniversary, July 11, 2004. A slide show of this event can be found at: http://duel2004.weehawkenhistory.org/duel2004-1.mov.

2. Richard Brookhiser, *Alexander Hamilton, American* (Free Press, 1999).

3. Ibid.

4. "Code Duello: The Rules of Dueling," PBS.org, http://www.pbs.org/wgbh/amex/duel/sfeature/rulesofdueling.html.

5. Brookhiser, *Alexander Hamilton*.

6. *The Catholic Encyclopedia* (Encyclopedia Press, 1913) s.v. "Duel," http://www.newadvent.org/cathen/05184b.htm.

7. Joseph Wheelan, *Jefferson's Vendetta: The Pursuit of Aaron Burr and the Judiciary* (Carroll & Graf, 2005).

8. Brookhiser, *Alexander Hamilton*.

9. Susan Dunn, *Jefferson's Second Revolution: The Election Crisis of 1800 and the Triumph of Republicanism* (Houghton Mifflin, 2004).

10. Hatfield, *Vice Presidents*.

11. Ibid.

12. "March 2, 1805: Indicted Vice President Bids Senate Farewell," United States Senate Historical Minute Essays, http://www.senate.gov/artandhistory/history/minute/Indicted_Vice_President_Bids_Senate_Farewell.htm.

13. Ibid.

CHAPTER 4

1. Andrew Rosenthal, "Bush Encounters the Supermarket, Amazed," *New York Times*, February 5, 1992.

2. "Maybe I'm Amazed," *Urban Legends Reference Pages*, April 1, 2001, http://www.snopes.com/history/american/bushscan.htm.

3. William Seale, "About the Gold Spoon Oration," White House Historical Association, http://www.whitehousehistory.org/08/subs/08_b10.html.

4. Ibid.

5. "London," Samuel Johnson, *The Major Works* (Oxford University Press, 2000).

6. "Gold Spoon Oration," Wikipedia, http://en.wikipedia.org/wiki/Gold_Spoon_Oration.

7. "1840: One Hundred and Fifty Years Ago," *American Heritage*, http://www.americanheritage.com/articles/magazine/ah/1990/3/1990_3_40.shtml.

8. Seale, "About the Gold Spoon Oration."

9. Martin Van Buren, *The Autobiography of Martin Van Buren*, edited by John C. Fitzpatrick (Da Capo, 1973).

10. Ibid.

11. Robert V. Remini, *Martin Van Buren and the Making of the Democratic Party* (Columbia University Press, 1959).

12. Martin Van Buren, "Second Annual Message to Congress," Miller Center of Public Affairs, University of Virginia, http://www.millercenter.virginia.edu/scripps/digitalarchive/speeches/spe_1838_1203_vanburen.

13. Hatfield, *Vice Presidents*.

14. Remini, *Martin Van Buren*.

15. Ibid.

16. Robert V. Remini, *Henry Clay: Statesman for the Union* (Norton, 1991).

17. Sol Barzman, *Madmen and Geniuses: The Vice Presidents of the United States* (Follet, 1974).

18. Hatfield, *Vice Presidents*.

19. Clifton Johnson, "The *Amistad* Case and its Consequences in U.S. History," Amistad Research Center, Tulane University, http://www.tulane.edu/~amistad/amessays.htm.

20. Robert V. Remini, *Andrew Jackson and His Indian Wars* (Viking, 2001).

21. Niccolò Machiavelli, *The Prince*, trans. by George Bull (Penguin, 2003).

CHAPTER 5

1. Oliver Perry Chitwood, *John Tyler: Champion of the Old South* (American Political Biography Press, 2000).

2. Ibid.

3. Edward P. Crapol, *John Tyler, the Accidental President* (University of North Carolina Press, 2006).

4. Ibid.

5. Ibid.

6. Quoted in M. Boyd Coyner Jr., "John Tyler" in *Vice Presidents: A Biographical Dictionary*, 97.

7. Ibid.
8. Crapol, *John Tyler.*
9. Ibid.
10. Ibid.
11. For information on tours, see the plantation's Web site:
    http://www.sherwoodforest.org/.

CHAPTER 6
1. H. L. Mencken, *The Bathtub Hoax, and Other Blasts and Bravos from the Chicago Tribune* (Octagon, 1976).
2. Sandra Fleishman, "Builder's Winning Play: A Royal Flush," *Washington Post,* November 24, 2001, http://www.washingtonpost.com/ac2/ wp-dyn?pagename=article&node=&contentId=A7732-2001Nov23.
3. Cecil Adams, "Where Can I Join the Millard Fillmore Society?" http://www.straightdope.com/classics/a1_107.html.
4. Millard Fillmore, *Millard Fillmore Papers Vol. I* (Cornell, 1907).

CHAPTER 7
1. Hans L. Trefousse, *Andrew Johnson: A Biography* (Norton, 1989).
2. Ibid.
3. Howard Means, *The Avenger Takes His Place: Andrew Johnson and the 45 Days That Changed the Nation* (Harcourt, 2006).
4. Ibid.
5. Ibid.
6. Ibid.
7. Trefousse, *Andrew Johnson.*
8. Ibid.
9. Reflected in the end of the movie *Gangs of New York.*
10. Trefousse, *Andrew Johnson.*
11. Ibid.
12. John F. Kennedy, *Profiles in Courage: Decisive Moments in the Lives of Celebrated Americans* (HarperCollins, 2006).

CHAPTER 8
1. A pretty good account of this can be found in Kenneth D. Ackerman, *Dark Horse: The Surprise Election and Political Murder of President James A. Garfield* (Carroll & Graf, 2003).
2. Zachary Karabell, *Chester Alan Arthur* (Times Books, 2004).
3. Ibid.

CHAPTER 9

1. "The Destruction of USS *Maine*," Naval Historical Center, Department of the Navy, August 13, 2003, http://www.history.navy.mil/faqs/faq71-1.htm.

2. "Garret Augustus Hobart, 24th Vice President," United States Senate Web site, http://www.senate.gov/artandhistory/history/common/generic/VP_Garret_Hobart.htm.

3. David H. Burton, *Taft, Roosevelt, and the Limits of Friendship* (Fairleigh Dickinson University Press, 2005).

4. John Morton Blum, *The Republican Roosevelt*, 2nd ed. (Harvard University Press, 2004).

5. Hatfield, *Vice Presidents of the United States*.

6. William A. DeGregorio, *The Complete Book of U.S. Presidents*, 6th ed. (Barricade Books, 2005).

7. *Rough Riders* (Turner Home Entertainment, 2006), motion picture.

8. "Citizenship in a Republic," speech given at the Sorbonne, Paris, April 23, 1910, quoted in *Quotations of Theodore Roosevelt* (Applewood Books, 2004).

9. Speech given at Oyster Bay, New York, July 7, 1915, quoted in ibid.

10. Theodore Roosevelt, *The Rough Riders/An Autobiography* (Library of America, 2004).

11. DeGregorio, *The Complete Book of U.S. Presidents*.

12. *The American Heritage Dictionary of the English Language*, 4th ed. (Houghton Mifflin, 2000), http://www.bartleby.com/61/58/B0545800.html.

13. Roosevelt, *An Autobiography*.

14. David McCullough, *The Path Between the Seas: The Creation of the Panama Canal, 1870–1914* (Simon and Schuster, 1977).

15. John B. Judis, *The Folly of Empire: What George W. Bush Could Learn From Theodore Roosevelt and Woodrow Wilson* (Oxford University Press, 2006).

16. But see "Credit 'Splendid Little War' to John Hay," John A. Gable, Letter to the Editor, *New York Times*, July 9, 1991.

17. David Greenberg, "Bhagwan Teddy: Explaining the Cult of Theodore Roosevelt," *Slate*, March 28, 2002, http://www.slate.com/id/2063795.

18. Edmund Morris, *Theodore Rex* (Modern Library, 2002).

CHAPTER 10

1. David J. Bennett, *He Almost Changed the World: The Life and Times of Thomas Riley Marshall* (AuthorHouse, 2007).

2. Ibid.

3. Ibid.

4. Ibid.

5. Hatfield, *Vice Presidents of the United States*.

6. Ibid.

7. Ibid.
8. Ibid.
9. Ibid.
10. Thomas R. Marshall, *Recollections of Thomas R. Marshall, Vice President* and *Hoosier Philosopher; a Hoosier Salad* (Bobbs-Merrill, 1925).

CHAPTER 11
1. David Greenberg, *Calvin Coolidge* (Times Books, 2006), 97.
2. Calvin Coolidge, *The Autobiography of Calvin Coolidge* (Cosmopolitan, 1929), 189–90.
3. Greenberg, *Calvin Coolidge*, 98.
4. For the definitive account of wartime regulation of radio, see Jesse Walker, *Rebels on the Air: An Alternative History of Radio in America* (NYU Press, 2004).
5. Greenberg, *Calvin Coolidge*, 142–50.
6. Ben Bernake "On Milton Friedman's Ninetieth Birthday," November 8, 2002, http://www.federalreserve.gov/BOARDDOCS/SPEECHES/2002/20021108/default.htm.
7. Robert Sobel, *Coolidge: An American Enigma* (Regnery, 1998), 186–90.
8. Paul L. Silver, "Calvin Coolidge" in *Vice Presidents: A Biographical Dictionary*, 268.
9. Greenberg, *Calvin Coolidge*, 142–50.
10. He did say something close to that but, as Thomas Silver argued, it was wrenched all out of context by several historians. See Thomas B. Silver, "Arthur Schlesinger in Calvin Coolidge" (Claremont Review of Books, Summer 2007), 23–24.

CHAPTER 12
1. Hatfield, *Vice Presidents of the United States*.
2. Ibid.
3. Pictures can be found at http://users.ntplx.net/~bbarker/deadprez/jng.htm.
4. Hatfield, *Vice Presidents*.
5. Ibid.
6. Ibid.
7. "Oral history interview with Jonathan Daniels," Truman Presidential Museum and Library, October 4–5, 1963, http://www.trumanlibrary.org/oralhist/danielsj.htm.
8. "Garner biography," John Nance Garner Museum, Center for American History, University of Texas at Austin, http://www.cah.utexas.edu/museums/garner_bio.php.
9. Nigel Rees, *Brewer's Famous Quotations: 5000 Quotations and the Stories Behind Them* (Sterling, 2006).

10. Gerald S. Strober and Deborah Hart Strober, *The Kennedy Presidency: An Oral History of the Era*, rev. ed. (Potomac, 2003).
11. Ralph Keyes, *"Nice Guys Finish Seventh": False Phrases, Spurious Sayings, and Familiar Misquotations* (HarperCollins, 1992).
12. Hatfield, *Vice Presidents*.
13. Franklin D. Roosevelt, "Can the Vice President Be Useful?" *Saturday Evening Post*, October 16, 1920.
14. Henry A. Wallace, "The Price of Free World Victory," Selected Works of Henry A. Wallace, New Deal Network, http://newdeal.feri.org/wallace/haw17.htm#15.
15. Hatfield, *Vice Presidents*.
16. Robert H. Ferrell, *Harry S. Truman: A Life* (University of Missouri Press, 1994).
17. David McCullough, *Truman* (Simon and Schuster, 1992).
18. "Oral History Interview with Jonathan Daniels."
19. Ibid.
20. Ibid.
21. Interview with Paul G. Kengor, May 11–12, 2007.
22. Ibid.

CHAPTER 13

1. Richard Nixon, *Six Crises* (Simon and Schuster, 1962).
2. Ibid.
3. Ibid.
4. Ibid.
5. Paul Kengor, *Wreath Layer or Policy Player: The Vice President's Role in Foreign Policy* (Lexington, 2002).
6. Ibid.
7. Ibid.
8. Daniel Patrick Moynihan, *Secrecy: The American Experience* (Yale, 1998).
9. See the "Checkers Speech" Appendix.
10. Ibid.
11. Kengor, *Wreath Layer or Policy Player*.

CHAPTER 14

1. *Scarface*, Universal Studios, 2003.
2. *The Right Stuff*, Warner Home Video, 2003, adapted from Tom Wolfe, *The Right Stuff* (Bantam Books, 2001).
3. Robert A. Caro, *The Path to Power*, (Knopf, 1982).
4. Ibid.
5. Robert Caro, "LBJ Had a Bright Side and a Dark Side," History News Network, April 22, 2002, http://hnn.us/articles/685.html.

6. David Wallechinsky and Irving Wallace, *The People's Almanac* (Doubleday, 1975).
7. T. Harry Williams, "Huey, Lyndon, and Southern Radicalism," *Journal of American History* 60, no. 2 (September 1973).
8. Doris Kearns Goodwin, *Lyndon Johnson and the American Dream* (Harper & Row, 1976).
9. Robert A. Caro, *Master of the Senate* (Knopf, 2002).
10. Goodwin, *Lyndon Johnson and the American Dream*.
11. Ibid.
12. Caro, *Master of the Senate*.
13. Robert A. Caro, *Means of Ascent* (Knopf, 1990).
14. Ibid.
15. See "LBJ's Lies About His War Record," History News Network, July 18, 2001, http://historynewsnetwork.org/articles/article.html?id=153.
16. Caro, *Master of the Senate*.
17. Ibid.
18. Theodore H. White, *The Making of the President, 1960* (Atheneum, 1961).
19. As quoted in Richard Nixon, *RN: The Memoirs of Richard Nixon* (Grosset & Dunlap, 1978).
20. Merle Miller, *Lyndon, an Oral Biography* (Putnam, 1980).

CHAPTER 15

1. William B. Welsh, "The Not-So-Imperial Vice Presidency," *Perspectives on Political Science*, Winter 1992.
2. Ibid.
3. Rowland Evans and Robert Novak, *Lyndon Johnson: The Exercise of Power* (New American Library, 1966).
4. Welsh, "The Not-So-Imperial Vice President."
5. Ibid.
6. Ibid.
7. Robert S. Strauss, Interview, Academy of Achievement, Washington D.C., www.achievement.org.
8. Alexander M. Haig, Jr., *Caveat: Realism, Reagan, and Foreign Policy* (Macmillan, 1984).
9. Welsh, "The Not-So-Imperial Vice President," "The quotes in this paragraph represent Lyndon Johnson's views as set forth in *The Vantage Point*" (Holt, Rinehart and Winston, 1971).
10. Donald Morrison, "Compromiser," *Time*, July 30, 1984, review of Carl Solberg, *Hubert Humphrey: A Biography* (Norton, 1984), http://www.time.com/time/magazine/article/0,9171,926736-1,00.html.

CHAPTER 16

1. Gerald R. Ford, "Address on Taking the Oath of the U.S. Presidency," *American Rhetoric*, http://www.americanrhetoric.com/speeches/geraldfordpresidentialoath.html.
2. David C. Whitney, *The American Presidents* (Doubleday, 1975).
3. "Nomination of Gerald R. Ford to Be Vice President of the United States: Hearings," Government Printing Office, 1973.
4. "The Second 1976 Presidential Debate, October 6, 1976," http://www.pbs.org/newshour/debatingourdestiny/76debates/2_b.html.
5. Richard Reeves, *A Ford, Not a Lincoln* (Harcourt, Brace, Jovanovich, 1975).
6. "Impeach Douglas?" *Time*, April 27, 1970, http://www.time.com/time/magazine/article/0,9171,909119-1,00.html.
7. Steven F. Hayward, *The Age of Reagan: The Fall of the Old Liberal Order, 1964–1980* (Forum, 2001).
8. Hatfield, *Vice Presidents of the United States.*
9. Douglas Brinkley, *Gerald R. Ford* (Times Books, 2007).
10. "Gerald Rudolf Ford," American President: An Online Reference Resource, Miller Center of Public Affairs, University of Virginia, http://www.millercenter.virginia.edu/academic/americanpresident/ford.
11. Nixon, *RN*.
12. James M. Cannon, *Time and Chance: Gerald Ford's Appointment With History* (University of Michigan Press, 1998).
13. Nixon, *RN*.
14. Alexander M. Haig, Jr., *Inner Circles: How America Changed the World: A Memoir* (Warner Books, 1992).
15. Ibid.
16. Hatfield, *Vice Presidents of the United States.*
17. Ibid.
18. Ibid.
19. Ibid.
20. Patrick J. Buchanan, *Right from the Beginning* (Little, Brown, 1988).
21. Spiro Agnew, "Television News Coverage," speech given at Des Moines, Iowa, November 13, 1969, http://www.americanrhetoric.com/speeches/spiroagnewtvnewscoverage.htm.
22. Ibid.
23. Ibid.
24. Nixon, *RN*.
25. Ibid.
26. Richard M. Scammon and Ben J. Wattenberg, *The Real Majority* (Coward-McCann, 1970).
27. Nixon, *RN*.
28. Ibid.

29. "Successful Student Project: Make Agnew Pay Up," United Press International, January 6, 1982.

30. Spiro T. Agnew, *Go Quietly . . . or Else* (Morrow, 1980).

31. Hatfield, *Vice Presidents of the United States*.

32. Ibid.

33. Peter Collier and David Horowitz, *The Rockefellers: An American Dynasty* (Holt, Rinehart and Winston, 1976).

34. Ibid.

35. Nixon, *RN*.

36. Hatfield, *Vice Presidents of the United States*.

37. Ibid.

38. Leroy G. Dorsey, "Nelson A. Rockefeller," in L. E. Purcell, ed., *The Vice Presidents: A Biographical Dictionary* (Facts on File, 1998).

CHAPTER 18

1. For more on the exploding bullet, see Lawrence K. Altman, "The Doctor's World," *New York Times*, May 25, 1982.

2. For a good account of what went on in the White House that day, see Richard V. Allen, "The Day Reagan Was Shot," *Hoover Digest*, no. 3 (2001), http://www.hoover.org/publications/digest/3468001.html.

3. L. Edward Purcell, "George Herbert Walker Bush" in *Vice Presidents: A Biographical Dictionary*, 390.

4. Dan Quayle, *Standing Firm* (HarperCollins, 1994).

5. Ibid.

6. Dan Quayle, "Address to the Commonwealth Club of California," http://www.vicepresidentdanquayle.com/ speeches_StandingFirm_CCC_1.html.

7. William F. Buckley Jr., *Let Us Talk of Many Things: The Collected Speeches* (Forum, 2001).

8. Al Gore, *Earth in the Balance: Ecology and the Human Spirit* (Plume, 1993), 275.

9. Al Gore, *The Assault on Reason* (Penguin, 2007), 162–63.

CHAPTER 19

1. Mike Weiss, "Landing the Lineman," *San Francisco Chronicle*, October 3, 2004.

2. James Carney, "7 Clues to Understanding Dick Cheney," *Time*, December 22, 2002.

3. "George W. Bush Selects Dick Cheney as Running Mate," GeorgeBush.com, July 25, 2000.

4. Dan Ackman, "Cheney's Done So Well He Can Afford to Do Good," *Forbes*, July 27, 2000.

5. Dana Milbank, "The Day of the Attack," *Washington Post*, June 18, 2004.

6. Larry King Phone Interview with Cheney, CNN, November 22, 2000.

7. Timothy Noah, "Wolfowitz's Overconfidence," *Slate*, March 24, 2004.

8. "Resolution Impeaching Richard B. Cheney, Vice President of the United States, for High Crimes and Misdemeanors," 110th Congress, 1st session.

9. Tim Harper, "Cheney Argues for Nixon-Era Powers," *Toronto Star*, December 21, 2005.

10. Peter Baker and Jim VandeHeim, "Clash Is Latest Chapter in Bush Effort to Widen Executive Power," *Washington Post*, December 21, 2005.

11. Charlie Savage, "Cheney Aide Is Screening Legislation," *Boston Globe*, May 28, 2006.

12. "The Dark Side—Cheney in His Own Words," *Frontline*, PBS, June 20, 2006.

13. Ibid.

14. "The Legal Significance of Signing Statements," Memorandum for Bernard N. Nussbaum, U.S. Department of Justice, November 3, 1993.

15. Brian Williams, *Nightly News*, NBC, February 13, 2006.

16. Seymour M. Hersh, "The Next Act," *New Yorker*, November 27, 2006.

INDEX